# Faithfully Thought Out and Patiently Evolved

## The Work of M. Louise Stowell and Harvey Ellis

Edited by Kerry Schauber and Lauren Tagliaferro

RIT Press

Rochester, New York

Published and distributed by:
RIT Press
90 Lomb Memorial Drive
Rochester, New York 14623
https://press.rit.edu

Printed in the United States of America

ISBN 978-1-956313-22-2 (print)
ISBN 978-1-956313-05-5 (electronic)

Library of Congress Cataloging-in-Publication Data

Names: Schauber, Kerry, editor. | Tagliaferro, Lauren, editor. | University of Rochester. Memorial Art Gallery.
Title: Faithfully thought out and patiently evolved : the work of M. Louise Stowell and Harvey Ellis / edited by Kerry Schauber and Lauren Tagliaferro.
Description: Rochester, New York : RIT Press, Memorial Art Gallery, [2024] | Includes bibliographical references.
Identifiers: LCCN 2024033177 (print) | LCCN 2024033178 (ebook) | ISBN 9781956313222 (paperback) | ISBN 9781956313253 (pdf)
Subjects: LCSH: Stowell, M. Louise, 1861–1930–Criticism and interpretation. | Ellis, Harvey, 1852–1904–Criticism and interpretation. | Artistic collaboration–New York (State) –Rochester.
Classification: LCC N6537.S773 F35 2024 (print) | LCC N6537.S773 (ebook) | DDC 709.2/2–dc23/eng/20240719
LC record available at https://lccn.loc.gov/2024033177
LC ebook record available at https://lccn.loc.gov/2024033178

We gather on the traditional territory of the Onöndowa'ga:' or "the people of the Great Hill." In English, they are known as Seneca people, "the keeper of the western door." They are one of the six nations that make up the sovereign Haudenosaunee Confederacy.

We honor the land on which RIT was built and recognize the unique relationship that the Indigenous stewards have with this land. That relationship is the core of their traditions, cultures, and histories. We recognize the history of genocide, colonization, and assimilation of Indigenous people that took place on this land. Mindful of these histories, we work towards understanding, acknowledging, and ultimately reconciliation.

Cover images: Top: Detail of Harvey Ellis, *Farm at Twilight*, 1900. Gift of the Estate of Emily and James Sibley Watson, 1951.107. *See page 86 for full image.*
Bottom: Detail of M. Louise Stowell, *The Bridge*, 1900. Memorial Art Gallery: Virginia Jeffrey Smith Fund, in honor of Grant Holcomb and Marie Via, 2016.97. *See page 6 for full image.*

# Contents

# Foreword

Sarah Jesse

Works by Harvey Ellis have been a part of the Memorial Art Gallery collection since our second year of operation, 1914, and rightly so—he was one of Rochester's leading nineteenth-century artists.

Significantly, although Ellis and M. Louise Stowell were so alike in their interests, subject matter, and technique that their unsigned works are often credited to one another, it would be another four decades before we acquired her works.

When 231 works by Stowell and Ellis became available at the same time in 2016, we leaped to acquire them. Not merely because Stowell's works would help correct the gender imbalance of our collection (a problem shared by every other major museum), but because their paired works illustrate something fundamental to the understanding of art.

Although the artistic process is necessarily solitary—one person facing a canvas, alone—artists are rarely truly isolated. They are almost always part of an artistic scene, seeking solace, comradeship, and inspiration from other artists.

Considered together, the work of Stowell and Ellis reminds us that every artwork is a product of its context. Ellis's works would not appear exactly as they do were it not for the influence of Stowell, and vice versa. And neither could exist outside of the fascinating and fecund fin de siècle Rochester art scene.

The exhibition *Faithfully Thought Out* and this accompanying publication were conceived and organized by Kerry Schauber and Lauren Tagliaferro, whose study of Ellis's and Stowell's work has generated new scholarship. They assembled an outstanding group of scholars to contribute essays to this book: Patrica Tice, who provides insight into the life and career of Stowell; Susan Futterman, who contextualizes the work of Stowell and Ellis within Rochester's artistic landscape; and Patricia Hamm, whose essay explores the artists' shared materials and techniques. Andy Olenick photographed the collection. MAG staff provided considerable expertise to bring the exhibition to fruition: Carol Acquilano, Courtney DiMartino, Travis Johansen, Nick Marshall, Jessica Marten, and Adam Ranz. Thanks are due to staff in the Department of Rare Books, Special Collections, and Preservation at the University's River Campus Libraries for their assistance in examining, photographing, and exhibiting their materials. The exhibition was supported by the MAG Council and Charlotte and Raul Herrera. Finally, neither project would have been possible without the support of the Institute of Museum and Library Services and the Greater Hudson Heritage Network.

*Sarah Jesse*
*Mary W. and Donald R. Clark Director*
*Memorial Art Gallery of the University of Rochester*

Detail of: M. Louise Stowell, *The Bridge*, 1900. Watercolor, charcoal, and black ink on laid paper. Memorial Art Gallery: Virginia Jeffrey Smith Fund, in honor of Grant Holcomb and Marie Via, 2016.97.
*See page 6 for full image.*

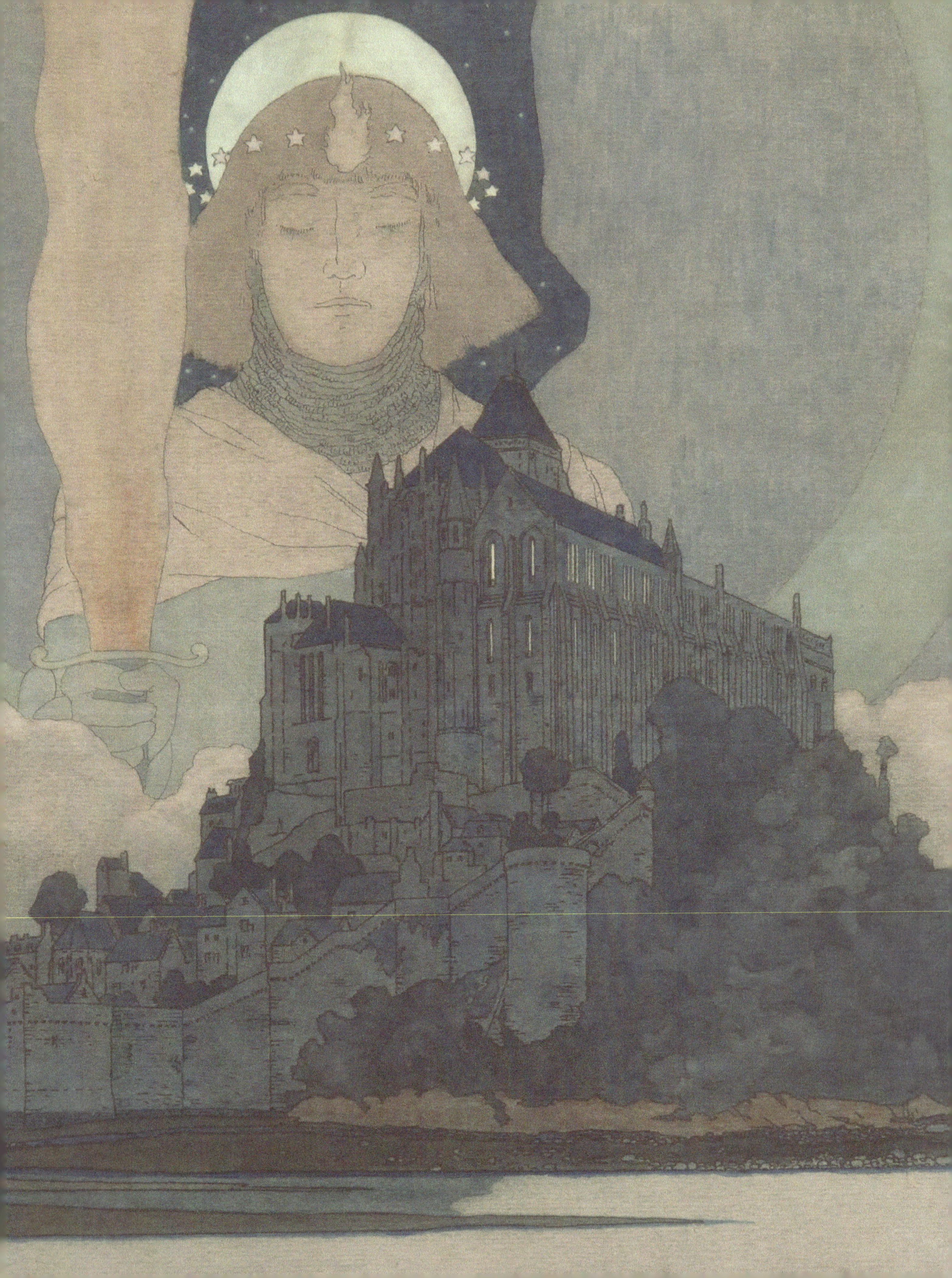

# Faithfully Thought Out and Patiently Evolved

# Introduction

Kerry Schauber

An instructive article M. Louise Stowell wrote in 1892 for the *Educational Gazette*, a periodical for teachers, advised: "Nothing should be careless in ornament or design, but should be faithfully thought out and patiently evolved." The work examined here, executed over two decades, demonstrates this patient forethought.

Anyone who read a newspaper in Rochester, New York, in the late 1890s would have been familiar with the names of M. Louise Stowell (1861–1930) and Harvey Ellis (1852–1904). Friends, colleagues, and studio neighbors, they constantly featured in reviews of exhibitions, mentions of current projects, and descriptions of their travels. Their artistic exploits reached beyond Rochester as well, with reviews in newspapers in New York, Philadelphia, and Chicago and in national magazines. Stowell taught drawing, composition, and color at the Mechanics Institute (later Rochester Institute of Technology); Ellis was an established architect and designer with a national reputation. They were both members of the Rochester Art Club, and together they founded the Rochester Arts and Crafts Society, the first in the nation. While teaching, writing, judging art competitions, and arranging exhibitions, they each created works of art that they showed locally, nationally, and internationally. Synthesizing compositional elements found in Japanese woodblock prints, Symbolism, the Pre-Raphaelite movement, and the work of others of their peers, Stowell and Ellis seemed to work in tandem, sharing techniques, themes, and source material to produce a distinctive visual style.

In 2016, curators at the Strong National Museum of Play contacted the Memorial Art Gallery to offer more than 200 works by Stowell and Ellis formerly in their collection. MAG eagerly accepted the offer to purchase the group, as the Strong's thoughtful once-in-a-lifetime offer ensured the collection—largely assembled by Margaret Woodbury Strong, an advocate for Rochester artists—would remain together, in the artists' hometown, and available to the public. MAG had the works examined by a conservator, and thanks to grants from the Greater Hudson Heritage Network and the Institute of Museum and Library Services, several of the works underwent treatment to repair, clean, and stabilize them. Once this work was complete, all the works were rephotographed. Added to the artwork already at MAG, the permanent collection now includes more than 250 pieces by these two significant artists.

At the same time, an invaluable cache of archival material was acquired from the Strong Museum by the Department of Rare Books, Special Collections, and Preservation, part of the River Campus Libraries at the University of Rochester. Examining and comparing all this material revealed a wealth of connections: preparatory works and their finished versions, shared subject matter and source material, and annotations that inform and enlighten.

The authors included here provide a variety of viewpoints on the artists and their work. Patricia Tice writes with particular insight into Stowell's scrapbooks of source material; Susan Futterman puts Stowell and Ellis into the context of Rochester's art scene as well as the larger American and international art movements of the day; and Patricia Hamm, who conserved these works for MAG, writes a brief explanation of the artists' preferred media and technique.

Although Ellis's name is still known today as an architect and designer, Stowell's name has nearly vanished from scholarship. This book aims to explore their characteristic shared technique and to illustrate the playful artistic partnership of two artists at the height of their artistic powers, but most of all it aspires to return Stowell to the recognition she received during her lifetime. Due to the light-sensitive nature of works on paper, these works are not often exhibited, and many are reproduced here for the first time. Their subtle use of color and shading and the fusion of the styles the artists absorbed make the artwork as remarkable as the newspapers found it when it was first made.

Detail of: Harvey Ellis, *Mont St. Michel*, 1901. Watercolor, ink, and pastel on paper. 2016.16.
*See page 95 for full image.*

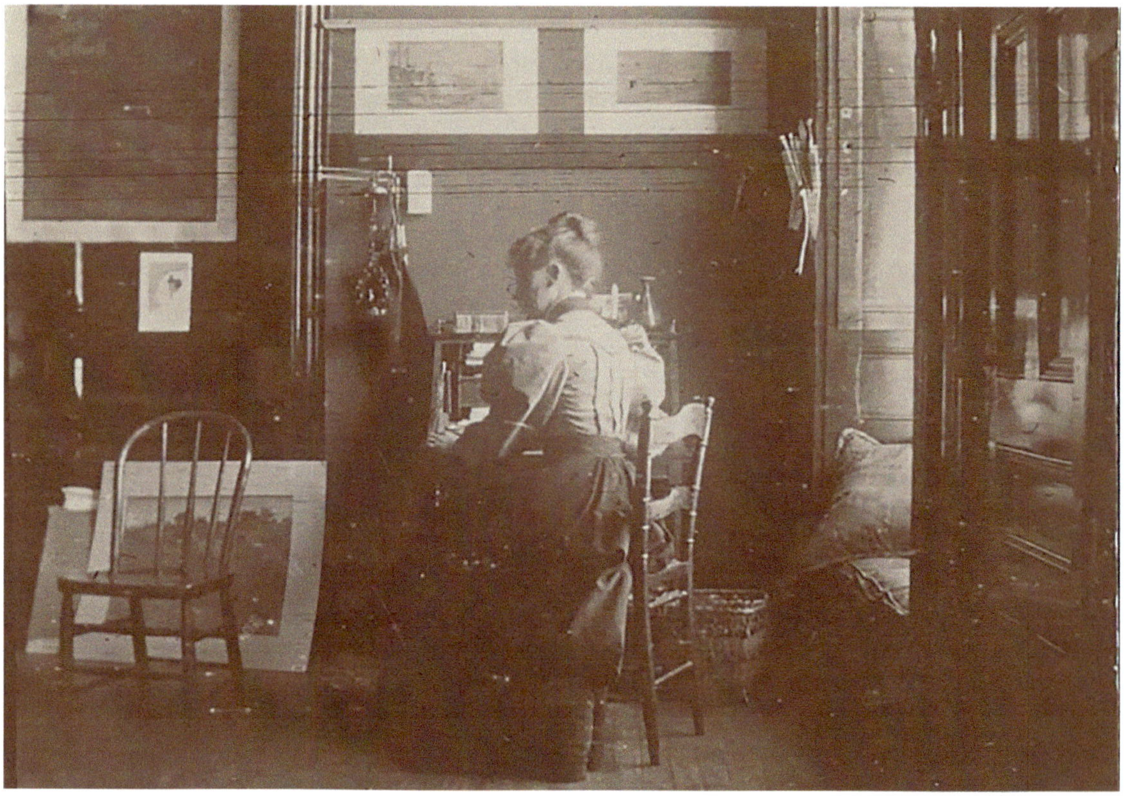

Photograph of M. Louise Stowell in her studio, undated. M. Louise Stowell Papers, D.506, Rare Books, Special Collections, and Preservation, River Campus Libraries, University of Rochester.

# "A High Order of Talent..."

Patricia Tice

Once well known, now forgotten, M. Louise Stowell (1861–1930) was an artist, teacher, writer, collector, Arts and Crafts enthusiast, and business owner who earned significant recognition for her art work between 1896 and 1910.

She exhibited paintings at the New York Water Color Club, the Art Institute of Chicago, and the Pennsylvania Academy of Fine Arts. She handily won honorable mention for her poster design at an international poster contest in Leipzig, Germany, in 1896, and her work hung at the 1904 St. Louis World's Fair. A critic wrote in the national publication *Brush and Pencil*: "This artist has a high order of talent and excites our admiration."[1]

Within ten years of her World's Fair triumph, however, an unidentified illness rendered Stowell an invalid, curtailing her artistic and teaching career. She left behind a body of paintings, drawings, posters, and voluminous scrapbooks that offer a glimpse into her world and her art.

Much remains a mystery about this Rochester, New York, artist. The 1865 federal census lists her as "Mary," but the 1880 census and church confirmation records list the nineteen-year-old as "Minnie." As an artist, she signed her works "M. Louise Stowell," but she called herself Louise Stowell when enrolling in art courses, conducting interviews, or answering census surveys as the head of her own household. Her friend May Bragdon sometimes called her "Mame"; her 1930 death certificate listed her as "Marie." Surviving friends and family members evidently had the last word, for her headstone in Rochester's Mount Hope Cemetery reads Mary Louise Stowell.[2]

M. Louise Stowell was born in Hornell, New York, on June 16, 1861, into a divided nation facing the Civil War. Her parents were Thomas Pollard Stowell (1819–1896) and Henrietta L. Fowler Stowell (1829–1902). Stowell's father hailed from a farming family in Pine Creek, Pennsylvania, but eventually sought employment with the Erie Railroad as a station agent, first in Oswego, New York, around 1851, and later in Hornell, New York, in 1856. In 1863, Stowell accepted a position with the Aetna Fire Insurance Company and moved his family to Rochester, where they lived on Atkinson Street in Rochester's Corn Hill district.

M. Louise Stowell was the youngest of five surviving siblings in a family of high achievers. Her father collected rare mathematical texts and frequently wrote for mathematical journals. The artist's three brothers, Calvin (1845–1920), Henry (1846–1919), and Charles (1853–1933), found success in business, medicine, and engineering, respectively. Little is known about Stowell's older sister, Anna (1849–1896), who lived in the family home until her death at forty-five.

For that matter, little is known about the early endeavors of M. Louise Stowell herself. The young artist may have taken art lessons at the Ladies Art Exchange and the Rochester Art Club, two organizations that formed in 1879. Until the two merged in 1881, members of the Rochester Art Club taught classes in charcoal, drawing, painting, sketching, and figure drawing for the Ladies Art Exchange, as well as for Rochester Art Club members. Interestingly, one of those members who gave art lessons was Stowell's future colleague, Harvey Ellis, although it is not known if their paths crossed at this time. All art classes ceased after the Rochester Mechanics Institute (now Rochester Institute of Technology) formed in 1885. In 1886, the Mechanics Institute launched their fine arts program, offering formal instruction in drawing, painting and modeling, and design, and unlike the University of Rochester, the Mechanics Institute admitted women. One of those women was twenty-five-year-old M. Louise Stowell, who enrolled in drawing, painting, and modeling classes, earning an "E" for "excellence" in watercolors and drawing. By 1889, Stowell was an assistant teacher, and in 1890, she became an instructor teaching form study, drawing, color, and composition, including some children's Saturday morning art classes. She continued to teach intermittently at the Mechanics Institute until 1908.

For Stowell, and for many other women, studying art offered not only personal development, but also employment opportunities within culturally accepted norms that saw drawing, painting, handicrafts, and teaching art as suitable pursuits

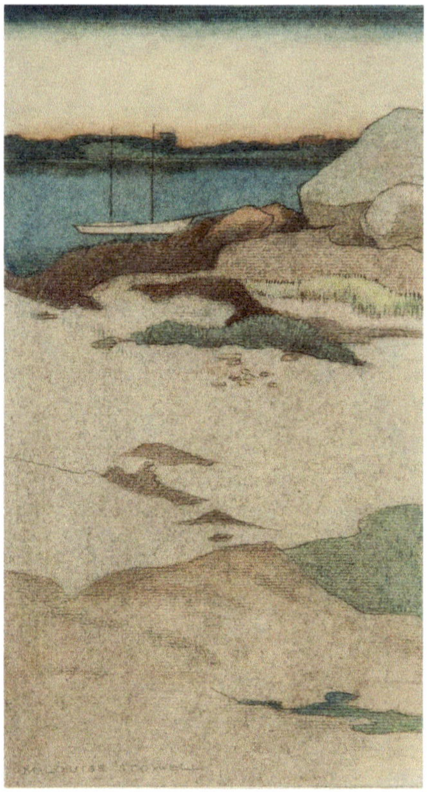

M. Louise Stowell, *Dunes with Boat*. Watercolor and charcoal on laid paper. Memorial Art Gallery: Virginia Jeffrey Smith Fund, in honor of Grant Holcomb and Marie Via, 2016.96.

for women. By the late nineteenth century, more women had begun to distinguish themselves as professional studio artists as well as illustrators, meeting the surging demand for greeting cards, advertisements, and catalogs, particularly in Rochester, where a thriving printing industry churned out illustrated seed and nursery catalogs.

In 1892, Stowell discovered a different approach to art, which she described to *The Artist* magazine: "In Boston, last winter, a new school of art was founded. . . . The new school conceives the synthetic treatment of line, color, and dark and light as fundamental truths, underlying all good designing, decorating and illustrating. Its aim is the development of the creative faculty in its pupils; and from the first, they are trained to observe, to discriminate, to select."[3] Stowell was referring to art classes taught by painter and printmaker Arthur Wesley Dow (1857–1922) based on the theories of Ernest Fenollosa (1853–1908), curator of Oriental art at Boston's Museum of Fine Art and a leading expert on Japanese art and culture. Dow would later join the museum as Fenollosa's assistant curator of Japanese art in 1893 and publish these theories in 1899 in his book *Composition*, which served as the standard text used by art teachers and students for years thereafter.[4]

Stowell attended Dow's Ipswich Summer School outside Boston in 1892 and 1893, where Dow taught students Japanese design principles and then sent them outdoors to paint and sketch. The goal was not to slavishly copy nature, but to compose and abstract it; the artist's observation and experience of a site was an important component of the work. Dow's teaching encouraged Stowell to explore new possibilities in landscape painting. In 1895, *Rochester's Union and Advertiser* reported, "Miss Stowell, whose exquisite watercolors and black and whites are so universally admired . . . studied outdoor painting under Mr. Arthur Dow of Boston, to whom she owes a great deal of her success as an interpreter of landscapes."[5]

Dow enthusiastically promoted the theories of the Arts and Crafts movement, a social, artistic, and design reform that swept across Great Britain, Europe, and the United States in the late nineteenth century. A reaction to the Industrial Revolution, the Arts and Crafts movement advocated for the integration of beauty into daily life, favoring handmade domestic objects imbued with the spirit of their creators. A few years later, Stowell became deeply involved in the Rochester Arts and Crafts Society, the first of its kind in the United States, a topic discussed further in Susan Futterman's essay.

While Dow and Fenollosa were both intensely interested in Japanese prints, it is Fenollosa whom Stowell credited with her knowledge of Japanese art and printmaking techniques. Fenollosa delivered a series of lectures on

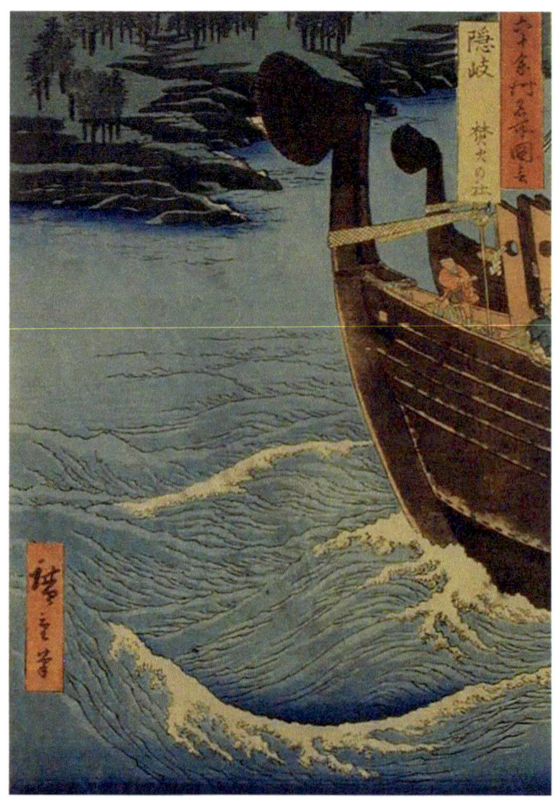


Utagawa Hiroshige, *Shrine of the Bonfires in Sanuki*, 1855. Color woodcut. Memorial Art Gallery: Gift of Margaret Sterling in memory of M. Louise Stowell, transfer from the Art Department of the University of Rochester, 1997.195.

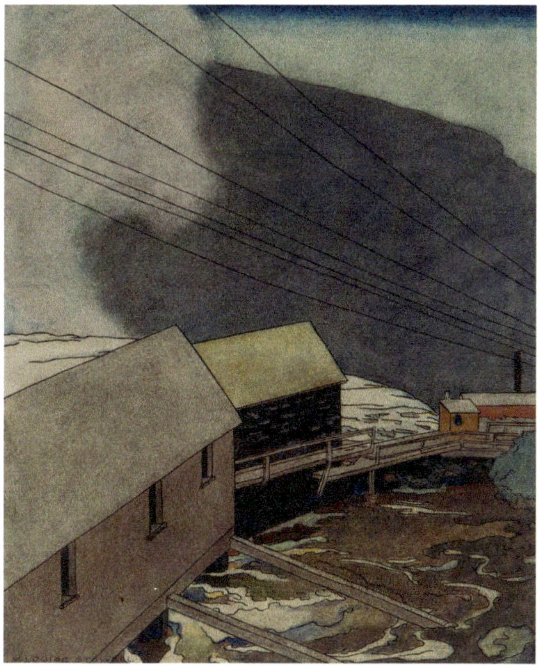

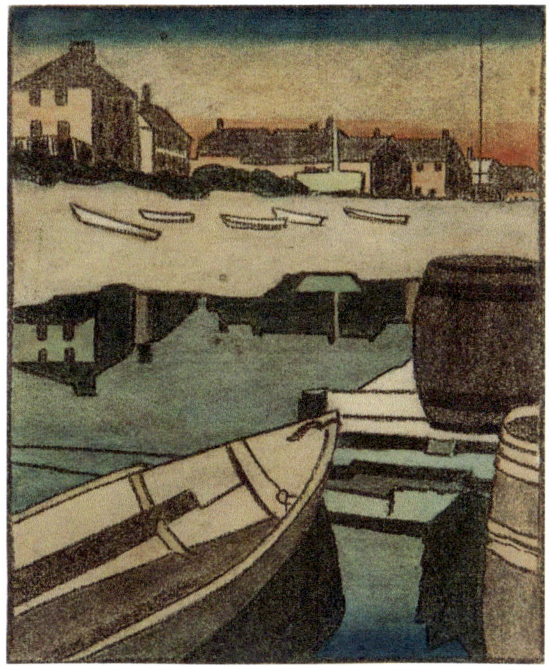

Left: M. Louise Stowell, *The Mill by the Falls, Rochester*, ca. 1905. Watercolor, charcoal, and black ink on paper. Memorial Art Gallery: Virginia Jeffrey Smith Fund, in honor of Grant Holcomb and Marie Via, 2016.116.

Right: M. Louise Stowell, *Boats on the Sand*. Watercolor and charcoal on paper. Memorial Art Gallery: Virginia Jeffrey Smith Fund, in honor of Grant Holcomb and Marie Via, 2016.140.

Japanese art during the winter of 1892 when Stowell was in Boston, and it is possible that she attended them. When Fenollosa visited Rochester in 1893 to lecture on Japanese art, Stowell wrote an insightful promotional piece for his lectures for *The Artist*, noting that these lectures were the same talks delivered by the curator in Boston during the previous winter.[6]

Like many Western artists, Stowell fell under the spell of Japan. Sharing her family's collecting passion, Stowell built what was considered the most comprehensive collection of Japanese prints in Rochester. In 1905, the *Rochester Post Express* commented that "Miss Louise Stowell . . . is an American girl so steeped in what the French would call 'Japaneseries,' that, if it were not for her saving grace of American humor, you would suspect her of being a changeling—a Japanese baby left in an American cradle by fairies from the Orient. . . . They are her hobby, those prints, and her studio on the seventh floor of Powers Building a sort of sanctuary of Eastern Art."[7]

Rochester's *Democrat and Chronicle* also praised Stowell, calling her "possibly the best connoisseur of Japanese Art in Rochester."[8] She exhibited her collection, lectured, and wrote articles on the subject, including one published in *The Craftsman* in October 1903. Some of Stowell's Japanese prints are now in the Memorial Art Gallery's collection, including *Shrine of the Bonfires in Sanuki* by Utagawa Hiroshige (1797–1858), which Stowell reproduced in a 1903 article for *The Craftsman*.

Japanese influence pervades some of Stowell's landscapes, and Stowell admitted that she owed "what there may be good in her work to the Japanese."[9] Those Japanese elements include a thin band of blue sky at the upper edge, broad flat spaces that balance detailed areas, contrasting areas of light and dark, and often a cropped, radical view that presents the viewer with an angled vantage point.

Stowell continued studying art, attending the Art Students League in New York from January through May 1894, taking drawing, sketching, and figure-study classes. At night, she attended the Metropolitan School of Art, then associated with the Metropolitan Museum of Art.

It was also in 1894 that the brilliant architect and draftsman Harvey Ellis returned to his native Rochester after several years spent working in the Midwest. He resumed his architectural work with his brother Charles Ellis in a studio on the seventh floor of the Powers Building downtown. A founding member of the Rochester Art Club, Ellis still found time to paint and teach at the Mechanics Institute, where he collaborated with Stowell and fellow architect Claude Bragdon (1866–1946). Stowell greatly admired Ellis, describing the charismatic artist in an article written several years after his death as: "A man of large generosity, Harvey Ellis' greatest delight was to help art workers by example and precept. His knowledge, his time and his pictures were given freely to students . . . so ingenious were the arguments spun out by the nimble intellect of this man that if he started to persuade you that black was white you invariably ended by conceding that it was at least light grey."[10]

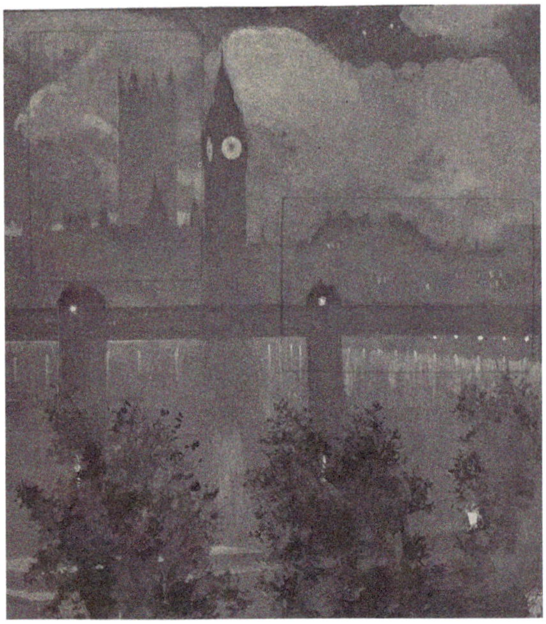

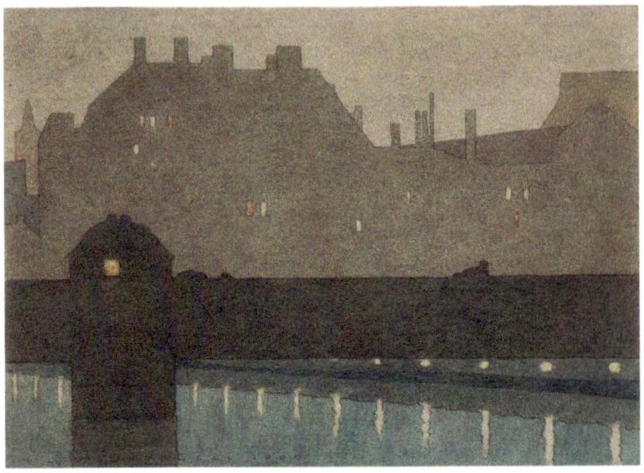

Left: Unidentified artist, painting of Westminster Bridge. Magazine clipping from one of Stowell's scrapbooks. M. Louise Stowell Papers, D.506, Rare Books, Special Collections, and Preservation, River Campus Libraries, University of Rochester.

Right: M. Louise Stowell, *The Bridge*, 1900. Watercolor, charcoal, and black ink on laid paper. Memorial Art Gallery: Virginia Jeffrey Smith Fund, in honor of Grant Holcomb and Marie Via, 2016.97.

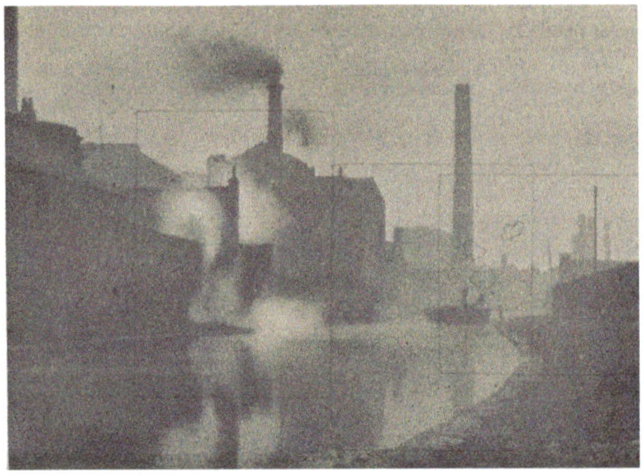

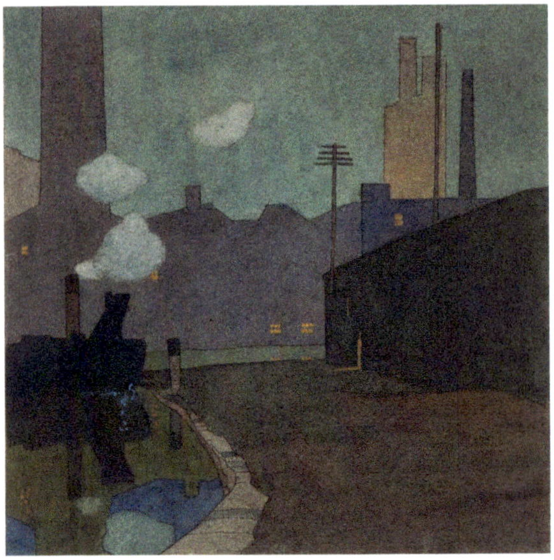

Left: Ward Muir, *Strife*. Magazine clipping from one of Stowell's scrapbooks. M. Louise Stowell Papers, D.506, Rare Books, Special Collections, and Preservation, River Campus Libraries, University of Rochester.

Right: M. Louise Stowell, *Factories Along the Canal, Night*. Watercolor, charcoal, black ink, and gouache on laid paper. Memorial Art Gallery: Virginia Jeffrey Smith Fund, in honor of Grant Holcomb and Marie Via, 2016.98.

Stowell and Ellis taught classes together at times, maintained neighboring studios in the Powers Building, served on the same committees, and exhibited their artwork together in New York, Chicago, and Philadelphia, as well as in Rochester. Their first exhibition together may have been a group exhibition of works in charcoal held in Rochester in March of 1896. Stowell and Ellis often worked in charcoal, a medium capable of producing a range of shadows and light. However, as Stowell later recalled, she and her colleagues sought to combine the techniques and effects of charcoal with watercolor. "A group of artists living in Rochester, N.Y., becoming dissatisfied with the existing methods of water color painting, experimented together with the view of evolving some way of using that medium to achieve full, rich and low-keyed color, breadth of execution and the sureness of procedure which the ordinary way of handling water color lacks."[11] This shared technique yielded very similar works, compounded by Stowell and Ellis's preferences for similar subjects, and unsigned works can be difficult to attribute to one or the other artist. Despite Stowell's mention of "a group of artists," only Stowell and Ellis are known to have used this technique.

For her part, Stowell found inspiration for some of her paintings quite literally at her fingertips. She compiled copious scrapbooks brimming with images cut from newspapers, art magazines, women's magazines, and avant-garde publications such as *Camera Work*. Through these publications, she was exposed to national and international art movements and trends. Stowell believed "wherever you are is your studio."[12] Perhaps for that reason, Stowell did not believe it was necessary for American artists to study in Europe; indeed, she thought that some artists had lost their originality through overexposure to foreign influences. Stowell was also wary of her own influence as a teacher, noting: "In my own classes, I am afraid to meddle overmuch with my pupil's mode of expression. I will not rob him of his precious bit of individuality."[13]

Whether she used these scrapbooks for teaching purposes or solely for her own use is unknown. Nevertheless, she selected details from several of these images and reinterpreted them in watercolor and charcoal.[14] For Stowell, the real challenge for an artist was knowing how to discern and select—and what to eliminate. "The outcome of art," she insisted to an interviewer in April 1897, "is to reproduce the essence, the type, the ideal. . . . I do not aim to render the blossom which lies before me, but a rose which shall make you think of all the roses you have ever seen."[15]

At times, Stowell drew lines or boxes on the clippings to focus the composition. In one album, a photo of an unidentified painting of Westminster Bridge shows carefully penciled lines around buildings on the right-hand side, creating a detail used as a source for her work *The Bridge*.

Another source was *Strife*, a photo of a factory taken by British author and photographer Ward Muir (1878–1927), whose pictures appeared in *Camera Work*. A close look at Stowell's clipping of *Strife* reveals the pencil lines that she drew on the image, effectively cropping the composition. She drew three puffs of smoke in the right side, echoing the three bursts of steam or smoke that appear on the left. The cropped right section inspired her painting now known as *Factories Along the Canal, Night*.

Stowell also used an unidentified image of pollarded willow trees for other paintings. Willows that had been pollarded, or severely cut back, were a popular subject among Dutch and French artists, including Jean-Baptiste-Camille Corot (1796–1875) and Vincent van Gogh (1853–1890). Symbolic of regeneration, pollarded willows were a mainstay of traditional land management, and willow branches were used in the crafts so revered by Arts and Crafts practitioners. Folklore and popular literature from *Jane Eyre* (1847) to *War of the Worlds* (1895–1897) also associated the gnarled, humanesque forms of pollarded willows with the supernatural, making pollarded willows a romantic subject for painters. On the left side of the photo clipping is a willow in the foreground with a hollowed trunk corresponding to *Landscape with Willows*; on the right are the distinctly shaped willows seen in *Willows by the River*. The latter work, then titled *Pollard Willows*, hung next to Harvey Ellis's *Silhouettes* in the 1899 exhibition of the New York Water Color Club.[16] The *Art Amateur* reviewed the exhibit, stating: "There are a number of clever things in flat tints by Harvey Ellis and M. Louise Stowell of which the latter's "'Pollard Willows' and the former's 'Silhouettes' of fishing boats by moonlight seem to justify the treatment."[17] The *New York Evening Post* opined on November 6, 1899: "Miss Stowell . . . seemingly draws her inspiration from the same source as Mr. Ellis, and yet in two of her contributions, at least, she comes closer to nature and is more thoughtful."[18]

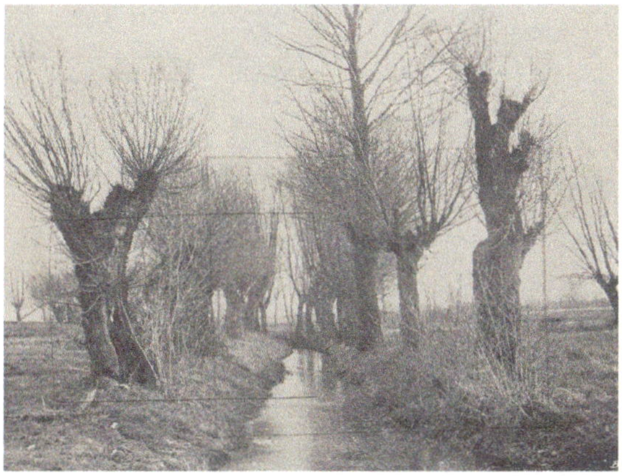

Photograph of pollarded willows from one of Stowell's scrapbooks. M. Louise Stowell Papers, D.506, Rare Books, Special Collections, and Preservation, River Campus Libraries, University of Rochester.

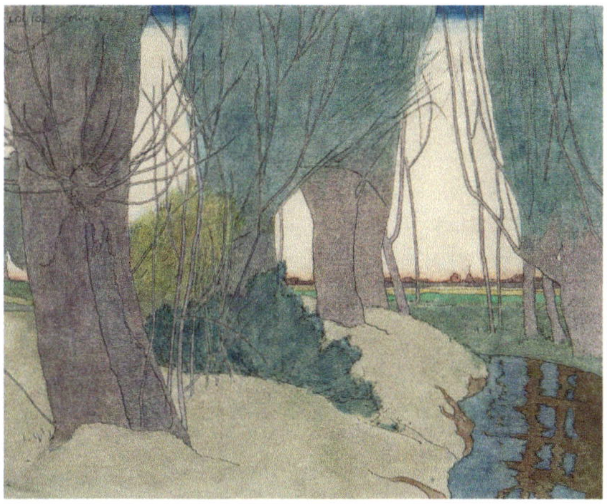

M. Louise Stowell, *Landscape with Willows*, 1899. Watercolor, charcoal, and black ink on laid paper. Memorial Art Gallery: Virginia Jeffrey Smith Fund, in honor of Grant Holcomb and Marie Via, 2016.125.

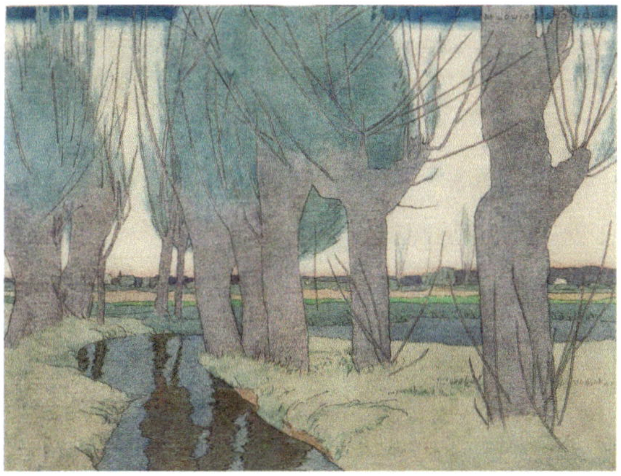

M. Louise Stowell, *Willows by the River*, 1899. Watercolor, charcoal, gouache, and black ink on paper. Memorial Art Gallery: Virginia Jeffrey Smith Fund, in honor of Grant Holcomb and Marie Via, 2016.88.

Stowell's use of photography as a creative aid was not unusual. Many late nineteenth-century artists, including Winslow Homer (1836–1910), Thomas Eakins (1844–1916), and Stowell's former teacher, Arthur Wesley Dow, relied upon photographs as a springboard for their own drawings, prints, and paintings. Photography allowed an

Left: Photograph of Stowell posing for *Philosophia*, from one of Stowell's scrapbooks. M. Louise Stowell Papers, D.506, Rare Books, Special Collections, and Preservation, River Campus Libraries, University of Rochester.

Right: M. Louise Stowell, *Study for Stained Glass Window: Seated Woman with Lily and Scroll*, ca. 1901. Watercolor, charcoal, and black ink with touches of gouache on laid paper. Memorial Art Gallery: Virginia Jeffrey Smith Fund, in honor of Grant Holcomb and Marie Via, 2016.139.2.

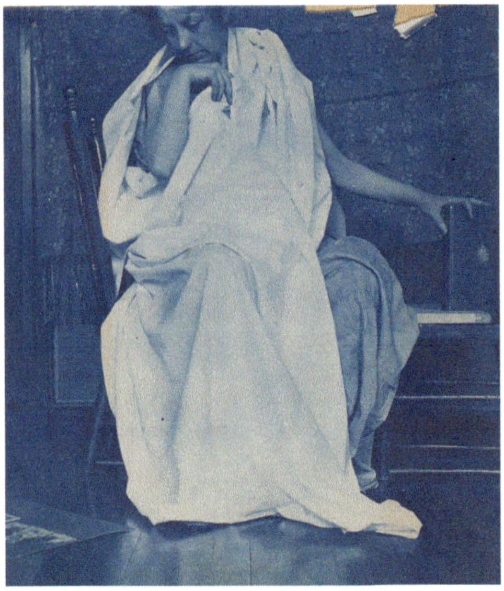

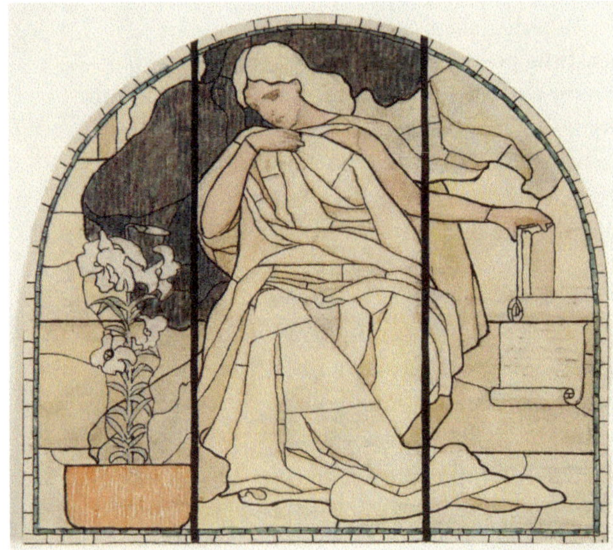

artist to arrange his subject in different poses and to correct the composition accordingly, before putting pencil to paper. Stowell also helped create these materials for others; in 1898, Stowell posed for a photo that Ellis used as a study for his allegorical work, *The Hour Glass*, reflecting their contention that paintings should be carefully composed, not copied from nature.

Stowell's scrapbooks include dozens of cyanotypes, an inexpensive and simple form of photography that produces a distinctive blue print. Arthur Wesley Dow took cyanotypes as sources for his paintings and prints and taught this photographic process in his Summer Institutes, so Stowell may have learned this technique there or at the Mechanics Institute. Stowell also used cyanotypes as studies for her own compositions, posing in some of them. Amateur photographer May Bragdon, sister of architect Claude Bragdon, may also have captured those images of Stowell. May Bragdon became well acquainted with her brother's friends and colleagues, including Ellis and Stowell, sharing an enthusiasm for bicycling and photography with the latter. Bragdon's diary entry for August 21, 1897, mentions that "Mame [M. Louise Stowell] & I went up to Hovey's to buy the Kodak."[19] On November 20, 1897, Bragdon notes that she visited Stowell's studio to see her "pictures & photographs & new camera."[20] Her diary entry for July 4, 1907, includes a cyanotype depicting a holiday outing with friends that includes "Mame with camera."[21]

An undated cyanotype in one of Stowell's scrapbooks illustrates M. Louise Stowell posing as *Philosophia*, a study for the stained glass window she designed in 1901 for her brother Calvin's family mausoleum in Mount Hope Cemetery. Considering the endeavors of the Stowell family in the arts and sciences, Philosophia—an allegorical figure for the love of wisdom—was a fitting theme. In 1902, Stowell transformed that composition into a related watercolor entitled *Philosophia*.

The allegory of Philosophia personified as an enthroned woman with a book descends from sixth-century iconography for Mary as the Seat of Wisdom, depicting the enthroned Virgin Mary holding the Christ Child, sometimes with a book of Gospels, white lilies, the emblem of purity, or a scepter topped with lilies. Around the twelfth century, artists secularized this image,

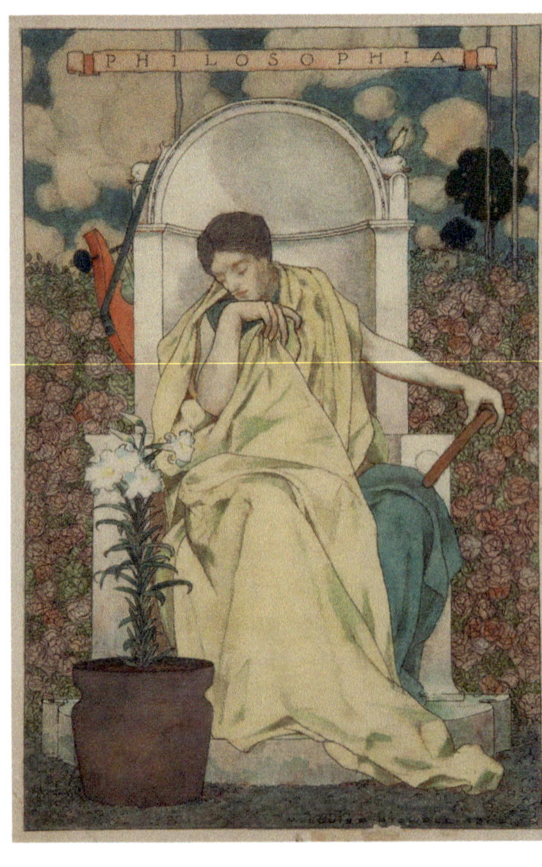


M. Louise Stowell, *Philosophia*, 1902. Watercolor, charcoal, black ink, and graphite on laid paper. Memorial Art Gallery: Virginia Jeffrey Smith Fund, in honor of Grant Holcomb and Marie Via, 2016.111.

replacing Mary with a classical figure holding books and white lilies. Stowell's 1902 version made Philosophia's throne grander and her book less obvious. She added a lyre, an ancient Greek symbol of wisdom and moderation, and a background of roses. This work reflects a broader cultural revival of classicism among architects and artists. This period, at the end of the nineteenth century and the beginning of the twentieth century, was one in which American culture drew heavily on the legacy of Greek and Roman humanism. Allegorical figures such as Philosophia were appearing in civic temples—neoclassical libraries and government buildings—being designed around this time, as Stowell would have known; an entire volume of her scrapbooks is dedicated to photos and clippings of murals, mostly in public buildings.

Stowell's 1899 *Court of Dreams* takes viewers into Greco-Roman mythology. These mystical, mythological scenes were popular in Arts and Crafts design. The seated, hooded figure represents Somnus, the Roman god of sleep. According to the Roman poet Ovid (43 BCE–17 CE), Somnus dwelt in a dark cave with red opium poppies growing around its entrance. Poppies were sacred to Somnus, because the blossoms yielded the sleep-inducing narcotic opium. In Stowell's version, the god of sleep abides in a stylish Arts and Crafts interior with wainscoting, frieze, and candle sconces. A brazier shaped like a giant poppy seed head wafts its potent smoke around each elegant yet languid attendant bearing a red opium poppy. As Stowell explained in *Palette and Bench in*August 1910, "Somnus nods on his ebony throne while the maidens of his court holding poppies stand drowsily waiting to be sent out as dreams."[22]

Stowell and her colleagues Bragdon and Ellis turned to poster design in the mid-1890s, inspired by the bright, colorful posters Bragdon had brought back from his studies in France. With her strong drafting skills, Stowell excelled in graphic design, creating posters for Rochester's *Union and Advertiser* newspaper and the rare-book shop belonging to her friend George Humphrey.

Her poster featuring a man on a bicycle won honorable mention at an international poster contest in Leipzig, Germany, in 1896; in 1897, *Maîtres de l'Affiche*, which issued posters to its subscribers, published *George P. Humphrey at the Sign of the "Old-Book Man,"* making her work known in Europe. A jubilant article in the local newspaper *Post Express* crowed over Stowell's success: "Miss M. Louise Stowell, of this city, who is becoming so well known on account of her posters, was the only woman to receive a prize at the recent German exhibition, where were represented the leading poster artists of the world."[23]

Stowell also won first prize for her poster for Rochester's Marie Antoinette Fete in January of 1897 and created a striking poster advertising a

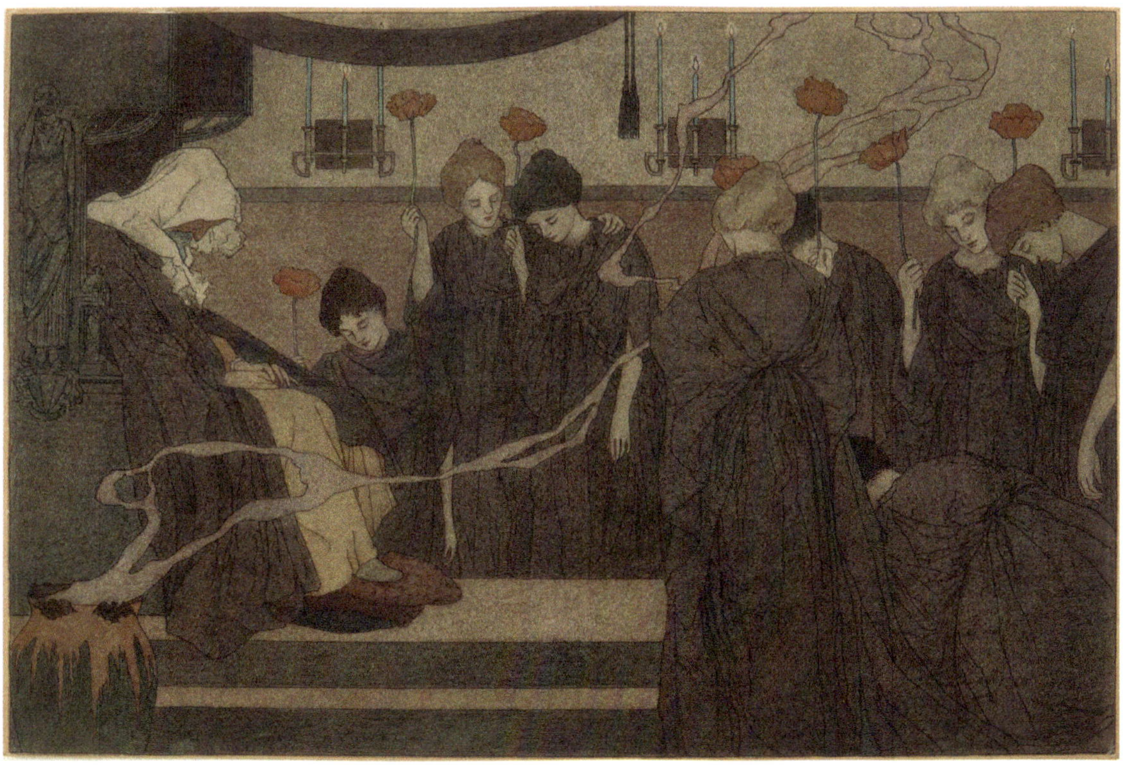

M. Louise Stowell, *The Court of Dreams*, ca. 1899. Watercolor and charcoal on laid paper. Memorial Art Gallery: Virginia Jeffrey Smith Fund, in honor of Grant Holcomb and Marie Via, 2016.160.

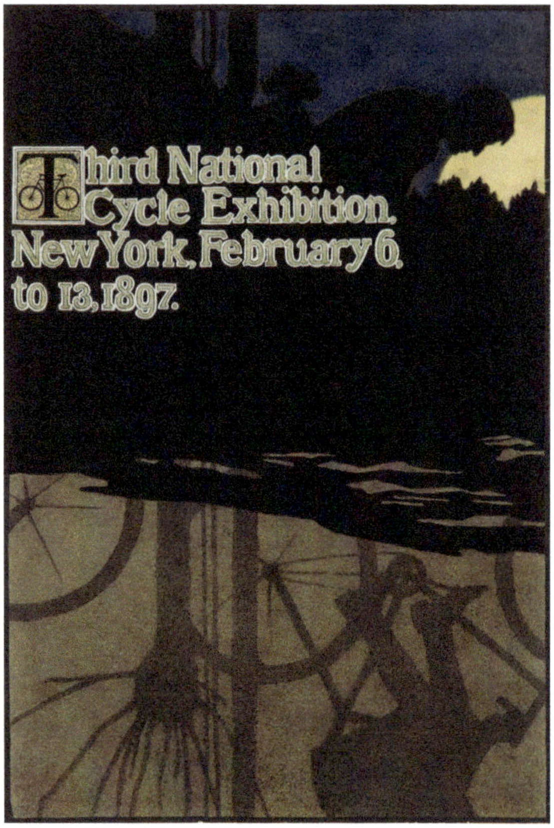


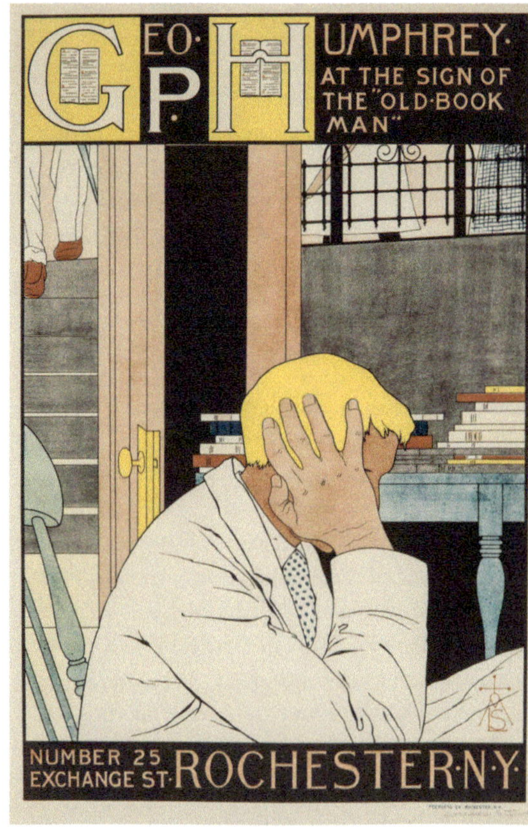


Left: M. Louise Stowell, poster for Third National Cycle Exhibition, 1897. Gouache, watercolor, charcoal, black ink, pastel, and graphite on paper. Memorial Art Gallery: Virginia Jeffrey Smith Fund, in honor of Grant Holcomb and Marie Via, 2016.65.

Right: M. Louise Stowell, *George P. Humphrey at the Sign of the "Old-Book Man,"* ca. 1895. Lithograph. Memorial Art Gallery: Anonymous gift, 1984.35.

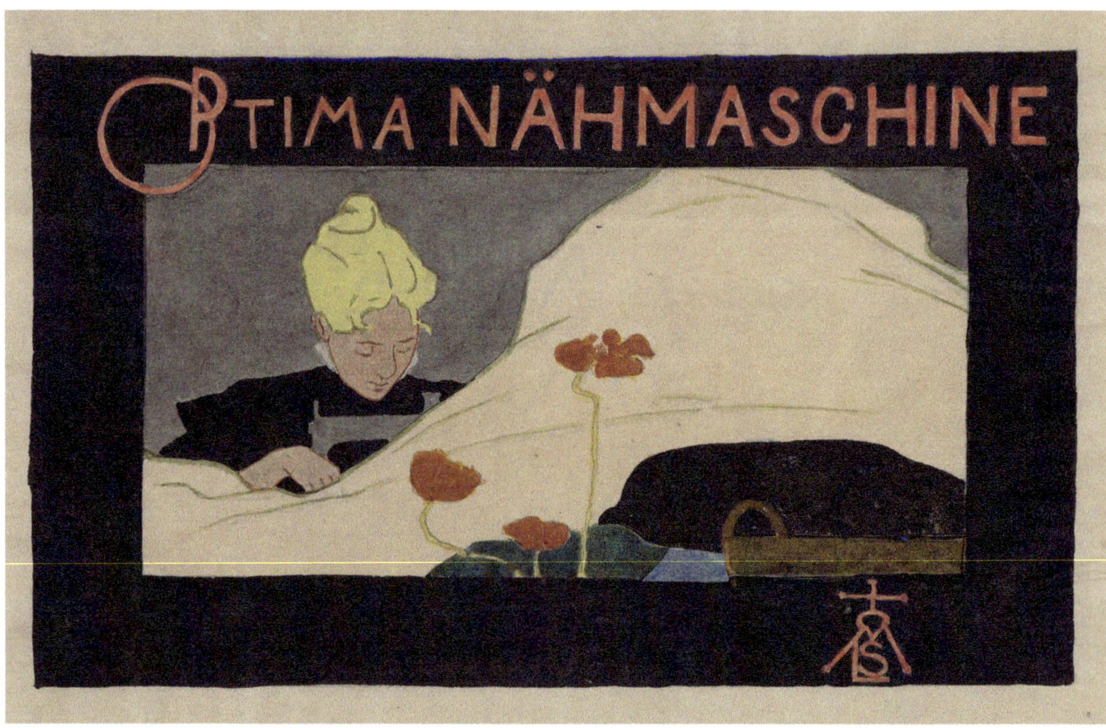


M. Louise Stowell, *Poster for Optima Nähmaschine*, 1897. M. Louise Stowell Papers, D.506, Rare Books, Special Collections, and Preservation, River Campus Libraries, University of Rochester.

German sewing machine, *Optima Nähmaschine*, using the same colors seen in *The Old-Book Man*. That color choice had less to do with aesthetics and more to do with the technology developed by French artist Jules Chéret (1836–1932). In the 1880s, Chéret developed the three-stone lithographic method for printing large-scale color posters, which produced designs with four colors—usually red, yellow, black, and white. Stowell was familiar with Chéret's work, as evidenced by the Rochester Arts and Crafts Society's first exhibition in the spring of 1897, which featured both modern French posters and Japanese prints. In creating *Optima Nähmaschine*, Stowell imitated Chéret's visual style through the collage medium, pasting the black and red elements onto her paper.

Stowell exhibited *The Old-Book Man, Optima Nähmaschine,* and *The Third National Cycle Exhibition* in the March 1897 poster exhibition at the Albany Club in Albany, New York. Albany's *The Argus* reported on March 30, 1897, that the exhibit included 750 French and American posters, adding that "American women have done a deal in the development of poster art and it is worth while for the student to look up the work of them at the Albany club. Ethel Reed, M. Louise Stowell, Blanche McManus, [and] Maud Humphrey . . . are among the American women whose work is shown at the exhibit." *The Argus* continued: "Miss Stowell's work included a sewing machine poster . . . a weird bicycle poster, which received honorable mention at the Leipzig competition last year, and a delightful "Old Book Man."[24] For the cycle exhibition poster, Stowell returned to her more customary dark palette in watercolors and charcoal.

According to newspaper reports, M. Louise Stowell resigned from the Mechanics Institute in 1908 due to poor health. A glance through the Rochester business directories suggests anything but a quiet retirement. From 1908 to 1922, Stowell was listed as an artist. By 1909, she had joined forces with bookbinder Margaret Sterling, whom she had met at Rochester's 1903 Arts and Crafts exhibition. Sterling became a boarder in the Stowell household, and the two artists formed the Masu Company, selling hair tonic. In 1910, Stowell curated a memorial exhibition of artwork by Harvey Ellis, who had died in 1904. She also reproduced several watercolors by Ellis and her former studio-mate Ada Howe Kent as hand-colored woodblock prints. In 1911, Stowell and Sterling opened the Far East Shop to sell exotic imported goods. In November of that year, May Bragdon noted in her journal: "We went to the Far East shop and spent an hour and some money. Miss S. had a lovely Chinese brocade with a blood stained dagger hole in!!"[25] *Dau's Blue Book for Rochester and Suburban Town*s for 1912 included a listing for the Far East Shop at 148 Cutler Building, Main Street East, along with an advertisement for the shop's "imported fabrics, laces, linen, blouses, jewelry and novelties from foreign lands." In 1914, Stowell and Sterling formed the Stowell and Sterling Company, which sold art supplies. Stowell continued listing herself as an artist as well as proprietor of the Masu Company, Far East Shop, and the Stowell and Sterling Company until the end of 1922. After that, a curtain drops on M. Louise Stowell's life until her death in 1930 from myocarditis, an inflammation of the heart sometimes triggered by a viral infection. Her obituary mentions that she suffered "an illness nearly 20 years ago which left her an invalid. Since that time she had centered most of her interest about the shop at her home which dealt in novelties and antiques."[26]

Research always produces as many questions as it answers. One such question concerns Stowell's production: her scrapbooks contain hundreds of clippings, perhaps sources for paintings for herself, Harvey Ellis, or her students, yet relatively few of her artworks are known today. Some are known only from titles listed in exhibition brochures; for example, what happened to the painting entitled *Between Two Bridges* that Stowell exhibited at the St. Louis World's Fair and other venues in 1904? Fairgoers purchased many of the works on exhibit, but the location of the work is unknown now. Are more Stowell paintings in private collections waiting to be discovered?

Stowell continued to list herself as an artist from 1908 to 1922, but only a few works date after 1912. While her health may have impacted her output, it may also be that the Arts and Crafts style and the mystical, religious subject matter she espoused after 1905 faded before the emerging styles of Modernism and Art Deco of the 1920s. Still, her artwork remains as evidence of a moment when she and Ellis created a body of work that drew from the international movements in the art world but remained unique to their own vision. Their high order of talent still, as the critics declared in 1899, "excites our admiration."

## Notes

1 James William Pattison, "Water-Color Exhibition at the Art Institute," *Brush and Pencil* IV, no. 3 (June 1899): 150–151. Pattison was an artist, educator, and critic.

2 Much research about this elusive artist was undertaken by Lynne Poirier-Wilson, the former vice president for collections and operations at Rochester's Strong Museum (now called Strong National Museum of Play), who aptly described Stowell as "an artist in the shadows" and who, through her research and public lectures, brought this figure "out into the light where she belongs." This essay is indebted to Poirer-Wilson's work and her meticulous Stowell genealogy summarized here.

3 *The Artist*, 1892, from scrapbook, M. Louise Stowell papers, D.506, Box 1, Rare Books, Special Collections, and Preservation, River Campus Libraries, University of Rochester, Rochester, New York.

4 Dow, Arthur Wesley, *Composition: A Series of Exercises in Art Structure for the Use of Students and Teachers* (Boston: J. M. Bowles, 1899).

5 "Artist's Studios," *[Rochester] Union and Advertiser*, March 16, 1895, 3.

6 *The Artist*, 1893, from scrapbook, Stowell papers, D.506, Box 1.

7 "Prints from Japan: Miss Louise Stowell Is a Devotee of Oriental Art," *[Rochester] Post Express*, January 27, 1905, 9.

8 "Japanese Prints on View," *[Rochester] Democrat and Chronicle*, February 10, 1910, 14

9 "Fair Woman's World" column, *[Rochester] Post Express*, April 10, 1897, 18.

10 Harvey Ellis, "Some Pictures," *Palette and Bench*, September 1910, 302.

11 M. Louise Stowell, "Water Color Over Charcoal," *Palette and Bench*, August 1910, 284. Conservator Patricia Hamm discusses this technique more fully on p. 25.

12 "Fair Woman's World."

13 "Fair Woman's World."

14 Harvey Ellis also used Stowell's scrapbooks as a resource; MAG research assistant Kerry Schauber has identified at least three Ellis watercolors in MAG's collection that were based on newspaper clippings in one of Stowell's albums, including *Port Scene* (2016.33), *The Old Mill* (2016.76), and *Farm at Twilight* (1951.107).

15 "Fair Woman's World."

16 See p. 18.

17 "The Water-Color Club," *Art Amateur*, December 1899, 6.

18 "New York Water-Color Club," *Evening Post* (New York), November 6, 1899, 7.

19 May Bragdon diaries, entry for August 21, 1897, Bragdon Family Papers, A.B81, Rare Books, Special Collections, and Preservation, River Campus Libraries, University of Rochester, https://maybragdon.lib.rochester.edu.

20 May Bragdon diaries, entry for November 20, 1897.

21 May Bragdon diaries, entry for July 4, 1907.

22 Stowell, "Water Color Over Charcoal," 285.

23 "Fair Woman's World."

24 "Albany's Poster Show," *[Albany] Argus*, March 31, 1897, 8. In the late nineteenth century, the word "weird" meant "eerie" or "supernatural," a fair description of the nocturnal cyclist and his ghostly reflection.

25 May Bragdon diaries, entry for November 15, 1911.

26 *[Rochester] Times-Union*, February 8, 1930.

# Kindred Spirits

Susan Futterman

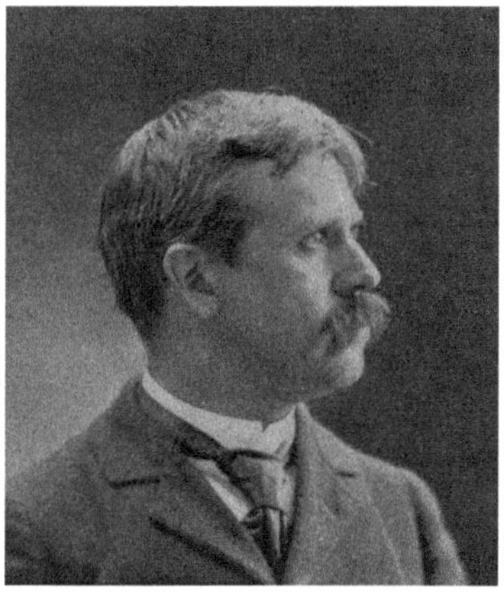

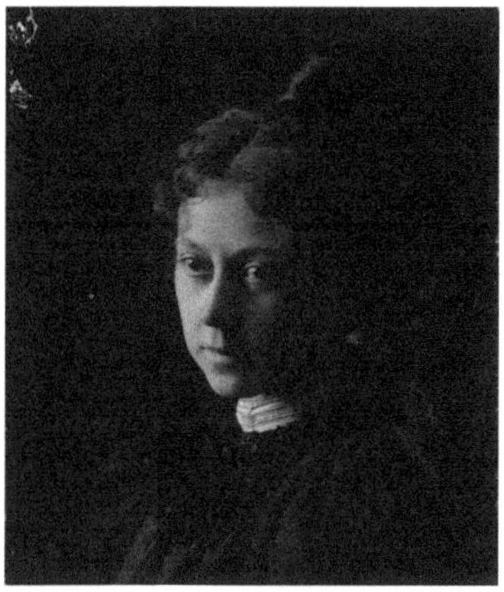

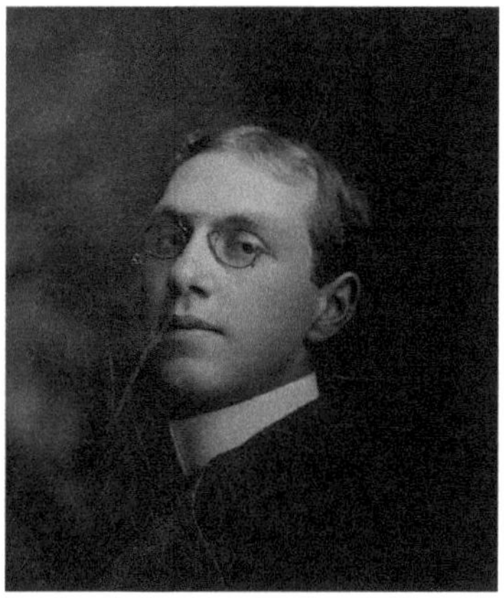

Left: Photograph of Harvey Ellis, 1897. Taken from *The Brochure Series of Architectural Illustration*, September 1897. From May Bragdon diaries, entry for August 22, 1897, Bragdon Family Papers, A.B81, Rare Books, Special Collections, and Preservation, River Campus Libraries, University of Rochester.

Center: Photograph of M. Louise Stowell, undated. M. Louise Stowell Papers, D.506, Rare Books, Special Collections, and Preservation, River Campus Libraries, University of Rochester.

Right: Photograph of Claude Fayette Bragdon, undated. Bragdon Family Papers, A.B81, Rare Books, Special Collections, and Preservation, River Campus Libraries, University of Rochester.

After a long absence, Harvey Clinton Ellis (1852–1904)—an architect by trade, an artist by choice—returned to his hometown of Rochester, New York. Ellis found common ground with the artist M. Louise Stowell (1861–1930) and the architect Claude Bragdon (1866–1946). For a brief period from 1893 to 1903, the lives of these three people were artistically intertwined through shared passions and ideals. They were all superb artists, theoretical thinkers, expansive readers, and able writers. Together and in pairs, they developed new approaches to art through their interpretation of the principles set forth by Arthur Wesley Dow and their understanding of the approach of Japanese printmakers to their subject matter. They established the Rochester Arts and Crafts Society, taught art classes, presented thought-provoking exhibitions, and wrote informative articles on topics such as Japanese prints and the emerging Arts and Crafts architecture and its color palette.

Rochester in the 1890s was a progressive city with awareness of racial tolerance influenced by Frederick Douglass, who lived there for decades. It was the birthplace of Susan B. Anthony, who advocated for social equality and women moving into the workforce. Manual training in schools was growing everywhere, and Rochester was no exception. The Mechanics Institute opened in 1885, with the goal of providing technical training for skilled laborers in industry. Following the city's egalitarian philosophy, the school from its onset welcomed both men and women in all classes, was free for the first year, and awarded scholarships. This was especially important, because women at that time had few options for post-primary education. The institute embraced the Arts and Crafts movement, especially the philosophy of Englishmen John Ruskin and William Morris. Women flocked to enroll, including M. Louise Stowell.

M. Louise Stowell had grown up in Rochester. Artistically gifted, she enrolled in one of the Mechanics Institute's first entering classes in the two-year art-study course in 1887, where her work was regularly included and praised in student exhibits. Upon receiving her two-year diploma, she was hired to teach freehand drawing, color, and composition, and went on to complete her advanced diploma in 1890. By 1892 she was showing her watercolor paintings in the Rochester Art Club exhibits. She proved herself to be an articulate writer, penning a series of articles directed toward teachers of art for the *Educational Gazette* beginning in 1892.[1] The first was a straightforward academic approach about geometry as the basis of all line designs, citing how units occurring in nature do so in regular patterns. The artist, she noted, has control over this regularity and the density of the patterning, and so must consider the principle of "a deliberate and wise rejection. The more artistic a person's nature, the more effectively will he employ this principle of rejection."[2]

In a subsequent article, Stowell wrote about "a New School," where rather than approaching art from a perspective of reproducing a scene, students should be encouraged "to observe, to

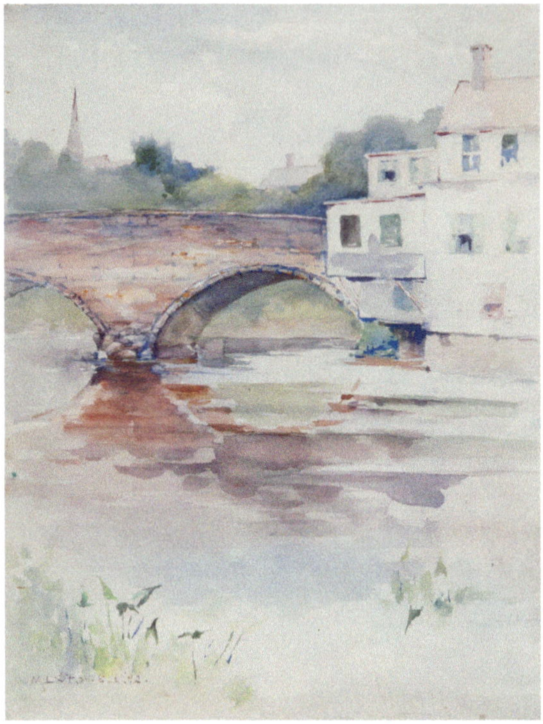

M. Louise Stowell, *Bridge, Ipswich Massachusetts*, 1892. Watercolor and graphite on paper. Memorial Art Gallery: Virginia Jeffrey Smith Fund, in honor of Grant Holcomb and Marie Via, 2016.104.

discriminate, to select."[3] She suggested that students should look to Japanese prints to understand these principles. Undoubtedly, she was writing of Arthur Wesley Dow (1857–1922) and his new Ipswich Summer School, which she attended in the summer of 1892.

The following winter, she wrote about the upcoming lectures in Rochester of Ernest Fenollosa (1853–1908), the curator of Oriental art at the Museum of Fine Arts in Boston. Stowell's teacher Dow, a painter and printmaker, had been strongly influenced by Fenollosa, who had spent twelve years living in Japan and studying the principles of its artwork. Rochester's lively art community soaked up Fenollosa's ideas at his series of lectures. He believed that certain principles were common to both Eastern and Western schools of art: line, dark and light, and color. However, he said, Western schools took a photographic approach to art, while Eastern schools took a more introspective approach. Artists should be encouraged to think about the subject matter and focus on the spirit or essential quality of what was before them. Fenollosa had conveyed these beliefs to Dow, who taught them in his summer painting classes. Judging by the tone of the articles, Stowell was already a convert to Dow's way of thinking and to an Eastern approach to art. Under Dow's influence, she began her collection of Japanese prints.

Stowell left teaching in 1894 and devoted herself to her own art, taking a studio space in the Powers Building in downtown Rochester with fellow artist Ada Howe Kent, who had studied in Paris with James McNeill Whistler and was a collector of Japanese prints as well. The building, with both offices and artists' studios, had been built by Daniel Powers, an art collector, who had opened several galleries exhibiting his art to the public.

Harvey Ellis is best known today as a furniture designer. During the last seven months of his life, he worked for Gustav Stickley's furniture company, the United Crafts, in Syracuse, New York.[4] He was largely responsible for influencing the United Crafts' migration from producing heavy, boxy furniture to lighter, more graceful styling, often decorated with brass inlays. But this multitalented individual lived a lifetime before his work with Stickley.

Ellis was a Rochester native who had always shown an interest in and an aptitude for drawing. By the time he was a young man, he was a capable artist and etcher, with clear artistic talents and interests. He attended West Point for fewer than seven months before he was dishonorably discharged. Bragdon described him as having "the dress, bearing, and manners of a gentleman, with a quiet dignity about him,"[5] but Ellis was genuinely unambitious for himself. Returning home, he wandered for a while, most probably working as a draftsman in New York City and studying art. Because Ellis hardly ever talked about himself, little is known about any formal

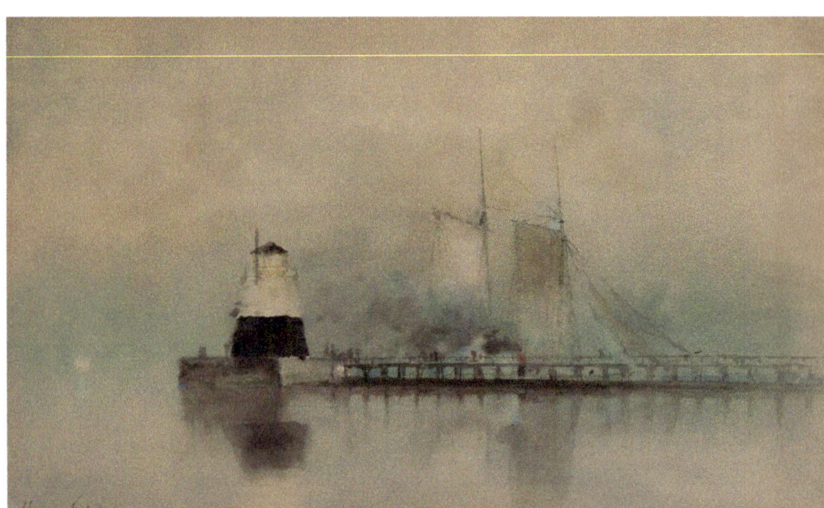

Harvey Ellis, *Summerville Pier and Lighthouse*, 1884. Watercolor on wove paper. Memorial Art Gallery: Gift of Charlotte Whitney Allen, 1964.38.

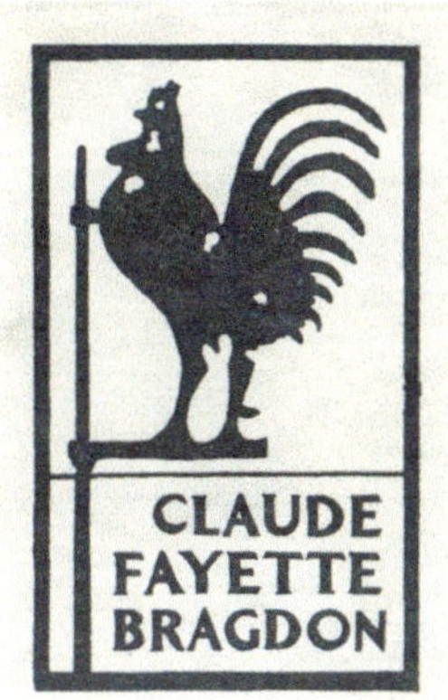


Claude Fayette Bragdon, bookplate. Bragdon Family Papers, A.B81, Rare Books, Special Collections, and Preservation, River Campus Libraries, University of Rochester.

training he had in either art or architecture. Nevertheless, with his innate artistic talents, his skill as a draftsman and artist developed.

In Rochester, he applied himself to painting and was a founding member, and later president, of the Rochester Art Club. He and his brother Charles formed an architectural firm and were moderately successful with a series of smaller buildings. Harvey did the designing and Charles attended to the business, until Charles was indicted for bribery in 1885, at which point Harvey left Rochester.

For almost a decade, Harvey worked throughout the Midwest for a series of architectural firms, some simultaneously. Ellis had a brilliant mind and the ability to quickly absorb different styles of architecture from the many articles in contemporary periodicals about the latest building styles and advances in construction techniques. He is sometimes described as a "paper" architect, but more appropriately, he was a "visionary" architect. He could envision a building in its entirety and place it beautifully on a piece of paper. It was rumored that Ellis's renderings alone could win a job for a firm. Most often, he would leave it to others to follow up with more detailed plans. Many of his early designs followed the styles of Henry Hobson Richardson, Louis Sullivan, and the Prairie School. He penned an illustration for a skyscraper years before a similar building was finally built. It was said that Ellis's sketch of a small bank building appeared in print and was pinned to a wall in Sullivan's office a decade before Sullivan's first "jewel box" bank was built.[6]

As Ellis was leaving his hometown, Claude Bragdon's family moved to Rochester. Bragdon was an architect who trained by working in a series of architectural firms in New York City, Buffalo, and Rochester, each time in a slightly higher position requiring a greater level of skill. He was an intellectual who had a passion for American and European graphic arts such as advertising posters, book covers, and bookplates.

Bragdon later wrote, "In architecture I was inspired by two masters: Harvey Ellis and Louis Sullivan who were both ahead of the times they lived in."[7] Ellis's influence on Bragdon began even before they met, when Bragdon went to work for Charles Ellis. "The office had been full of Harvey's drawings, which moved me to admiration, emulation, and despair, for he was one of the finest pen-and-ink draughtsman this country has produced. . . . And he was no less accomplished as a painter than as a draughtsman."[8] Bragdon found Ellis's drawings "everything that such drawings should be: unlabored, economical of line, brilliant, beautifully balanced, with far more color and body than is usual in pen drawings."[9] This was high praise from a fellow architect who already had strong professional accomplishments.

By the time Harvey returned to Rochester in 1894, he was deeply interested in the English Arts and Crafts movement, following John Ruskin, Edward Burne-Jones, and the Pre-Raphaelite artists, writers, and architects, William Morris being his favorite. He was always current on all the latest periodicals, including *International Studio*, *The Lark*, *The Chap Book*, and *The Philistine*. He resumed his architectural practice with his brother, Charles, in an office in the Powers Building.

Although fifteen years their senior, he naturally fell in with a jovial but intellectual group of professional men, including Claude Bragdon, who lovingly called themselves "The Vagabonds." They would regularly adjourn to the antiquarian bookstore of fellow Vagabond George Humphrey, either after lunch or before dinner to carry on

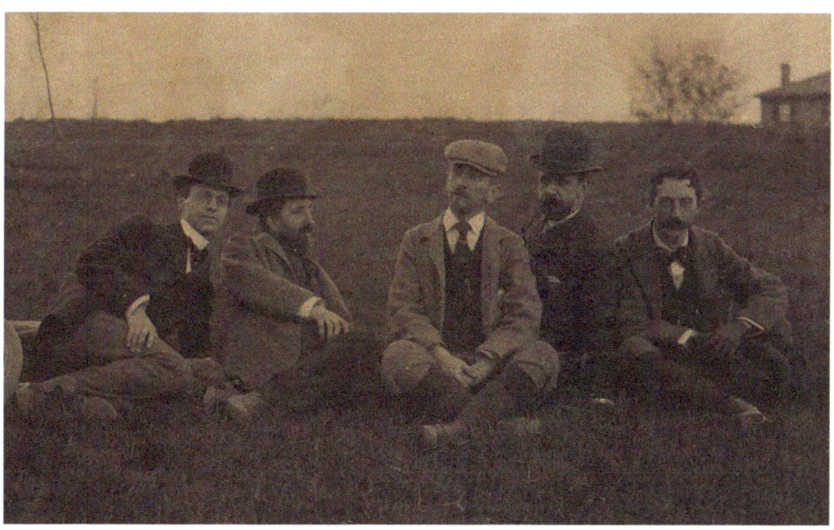

Photograph of the Vagabonds: Claude Bragdon, George Humphrey, John Dumont, Harvey Ellis, and Con Hillman. Bragdon Family Papers, A.B81, Rare Books, Special Collections, and Preservation, River Campus Libraries, University of Rochester.

Left: Claude Fayette Bragdon, cover design for *A Catalogue of American Book and Magazine Posters*, 1895. Bragdon Family Papers, A.B81, Rare Books, Special Collections, and Preservation, River Campus Libraries, University of Rochester.

Right: Photograph of Claude Bragdon in his studio. Bragdon Family Papers, A.B81, Rare Books, Special Collections, and Preservation, River Campus Libraries, University of Rochester.

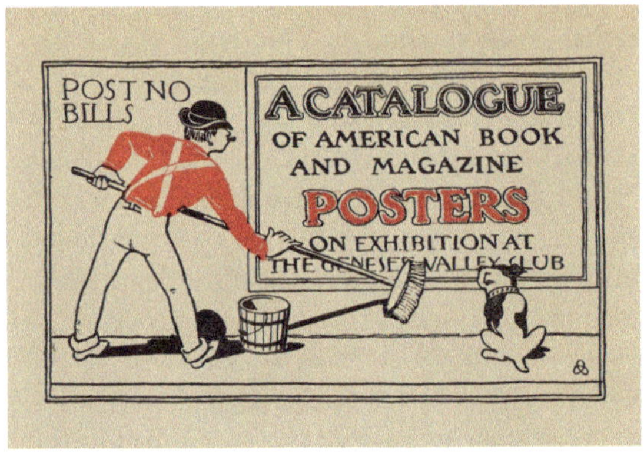


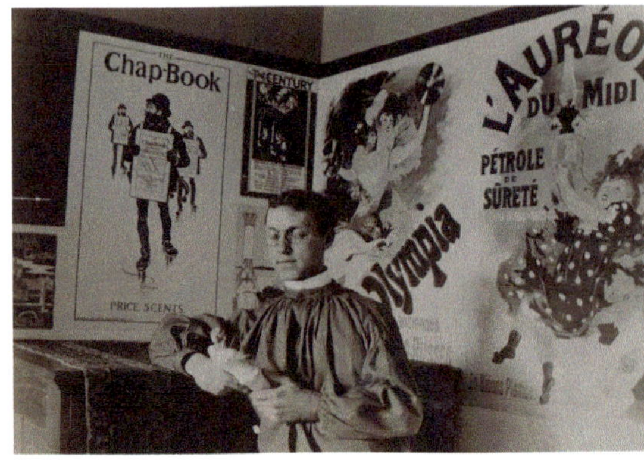


their discussions or debates, talking about everything and nothing. At the center of the discussions was Harvey Ellis. Bragdon later commented on Ellis's conversations: "His wonderful memory and powerful mental assimilation enabled him to talk with authority on almost any subject, though one could never discover where he picked up his knowledge, which perhaps after all was more wide than deep."[10]

Bragdon, as well, had a wide range of intellectual interests, often fed by the extensive home library of his family, which was especially strong in Eastern philosophy, mysticism, and Theosophy. Passionate about the bold graphic arts, he collected American magazine and book posters for some time, especially those of William Bradley, Maxfield Parrish, Edward Penfield, and Louis J. Rhead, along with the French artist Jules Chéret. He yearned to go to Europe to experience the architecture, and especially to see Chéret's posters in their original colors.

In May 1895, Bragdon mounted a comprehensive exhibition of American book and magazine posters at Rochester's Genesee Valley Club, including all of Edward Penfield's *Harper's Magazine* and Will Bradley's *Chap Book* and *Inland Printer* covers to date. Days later, he took a freighter to Europe for an extended stay.[11] First stopping in London, he moved on to Italy and finished with a month in Paris. He was dazzled with the posters he saw in Paris, eagerly seeking them out in cafés and bookstores. He returned to Rochester with a stash of thirty-five French posters, three full sketchbooks, and a portfolio of one hundred finished drawings. He quickly mounted a second exhibition at the Mechanics Institute made up of American, French, and English posters. Writing came easily to him, whether about his architectural projects or his personal theories. He published an account, complete with drawings, of his time in Italy,[12] as well as lecturing and selling many of his European sketches.[13]

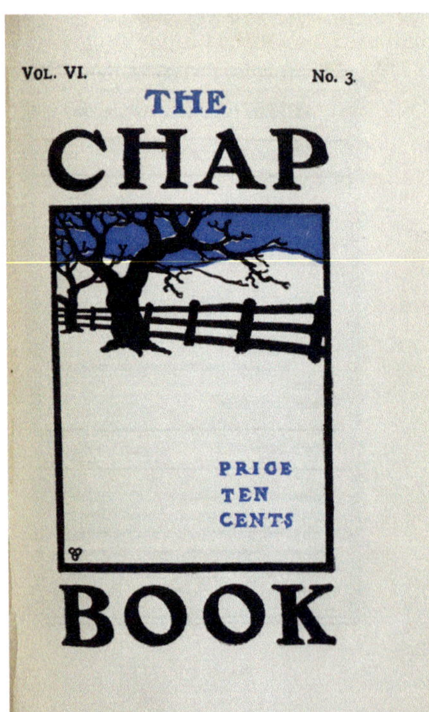


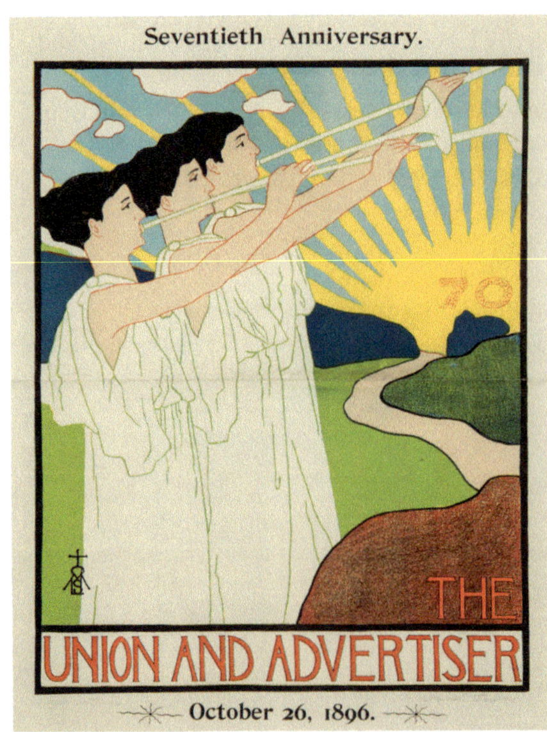


Left: Claude Fayette Bragdon, cover for *The Chap Book*, 1896. Bragdon Family Papers, A.B81, Rare Books, Special Collections, and Preservation, River Campus Libraries, University of Rochester.

Right: M. Louise Stowell, *Seventieth Anniversary of the Union and Advertiser*, October 26, 1896. Lithograph. Memorial Art Gallery: Anonymous gift, 1984.34.

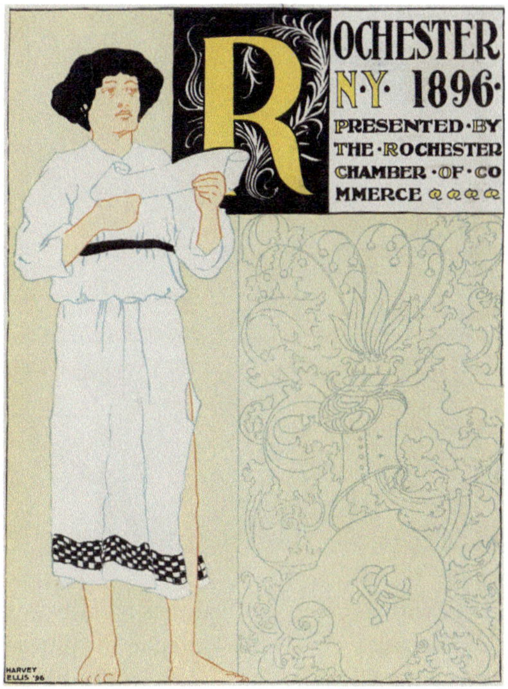


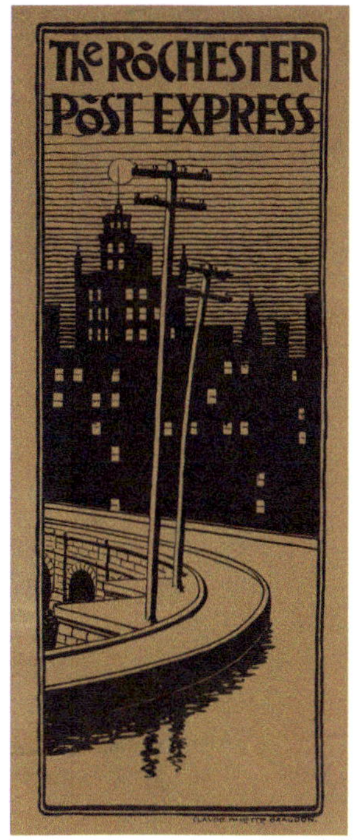


Left: Harvey Ellis, poster for the Rochester Chamber of Commerce, 1896. Lithograph. Harvey Ellis Papers, D.252, Rare Books, Special Collections, and Preservation, River Campus Libraries, University of Rochester.

Right: Claude Fayette Bragdon, poster for the *Rochester Post Express*, 1895. Lithograph. Bragdon Family Papers, A.B81, Rare Books, Special Collections, and Preservation, River Campus Libraries, University of Rochester.

Over time, he would become a prolific writer in topics ranging from Theosophy to theater.

On his return from Europe, Bragdon infused his two friends, Ellis and Stowell, with his passion for posters. They all eagerly became engaged in the graphic process of designing advertising posters as well as exhibition programs and posters. In quick succession, Bragdon designed three posters for *The Chap Book* (1895) and a cover design the year after, as well as posters for the local paper, the *Post Express*. The Rochester *Union and Advertiser* had Ellis design a poster in 1895, and Stowell in 1896, for its seventieth anniversary. Both Ellis and Bragdon would design for Scribner's. Poster design demands that the artist work in a flattened, two-dimensional style very similar to Japanese prints of the *ukiyo-e* style. This graphic art experience gave Ellis and Stowell the preparation for taking a flat, two-dimensional approach to their art. Stowell would state in an interview: "Posters are the fairy tales of art and fairy tales are a pleasant relief from more grave subjects. . . . A poster is an instantaneous view—something which one apprehends at a glance. The masses are broad and simple, all superfluous detail is lopped off and the imagination of the spectator is unconsciously set at work to supply the missing links."[14]

Around 1895, George Humphrey's bookstore became the subject of Stowell's poster, *George P. Humphrey at the Sign of the "Old-Book Man."* The work was chosen for inclusion in *Les Maitres de l'Affiche*, a highly respected French portfolio of 256 color posters issued by subscription to collectors. In 1896, Stowell entered an international poster competition in Leipzig, where she was the only American competitor and also the only woman. Her *Third National Cycle Exhibition* poster took honorable mention. These accolades brought a great deal of attention to Stowell both locally and internationally.

Just as he had with architecture, when Ellis first turned his energies back to painting, he rambled through a great many styles and subjects: marine scenes with guns blazing in deep saturated colors; tonalism (moody, deeply personal, spiritual); and mythical, religious, and medieval themes. At the same time, Stowell, working in watercolors, was beginning to apply to her own artwork what she had learned from two summers studying under Dow. They both were ready for an upheaval in their art.

When Stowell and Ellis came together artistically, they seemed to go through a metamorphosis, shedding their cocoons of Western art to conceive a fresh approach. They began to experiment with new techniques to help them adhere to Dow's and the Japanese principles of composition: line, color, and *notan*, the harmonious arrangement of darks and lights. Stowell readily credited the Japanese for her inspiration. "Theirs," she stated, "is the very essence of art, an art which is at once intellectual, emotional and spiritual but which is always dominated by reason."[15]

Stowell would later describe their method of working thus: "Some time ago a group of artists living in Rochester, N. Y., becoming dissatisfied with the existing methods of water color painting, experimented together with the view of evolving some way of using that medium to achieve full, rich and low-keyed color . . . which the ordinary way of handling water color lacks."[16]

Their creative process was labored, thoughtful, and original. They would first sketch on a piece of charcoal paper pasted on a drawing board. Then specific areas were shaded with the side of a

Left: Harvey Ellis, *Silhouettes–Boats*, 1899. Watercolor, charcoal, and black ink on paper. Memorial Art Gallery: Virginia Jeffrey Smith Fund, in honor of Grant Holcomb and Marie Via, 2016.31.

Right: Claude Fayette Bragdon, cover for the *Rochester Arts and Crafts Society Exhibition* catalog, 1897. Bragdon Family Papers, A.B81, Rare Books, Special Collections, and Preservation, River Campus Libraries, University of Rochester.

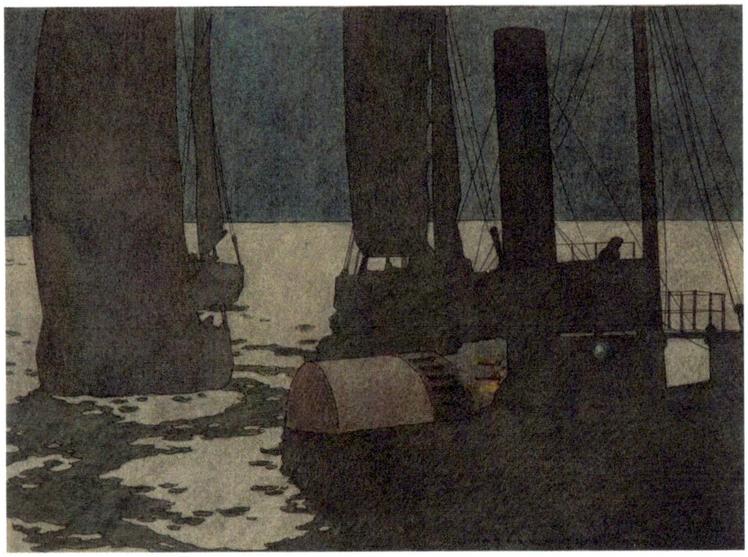

stick of charcoal, then smoothed out with a piece of chamois leather. Areas outside the shaded areas were cleaned up and sprayed with fixative, after which a transparent wash of some warm color was laid down. Finally, the artist applied many layers of watercolors over the carefully prepared charcoal images, producing deep, rich colors. The color palette of these paintings operated within a very narrow range, producing an almost tonal effect. The end result was a harmonious, evocative tone poem. Bragdon described them as "hauntingly beautiful"[17] and "with the depth and richness of a Persian rug."[18]

In these years, interest in the Arts and Crafts movement was growing nationwide, but especially in New York state. In April 1897, Stowell, Ellis, and Bragdon formed the Rochester Arts and Crafts Society, the first in the country. Ellis served as president, Bragdon as vice president, and Stowell as secretary. Its purpose was to hold exhibitions to educate the public about the ideals of the Arts and Crafts movement. Most groups dedicated to the movement came together to sell their handcrafts, but the group in Rochester was made up of artists mainly interested in exploring the theoretical foundations of the movement. Beginning with eighteen members, they held an exhibition of Japanese prints and modern French posters in a commercial space on Rochester's East Avenue. The exhibition featured seventy-three Japanese prints and sixty-five European prints, posters, and covers. The Japanese prints came mainly from the collections of Stowell and Ellis, and the French posters from Bragdon. The catalog contained an essay introducing Japanese prints by Mrs. Elizabeth Fenollosa, the first wife of Ernest Fenollosa. The focus of the essay was the artistic influence the Japanese aesthetic had on the philosophies of the Arts and Crafts movement.

This exhibition was followed in June 1897 by an exhibition of modern photography, with more than a hundred Pictorialist-style works by fifty

Left: Harvey Ellis, copyright label for John Dumont, photographer, 1897. Courtesy of Photoseed.com.

Right: M. Louise Stowell, *A Silver Moon*, 1905. Watercolor and charcoal on paper. Memorial Art Gallery: Virginia Jeffrey Smith Fund, in honor of Grant Holcomb and Marie Via, 2016.93.

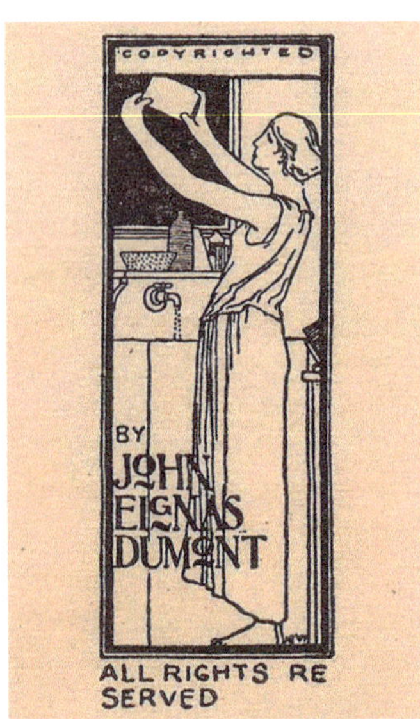


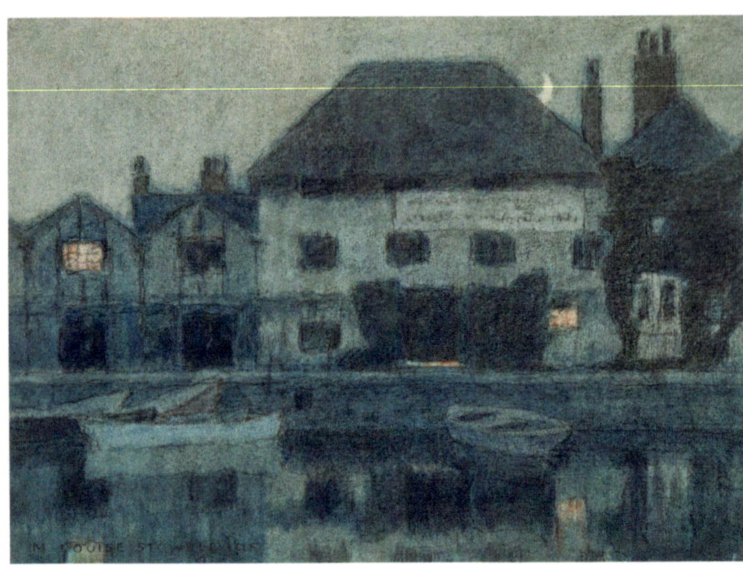

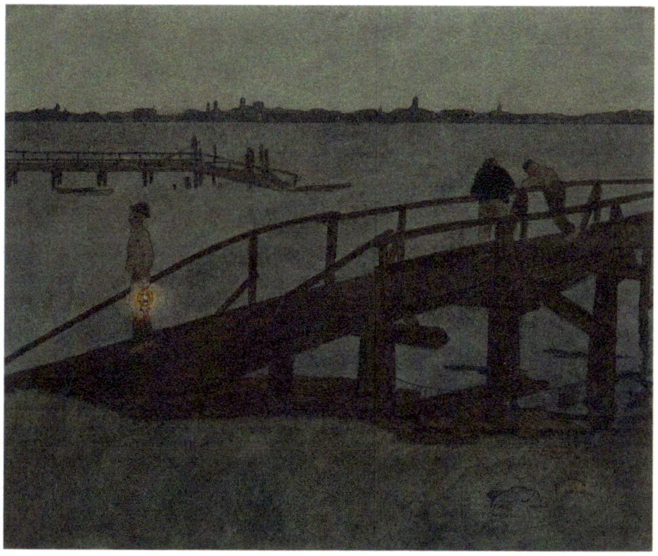

M. Louise Stowell, *Men on a Dock*. Watercolor, charcoal, black ink, and touches of gouache on laid paper. Memorial Art Gallery: Virginia Jeffrey Smith Fund, in honor of Grant Holcomb and Marie Via, 2016.108.

photographers from Europe and America. It was mainly organized by Harvey Ellis and John Dumont, a Rochester photographer and a member of the Arts and Crafts Society's executive committee.[19] The local paper declared, "To the layman the exhibition will be a revelation. In artistic photography the day of the glossy photograph with sharp and accentuated lines and minuteness of detail is a thing of the past."[20] This was a perfect exhibit for Rochester, since 1892 the home of Eastman Kodak. At a meeting of the society in 1898, Stowell herself gave a lecture on Japanese prints that was reviewed in the local news.[21]

Many of their pictures during this period depict scenes at twilight or evening, which allows saturated colors with a water element so that the reflections on the water mass bring balance to the composition. Structures, whether a boat, building, or pier, allowed them to articulate "line" in the massing of the areas, such as a pattern or mosaic of varying tones within the picture. Very often, there is a small, diffused light source such as an interior house light, a lantern, or a sliver of a moon, which adds a feeling of tranquility to the overall composition.

The work of Ellis and Stowell became almost interchangeable in these years. They often entered the same exhibitions, both locally and regionally. Critics grouped their work together and almost always recognized and noted the Japanese influence in their art. They were able to see the abstraction representing the essence of a scene and the overall harmony achieved in the composition. Many reviewers liked their work, while others, who were used to perspective and careful reproductions of nature, could not grasp what these two artists, so strongly influenced by Japanese *ukiyo-e* woodcuts, were attempting to do.

Only two artists from Rochester, Stowell and Ellis, were asked to show work in the Pan-American Exposition in Buffalo, held from May to November 1901. Stowell exhibited her *The Steps* (1900) and Ellis showed three watercolors: *Silhouettes—Boats* (1899), *The Burning Bush* (1896), and *The Towers* (date unknown). *The Steps* was also on view at the Watercolor Society exhibition in New York, where it was singled out for mention in *Harper's Bazar*. They both showed widely: the Art Institute of Chicago, New York Water Color Club, Philadelphia Watercolor Club, and the American Watercolor Society.

Bragdon's sister May was a diarist and a shutterbug, documenting all three artists at various times and helping both Stowell and Ellis in buying their own cameras. Here a rare glimpse is provided of how an artist can use photography in lieu of long sessions with live models. Stowell posed for Ellis in preparation for his painting *The Hour Glass* (1898). Then she posed for her own painting of Philosophia (1902) sitting on her throne. It is likely there were other examples that have not survived.

All three also designed stained glass windows. Bragdon designed a crow on a grapevine for the front door of his own house, which he called "Cro'Nest" in honor of the crows living nearby on the property. May Bragdon mentioned in her diary that she "had gone to see a very fine stained glass window (medieval) designed by Harvey."[22] Ellis also exhibited some designs for stained glass in 1903, and *The Craftsman* has many stained glass designs among Ellis's drawings for his articles. Stowell made a number of drawings and watercolor paintings for murals, friezes, and

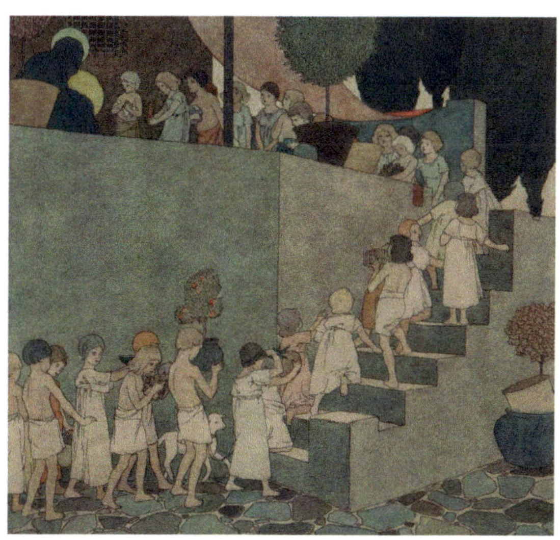

Stowell's *The Steps* was exhibited at both the Water Color Society's exhibition in New York and the Pan-American Exposition in Buffalo in 1901.
M. Louise Stowell, *The Steps*, 1900. Watercolor, pastel, charcoal, and ink on laid paper. Memorial Art Gallery: Virginia Jeffrey Smith Fund, in honor of Grant Holcomb and Marie Via, 2016.106.

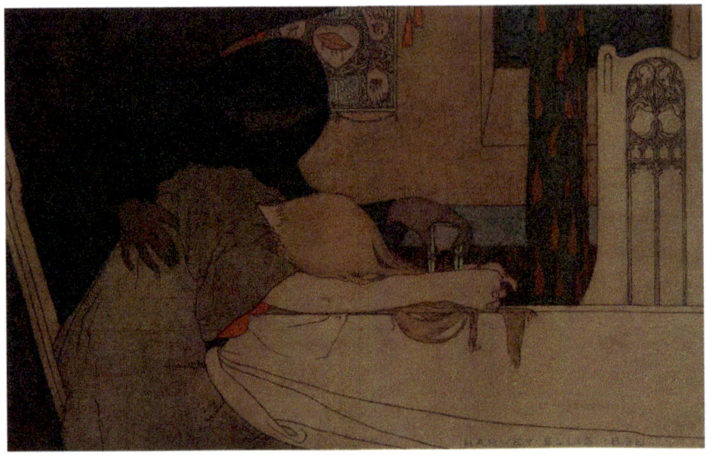

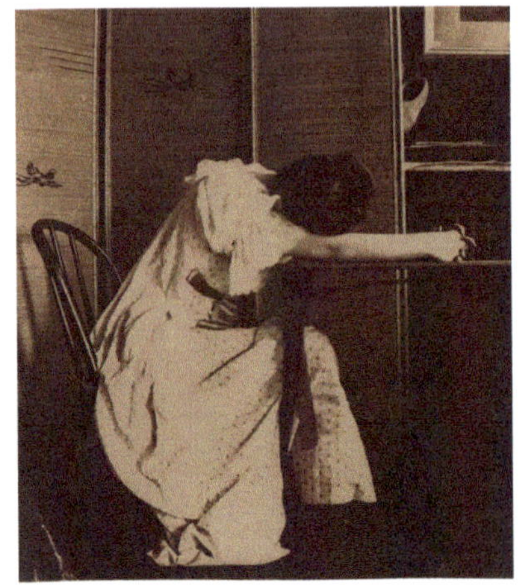

Left: Harvey Ellis, *The Hour Glass*, 1898. Watercolor, ink, charcoal, and gouache on laid paper. Memorial Art Gallery: Virginia Jeffrey Smith Fund, in honor of Grant Holcomb and Marie Via, 2016.27.

M. Louise Stowell posing for "The Hour Glass," 1898. Silver gelatin print. M. Louise Stowell Papers, D.506, Rare Books, Special Collections, and Preservation, River Campus Libraries, University of Rochester

stained glass, all bearing a religious theme. They may have been intended for her family's mausoleum in Rochester. Studies for mural paintings also occupied their creative endeavors for a while.

Different color palettes emerge for different periods and decorative trends: Victorian, French Impressionism, Pre-Raphaelite. While paints came in cakes and tubes ready-made by manufacturers, most artists liked to grind their colors themselves. Color occupied the minds of all three artists as well as their discussions. Stowell and Ellis would layer color over roughed-up paper to achieve their desired tones. Stowell's drawings often include marginal notes about potential color combinations. All three wrote about color, starting with Stowell's early essays for teachers. She would later write, "The Japanese artist does not consider the independent colors with the objects . . . but devotes his energies to the final result of his combinations . . . the outcome being the value of the separate combinations, plus the value of the sum total of their combinations."[23] Bragdon wrote that "[Ellis] learned to trust his instinct in the matter of color, and his instinct never played him false. . . . His color was never wrong, and it became clearer, fuller, more sonorous, with the passing years."[24]

Bragdon and Ellis had many discussions about the interiors of a simple bungalow—wall colors, ceiling colors, fireplace colors—especially around the building of Bragdon's own home. For their inspiration in the creation of a harmonious color palette, they drew from two sources: the surrounding nature of the dwelling and Japanese prints. Ellis wrote, "We shall find aid in our problem in the simple, restrained color schemes found in the better Japanese color prints. Here we have colors of the utmost subtlety combined frankly with that delicate appreciation of the intimate relations of tones."[25] Ellis and Bragdon wrote about these principles in their essays in *The Craftsman*, thus providing the unofficial guidelines for the Arts and Crafts color palette. A century later, their principles of harmonious combinations are still in use today in the Arts and Crafts revival movement.

In 1903, the Mechanics Institute utilized the talents of the leaders of the Arts and Crafts Society when it hosted an exhibition of Arts and Crafts furniture and accessories. All three artists would have been known to officials of the Mechanics Institute; at various times, they had all taught there (Stowell, 1890–1894; Ellis, 1897; and Bragdon, 1894–1897; Stowell and Ellis had jointly taught a regular Saturday art course open to the general

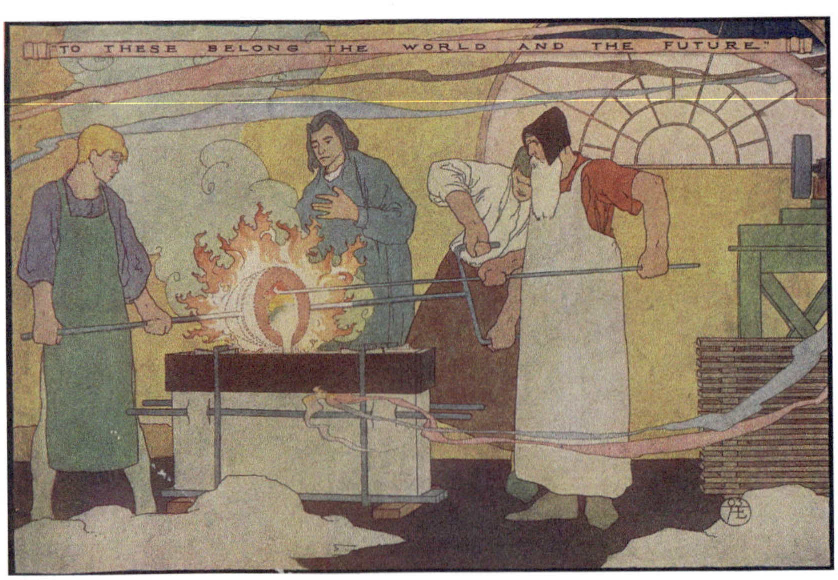


Harvey Ellis, *To These Belong the World and the Future*, 1903. Bragdon Family Papers, A.B81, Rare Books, Special Collections, and Preservation, River Campus Libraries, University of Rochester.

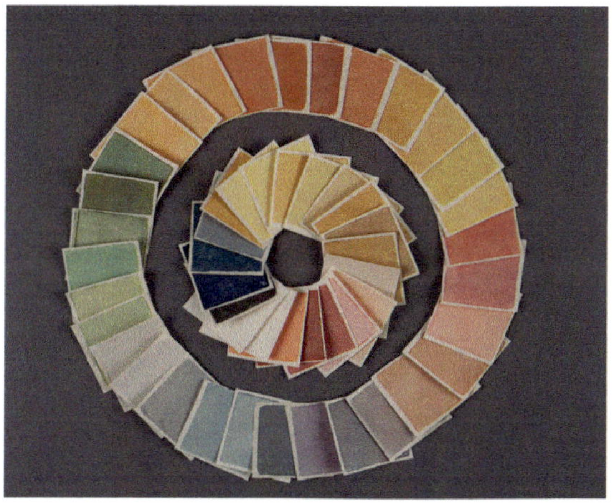

Color Samples, Ukiyo-e Print Colorant Database, Conservation and Art Materials Encyclopedia Online, Museum of Fine Arts, Boston, https://cameo.mfa.org/wiki/Ukiyo-e_Print_Colorant_Database, accessed May 15, 2024. Photograph © 2024 Museum of Fine Arts, Boston.

public in the 1890s). Gustav Stickley's intentions in mounting the exhibition in Syracuse to display the wares from his company, the United Crafts, were unabashedly commercial. However, the motives for the Rochester venue were primarily educational. Ellis was asked to take the lead role in staging the exhibition in Rochester, visiting Syracuse several times to familiarize himself with Stickley's exhibition. For Rochester, he redesigned the installation, changed the name from *Arts and Crafts Exhibition* to *Exhibition of Art Craftsmanship*, and designed the exhibition poster, while Bragdon created the program cover. Ellis, Stowell, and Bragdon worked together closely as they installed the exhibition, adding work by local artists, including some of their own.[26]

The *Exhibition of Art Craftsmanship at the Mechanics Institute* opened in April of 1903 and marked the swan song of the trio's work together in Rochester. Stickley had hired Ellis to come and work for his company, the United Crafts, in Syracuse. Both Claude's mother Katherine and sister May suggest in their respective diaries that Claude played a major part in Harvey's move to Syracuse through his brother-in-law Henry Wilkinson, a furniture designer for Stickley. Katherine wrote, "Claude has secured a position for Harvey with Stickley to design furniture."[27] However, Ellis had probably impressed Stickley with his talents on his own.

In any event, by May 1903, Ellis was ensconced in Syracuse, designing furniture, and writing and designing covers for *The Craftsman*. In a letter to his sister May in July, Bragdon wrote, "[Harvey] is working very hard and looks worn and old, but he's doing great stuff, as good as he has done in his life. The influence of Stickley is just what it should be—it subdues and chastens Harvey's naturally riotous fancy. He's designing a series of covers for *The Craftsman*."[28] He added, "*The Craftsman* and the furniture are vastly better by reason of his ministrations."[29]

Stickley never named a specific position for Ellis, but it is a widely held belief that Ellis engineered a design revolution in Stickley's furniture business, resulting in the more delicately scaled items and inlay decoration that began to appear mid-1903.[30] Ellis repeatedly drew chairs, dressers, and chests of drawers with curved aprons for the articles he wrote. His articles appeared from July through December, and he enlisted his friends to contribute, with Bragdon writing articles in August and September and Stowell contributing a major opus, "Japanese Color Prints and Some of Their Makers," in October. Meanwhile, Ellis's health declined. Bragdon reported to his mother, "Harvey is hopelessly ill in St. Joseph's Hospital with Brights disease, heart trouble, etc."[31] Bragdon visited him and brought money collected from friends, but by the beginning of January, Ellis was dead.

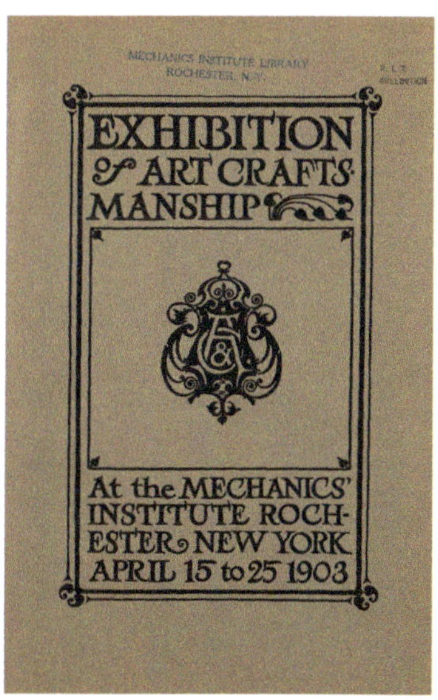


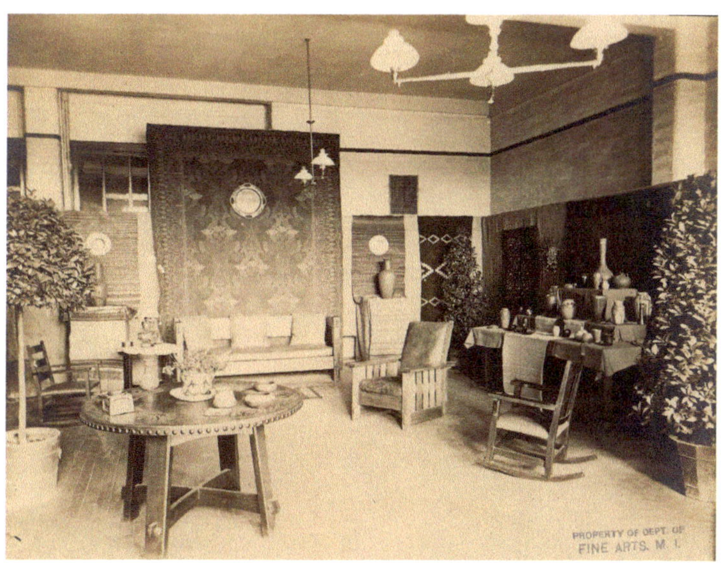


Left: Claude Bragdon, Poster for Exhibition of Art Craftsmanship, held at the Mechanics Institute, Rochester, NY, April 15 to 25, 1903. RIT Archives.

Right: Exhibition of Art Craftsmanship, held at the Mechanics Institute, Rochester, NY, in the Eastman Building, Plymouth Avenue, April 15 to 25, 1903. RIT Institutional Photograph collection.

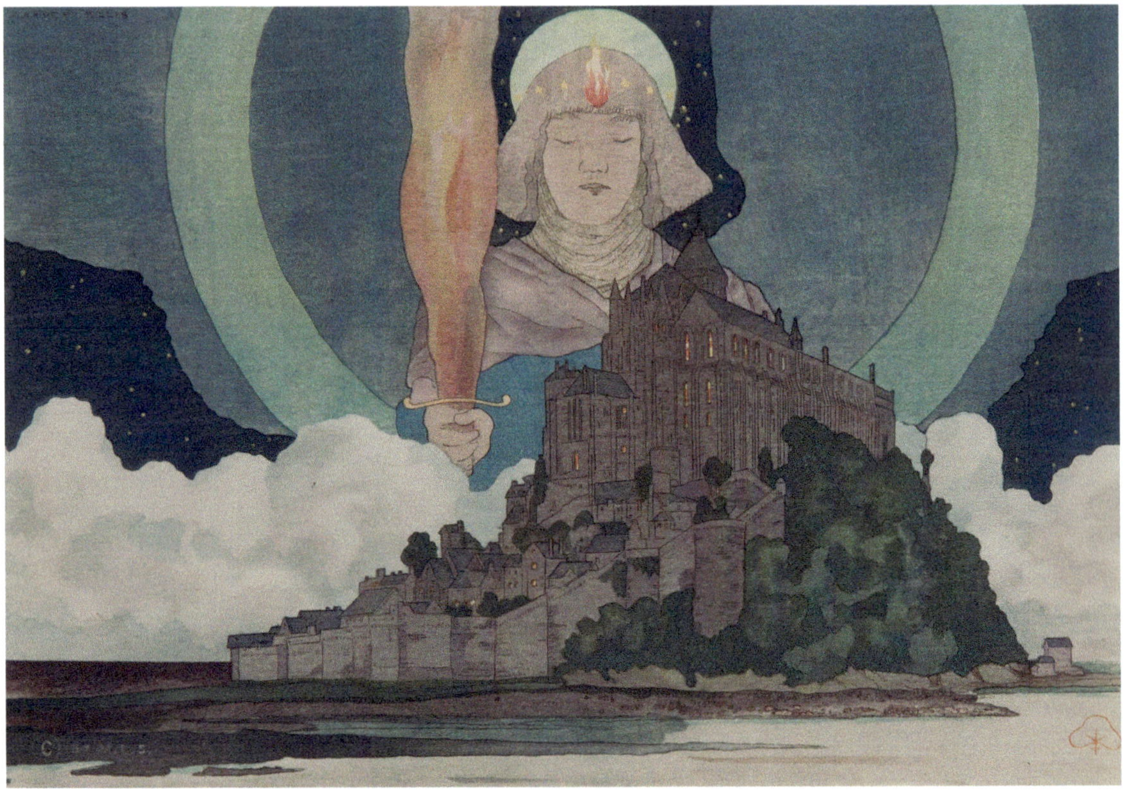

M. Louise Stowell and unknown Japanese artist, *Mont St. Michel* (after Harvey Ellis). Color woodcut. Memorial Art Gallery: Virginia Jeffrey Smith Fund, in honor of Grant Holcomb and Marie Via, 2016.178.

Later in 1904, Stowell returned to teaching at the Mechanics Institute in the newly formed School of Arts and Crafts. She taught there until 1908, when she retired due to health issues. In memory of Ellis, she wrote about him and mounted an exhibit of his work, and she had three of his paintings turned into woodcuts to honor her friend. Bragdon began to get major architectural commissions and became deeply involved in mysticism and Theosophy, becoming a prolific writer and lecturer on a range of topics. His commissions would continue to grow, culminating in 1914 with his designs for the New York Central Railroad Station in Rochester. He later turned all his energies to the New York theater. In 1905, the same Arts and Crafts team minus one—Stowell and Bragdon with Ada Howe Kent—helped to organize the *Exhibition of Art of Handicraft* under the auspices of the Mechanics Institute.[32]

Bragdon would say of Ellis, "I believe that Harvey possessed little real capacity for friendship. His friends chose him, rather than he them, and the burden to sustain the relation was theirs also."[33] But for a period of ten years, these three sustained a friendship that explored new ways to realize their artistic aspirations, established the Rochester Arts and Crafts Society, created thought-provoking exhibitions, and supported each other in exploring new ideas.

## Notes

1 M. Louise Stowell, "Decoration," *Educational Gazette*, 1892. *Educational Gazette* was a publication aimed at instructing art teachers. Stowell would continue to write articles for art teachers for several years.
2 M. Louise Stowell, "Decoration."
3 M. Louise Stowell, "The New School of Art," *The Artist*, 1892.
4 Stickley used the name "The United Crafts" as his company name from 1901 through September 1903, and then renamed it "Craftsman Workshops."
5 Claude Bragdon, "Harvey Ellis: A Portrait Sketch," *Architectural Review* XV, no. 7 (December 1908): 173.
6 Eileen Manning Michels, *Reconfiguring Harvey Ellis* (St. Paul, MN: Beaver's Pond Press, 2004), 180.
7 Claude Bragdon, *More Lives Than One* (Cosimo Classics, New York, 2006), 40–41.
8 Bragdon, *More Lives Than One*.
9 Bragdon, "Portrait Sketch," 176.
10 Bragdon, "Portrait Sketch," 175.
11 Although Bragdon would refer to it as his *wanderjahr*, his trip lasted from May 25 to September 29, 1895.
12 See his series of articles, "Everyday Italy," in *American Architect and Building News* LI (February 15, 1896): 71–74; VI (March 7, 1896): 107–109; VI (March 21, 1896): 127–130; and LII (April 4, 1896): 3–4.
13 Andrea Reithmayr, *Claude Bragdon & the Beautiful Necessity* (Rochester: Cary Graphic Arts Press, 2010), 102–3.
14 "Fair Woman's World" column, *[Rochester] Post Express*, April 10, 1897, 18.
15 "Fair Woman's World."
16 M. Louise Stowell, "Water Color Over Charcoal," *Palette and Bench*, September 1910, 284.
17 Claude Bragdon, "Harvey Ellis," *Brochure Series of Architectural Illustration*, September 1897, 139.
18 Bragdon, "Portrait Sketch," 173.
19 The inclusion of photography had become a common practice in Arts and Crafts exhibitions.
20 "To Give Remarkable Exhibition of Pictures," *Union and Advertiser* (Rochester, NY), June 19, 1897, 12.
21 *Post Express* (Rochester, NY), February 16, 1898, 10.
22 May Bragdon diaries, entry for June 29, 1897, Bragdon Family Papers, A.B81, Rare Books, Special Collections, and Preservation, River Campus Libraries, University of Rochester, https://maybragdon.lib.rochester.edu.
23 M. Louise Stowell, "Japanese Color Prints and Some of Their Makers," *The Craftsman* V, no. 1 (October 1903), 67.
24 Bragdon, "Portrait Sketch," 178.
25 Harvey Ellis, "A Note of Color," *The Craftsman* V, no. 2 (November 1903): 156.
26 May Bragdon diaries, entry for April 14, 1903. May noted in her diary, "Two weeks of 'Arts and Crafts' show . . . Claude had some good things in the show—also . . . Harvey, Miss Stowell &c."
27 Claude Bragdon to his mother, Katherine Bragdon, May 27, 1903, Bragdon Family Papers, A.B81, box 85, folder 7, Rare Books, Special Collections, and Preservation, River Campus Libraries, University of Rochester (per email from Andrea Reithmayr to Susan Futterman, September 23, 2013).
28 Claude Bragdon to his mother, Katherine Bragdon, July 26, 1903.
29 Claude Bragdon to Henry Wilkinson, July 20, 1903, Bragdon Family Papers, D.255.
30 Michels, *Reconfiguring Harvey Ellis*, 207.
31 Katherine Bragdon diaries, entry for December 2, 1902, Bragdon Family Papers, A.B81, box 85, folder 7, Rare Books, Special Collections, and Preservation, River Campus Libraries, University of Rochester.
32 Bruce Austin, *A Symbiotic Partnership* (Rochester: RIT Press, 2022), 55.
33 Bragdon, "Portrait Sketch," 174.

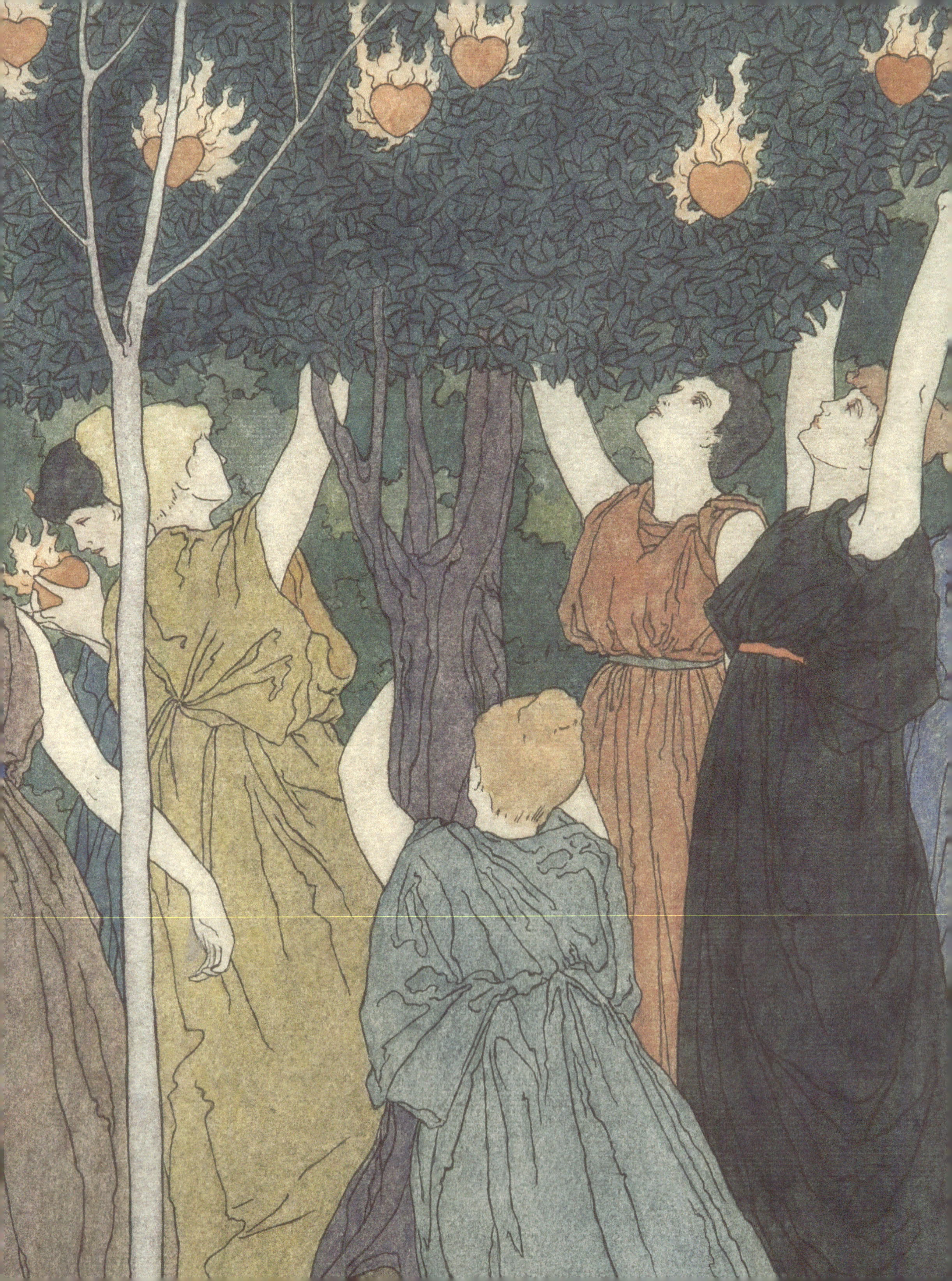

# M. Louise Stowell and Harvey Ellis: Characteristics of Their Artworks

Patricia D. Hamm

M. Louise Stowell and Harvey Ellis often worked closely together and inspired in each other a mutual creativity. In many cases, attempts to discern authorship of unsigned artworks can be challenging, if not downright impossible. As a conservator of fine art on paper, I have had the privilege of closely examining and treating several dozen artworks by both Ellis and Stowell and can claim some familiarity with their working techniques and aesthetic preferences. However, I also realize that in many cases, their working techniques overlap to such an extent that, without a signature, absolute discernment between them becomes unlikely. The following observations may help others to corroborate their own findings and observations.

Stowell's compositions tended to favor flatter designs using fewer details than Ellis. Ellis typically employed more detailed patterns in his compositions and tended to add many more small details. Ellis also appeared to exhibit a greater use of perspective and architectural details than Stowell.

Their similarities are more numerous than their differences. Both Stowell and Ellis shared the same laid paper as a support. The initial preparation of the laid paper was to apply an overall light layer of charcoal, thoroughly worked into the paper surface. (See further discussion of this technique in Susan Futterman's essay.) After about 1898, they both outlined the subject matter with black ink, thus providing crisper edges to their otherwise diffuse images. This technique relates to that used by Japanese woodblock print artists who used outlining to similar effect. Stowell and Ellis also both used a smudging technique to soften or eliminate drawn charcoal lines, adding to the challenge of detecting any signature style of underdrawing. On some artworks, they both borrowed a Japanese aesthetic for handling the distant sky of a landscape by employing horizontal bands of what appears to be Prussian blue pigment. Small details like windows containing spots of color or distant lampposts or lights add a wonderful sense of space and a liveliness in otherwise dimly lit scenes at dusk or night. They both refined their subject matter to pure patterns or forms and occasionally introduced patterns of bold color. This effect can be seen in some Japanese woodblock prints.

Throughout the history of art, artists have collaborated in various ways, whether as artist assistant/student/apprentice or through other more defined business relationships. Stowell and Ellis apparently did experiment and work side by side, using similar materials, techniques, and even subject matter. However, they did not mask the authorship of their art, as each signed their finished artworks. Definitively identifying authorship of the unsigned works will always remain challenging.

Detail of: M. Louise Stowell, *The Garden of the Hesperides*, 1900. Watercolor, pastel, charcoal, and ink on laid paper. 2016.122.
*See page 48 for full image.*

# Catalog of Images

Unless otherwise noted, images are from Memorial Art Gallery: Virginia Jeffrey Smith Fund, in honor of Grant Holcomb and Marie Via.

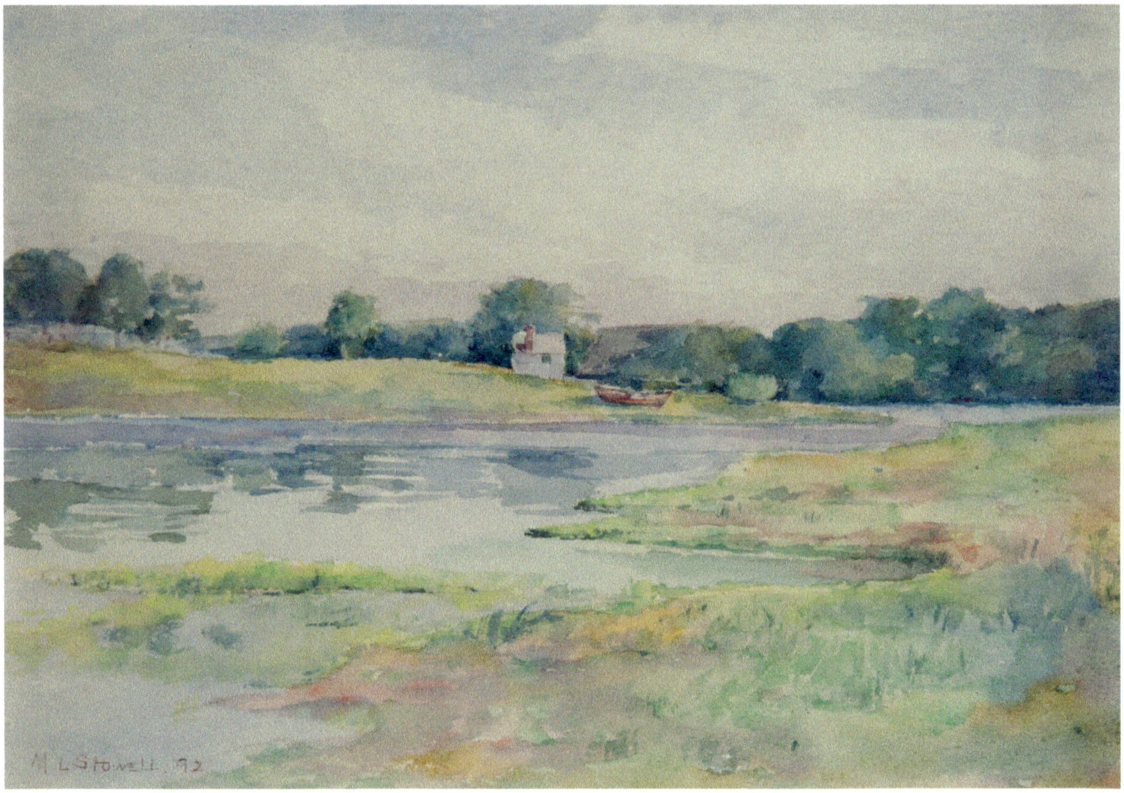

M. Louise Stowell, *Landscape with House and Boat*, 1892. Watercolor and graphite on paper. 2016.102

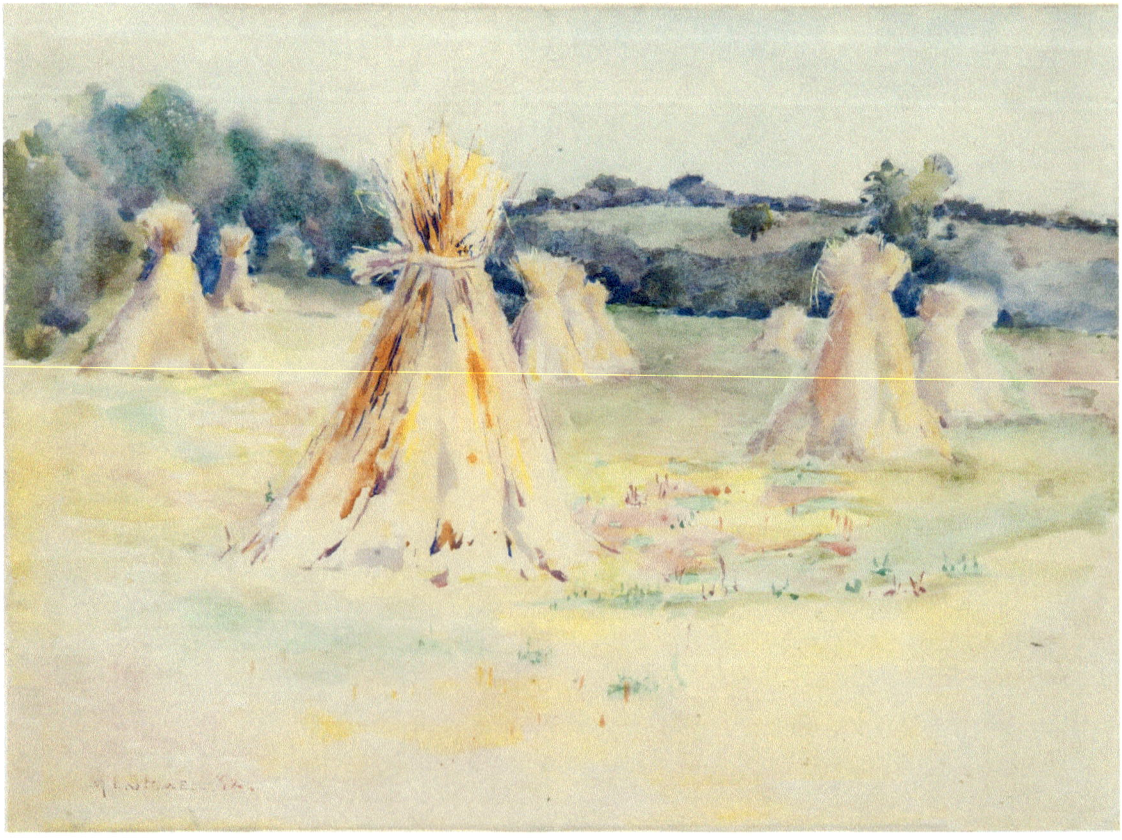

M. Louise Stowell, *Haystacks*, 1892. Watercolor and graphite on paper. 2016.105

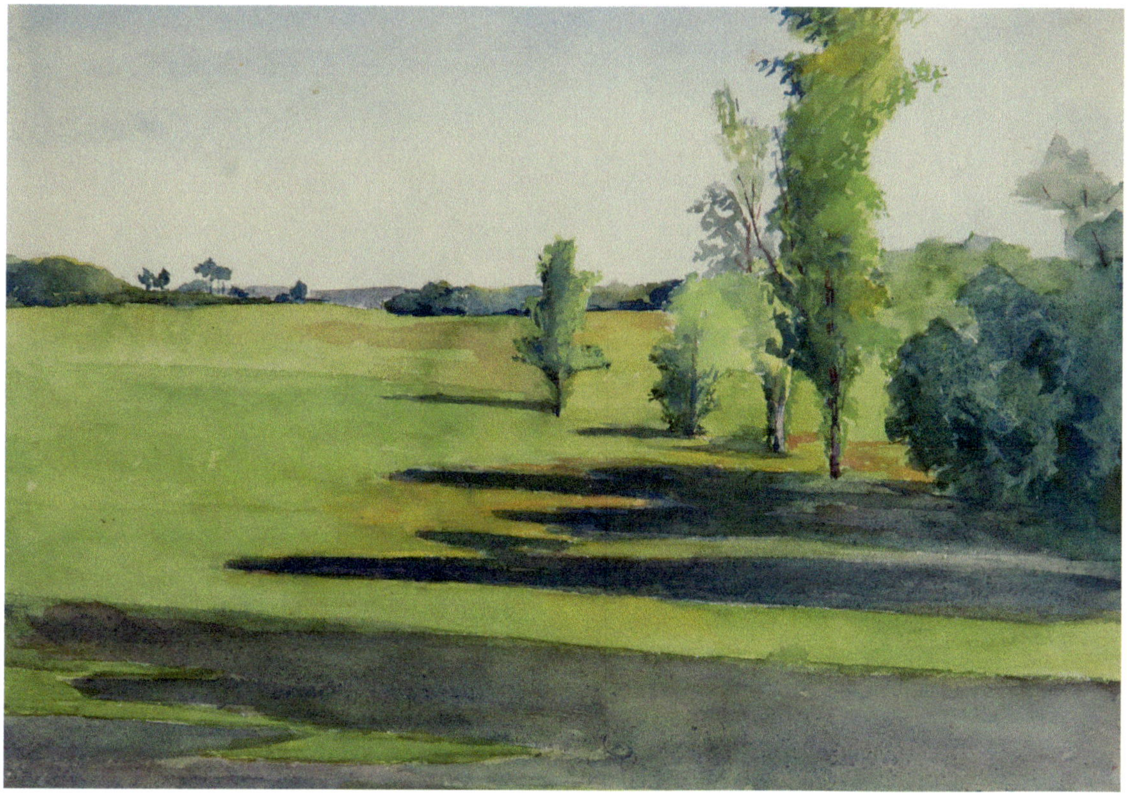

Attributed to M. Louise Stowell, *Grassy Landscape with Trees*, 19th century. Watercolor and pencil on paper. 2016.154

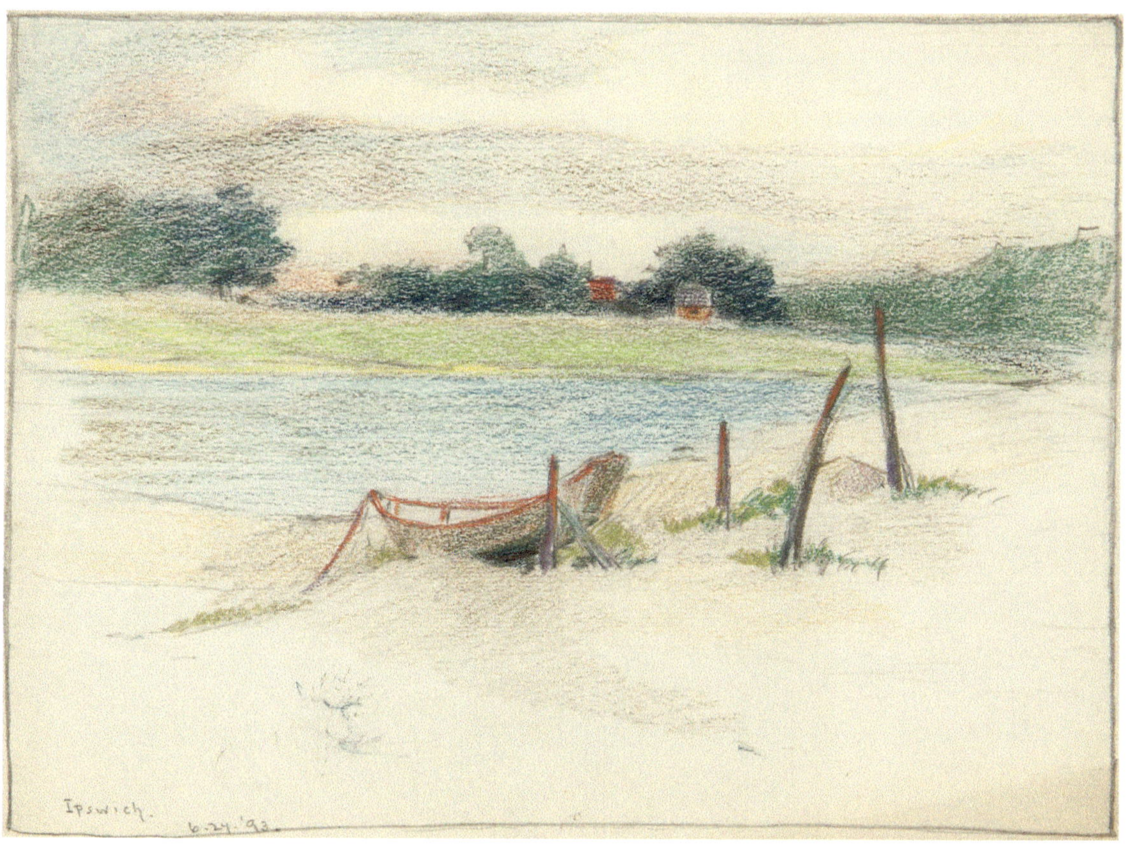


Attributed to M. Louise Stowell, *Landscape, Ipswich*, 1893. Colored pencil and graphite on paper. 2016.168

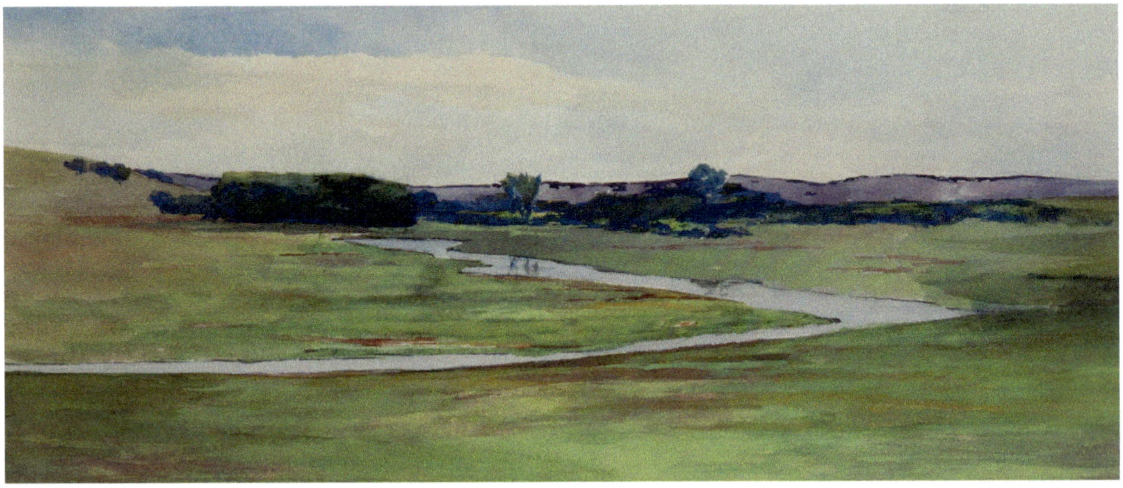

Attributed to M. Louise Stowell, *Landscape with Stream*, 19th–20th centuries. Watercolor on paper. 2016.152

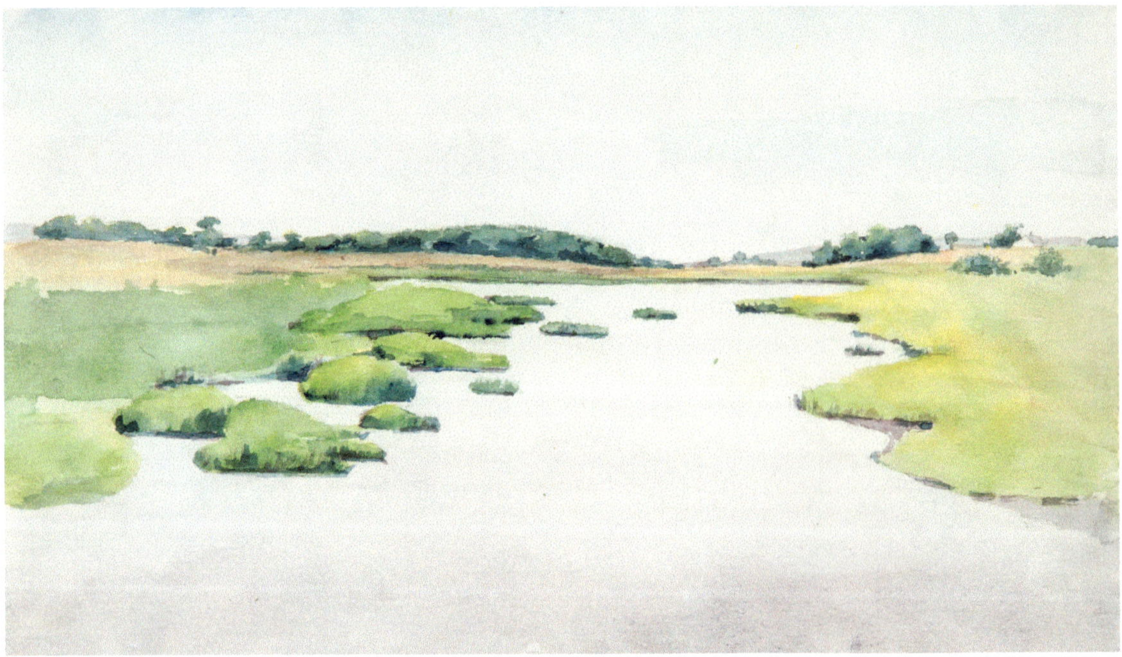

Attributed to M. Louise Stowell, *Marsh Scene*, 19th–20th centuries. Watercolor and graphite on paper. 2016.153

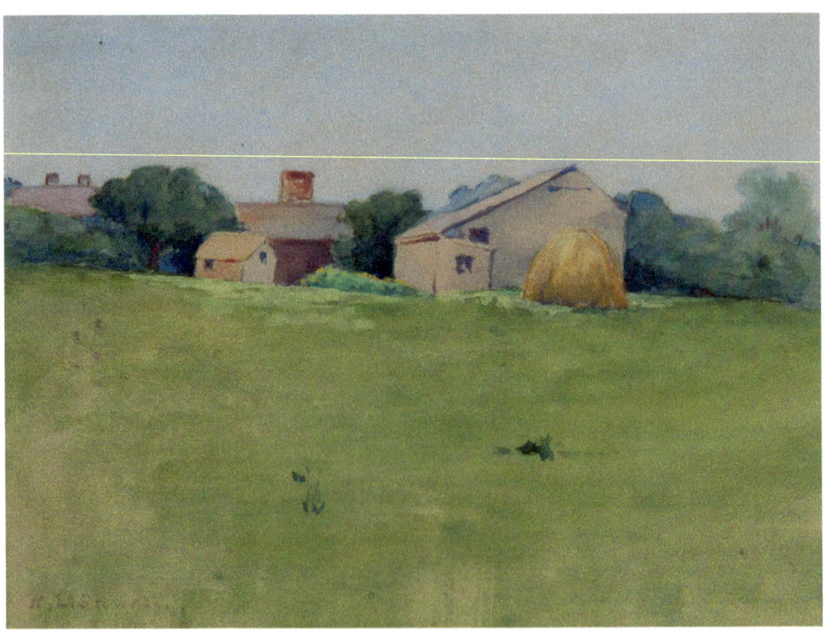

M. Louise Stowell, *Farmhouse Scene with Haystack*, 19th century. Watercolor and gouache on paper. 2016.134

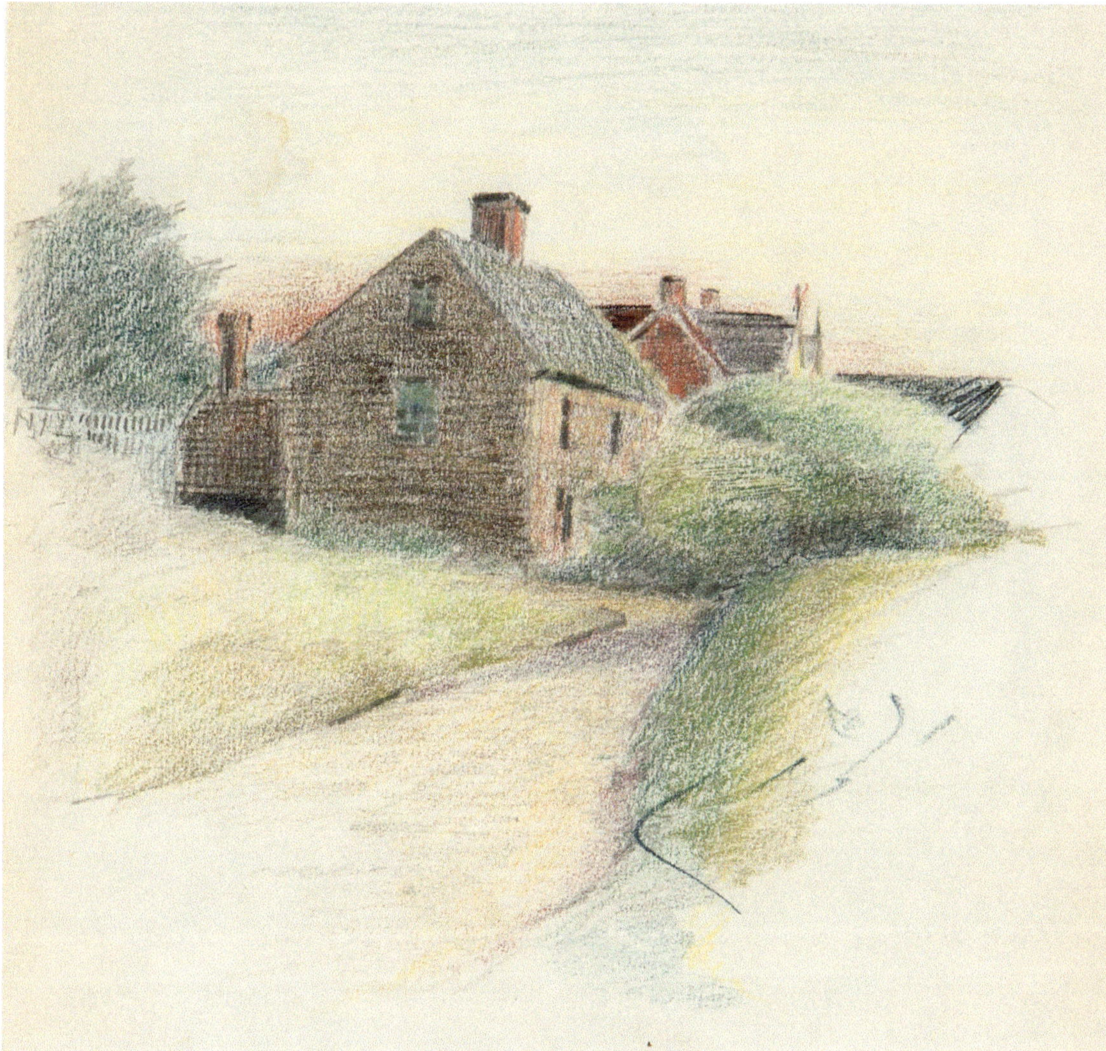

Attributed to M. Louise Stowell, *Landscape with Road to House*, 19th–20th centuries. Colored pencil and graphite on wove paper. 2016.167

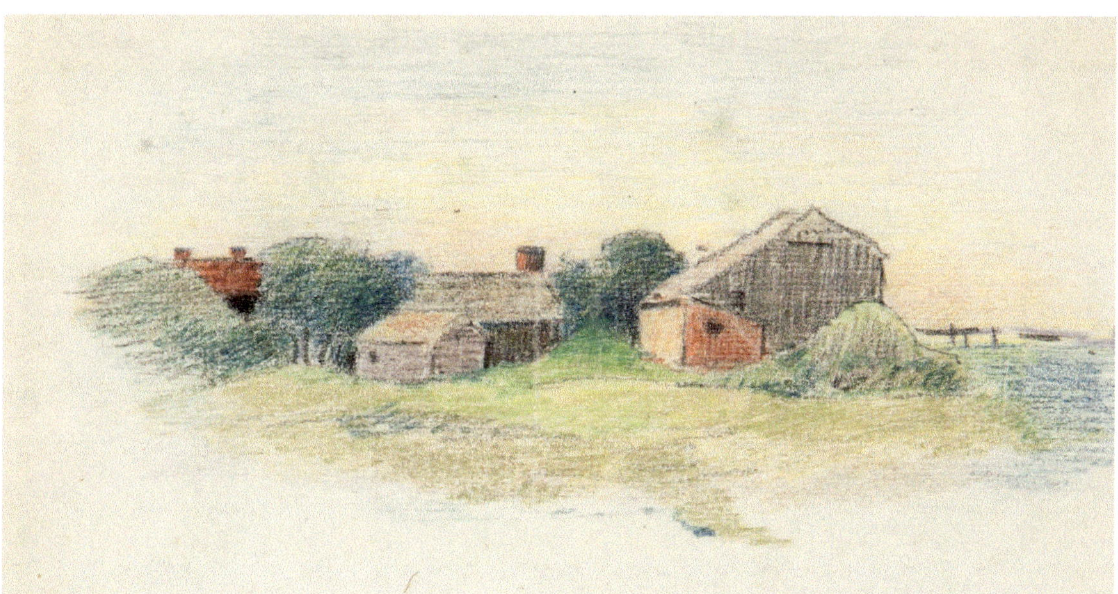

Attributed to M. Louise Stowell, *Rural Landscape with Distant Bridge*, 19-20th centuries. Colored pencil and graphite on paper. 2016.166

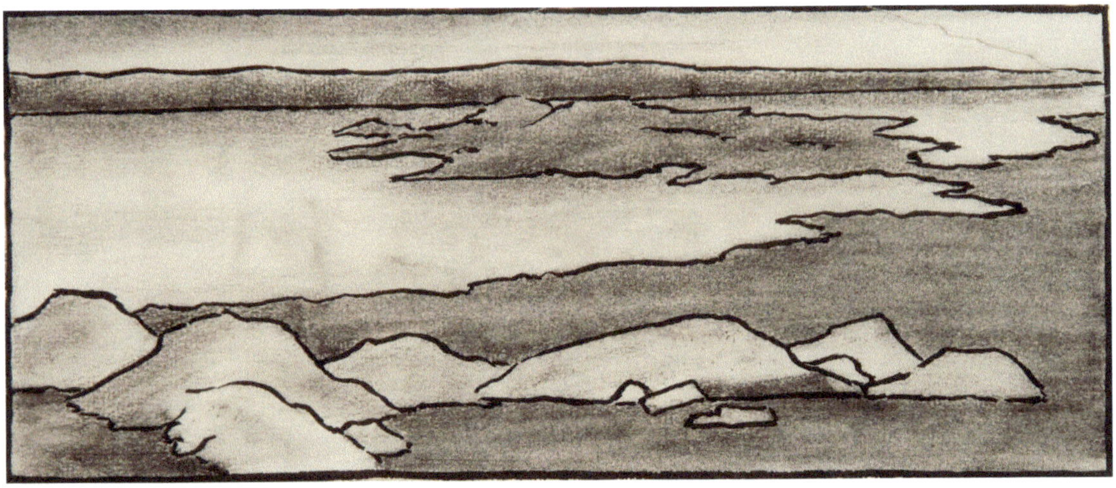

M. Louise Stowell, *Marshy Landscape*, 19th–20th centuries. Charcoal and black ink on paper. 2016.145

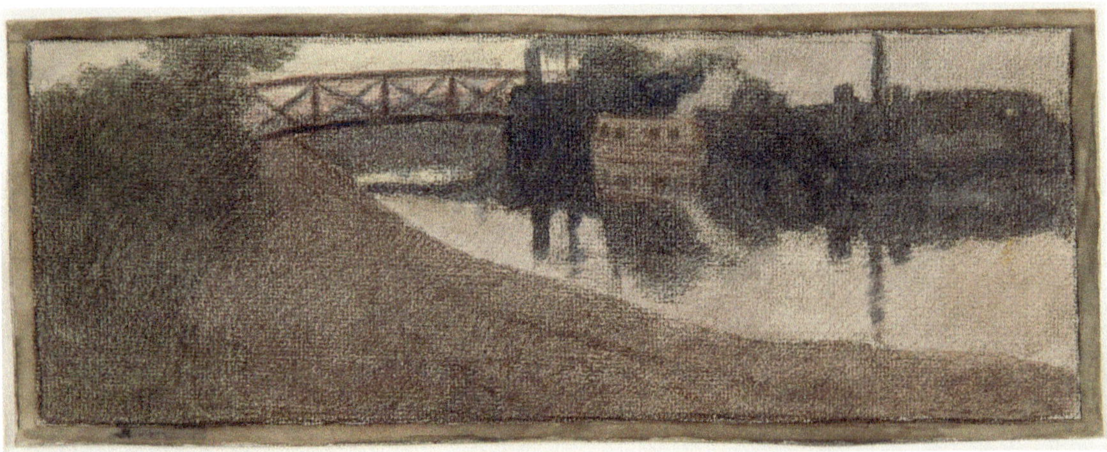

M. Louise Stowell, *Bridge over Canal*, 19th century. Watercolor and charcoal on paper. 2016.151

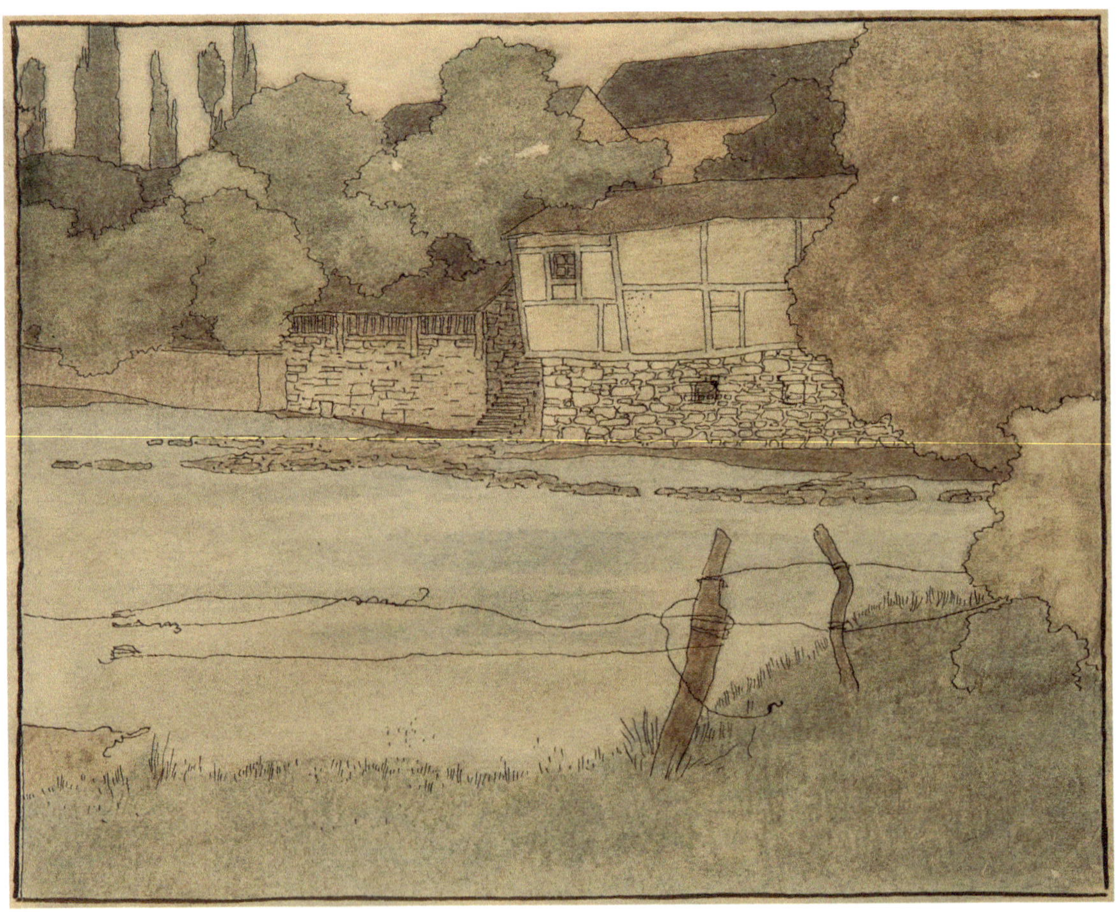

M. Louise Stowell, *Mill Building with Fence*, 19th century. Watercolor, pastel, charcoal, and black ink on paper. 2016.131

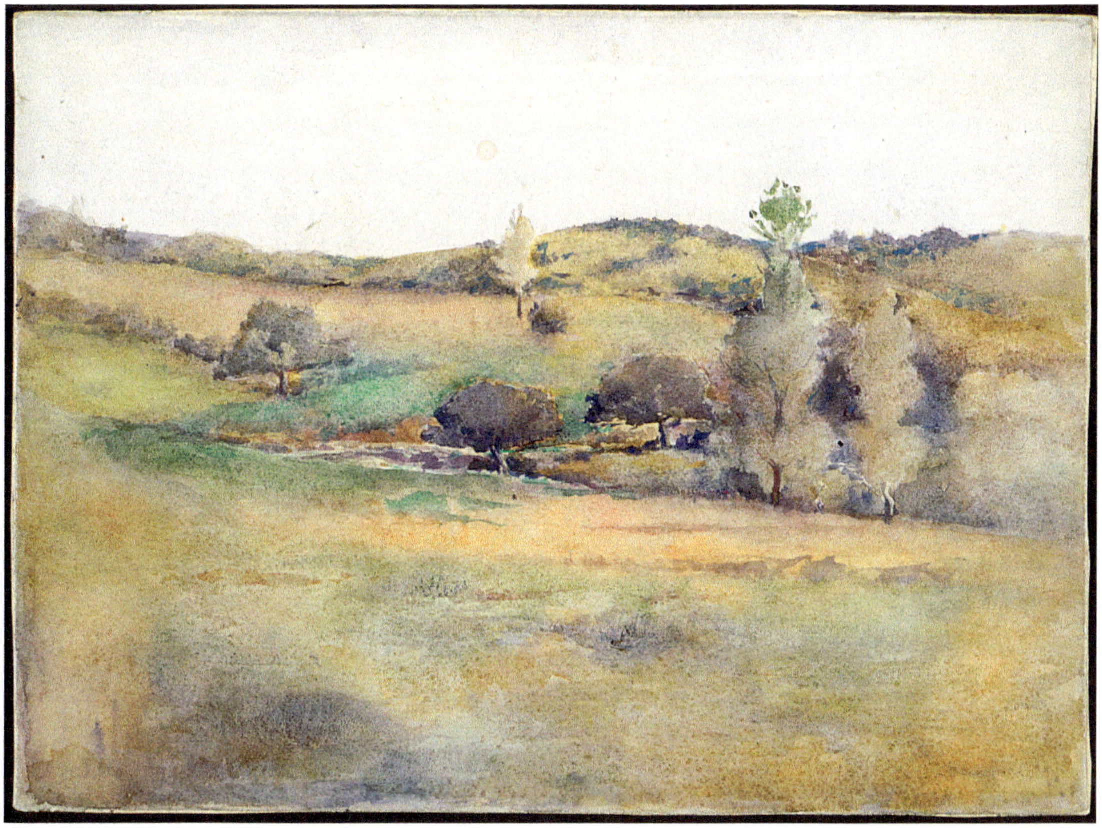

M. Louise Stowell, *Landscape with Trees*, 19th–20th centuries. Watercolor and graphite on paper. 2016.150

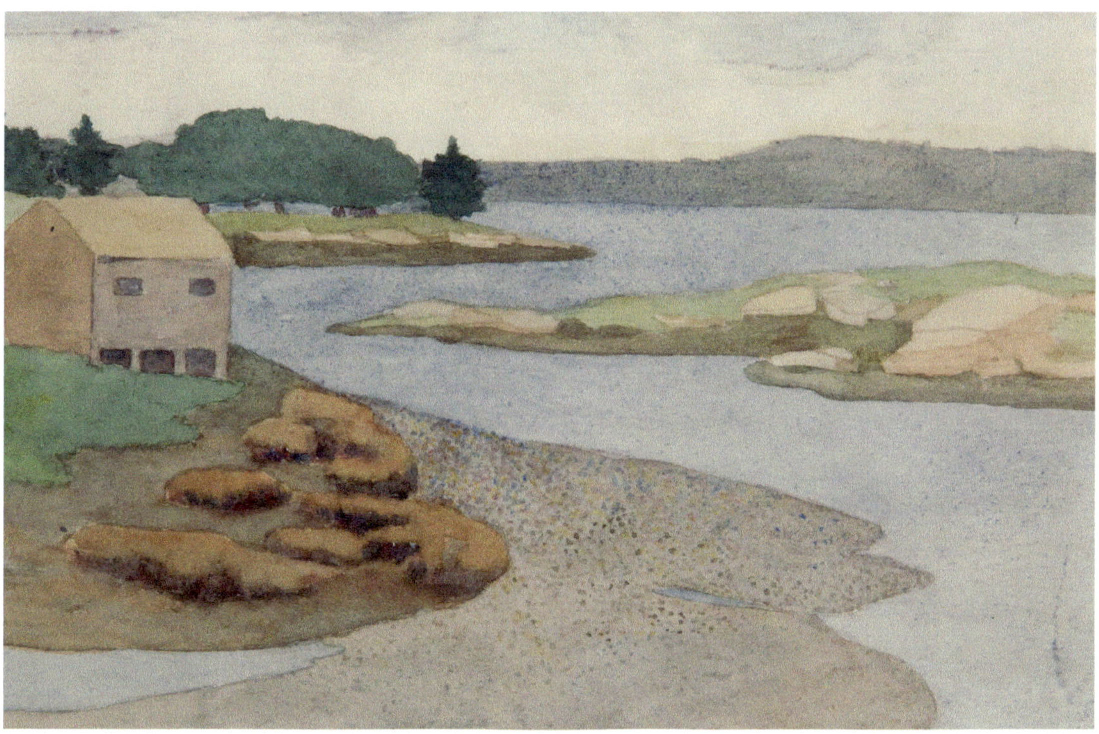

Attributed to M. Louise Stowell, *House on the Shore*, 19th–20th centuries. Watercolor and pencil on paper. 2016.173

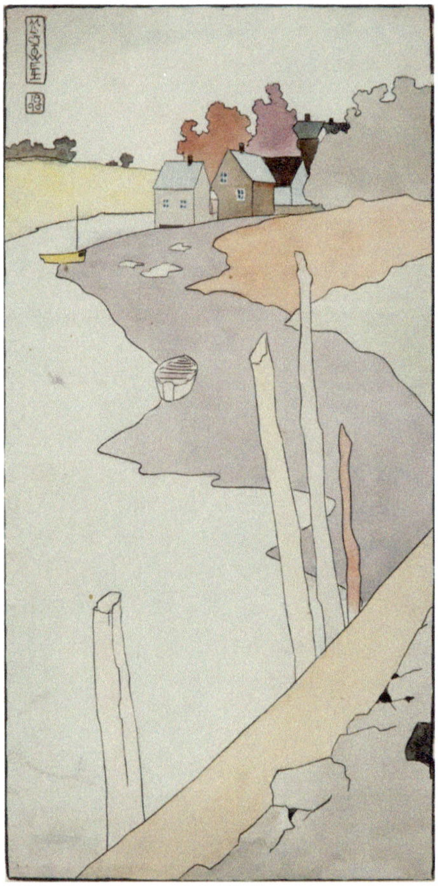

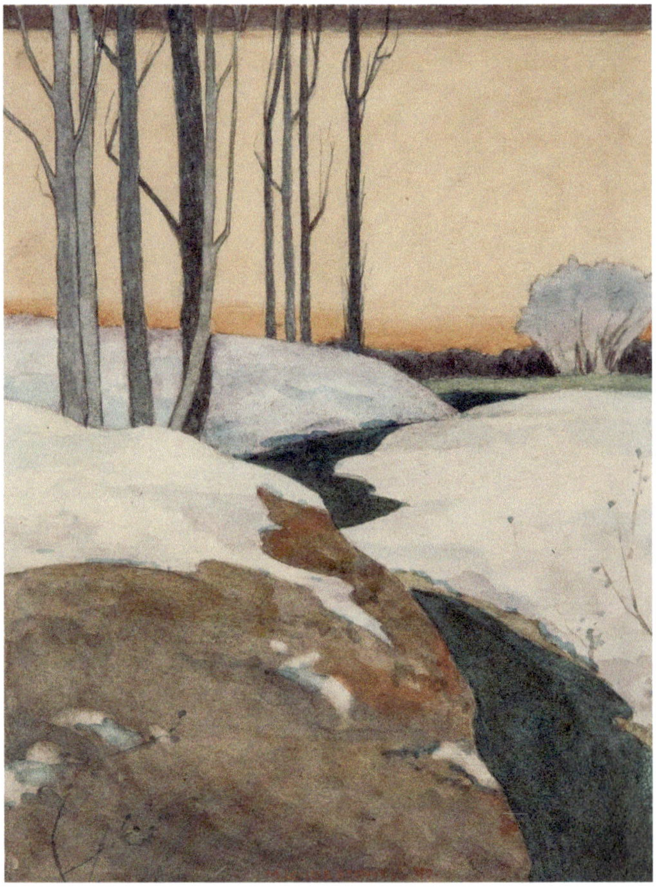

Left: M. Louise Stowell, *Dunes with Boat*, 1895. Watercolor, black ink, and graphite on paper. 2016.107

Right: M. Louise Stowell, *Winter Landscape*, 1897. Watercolor and graphite on paper. 2016.109

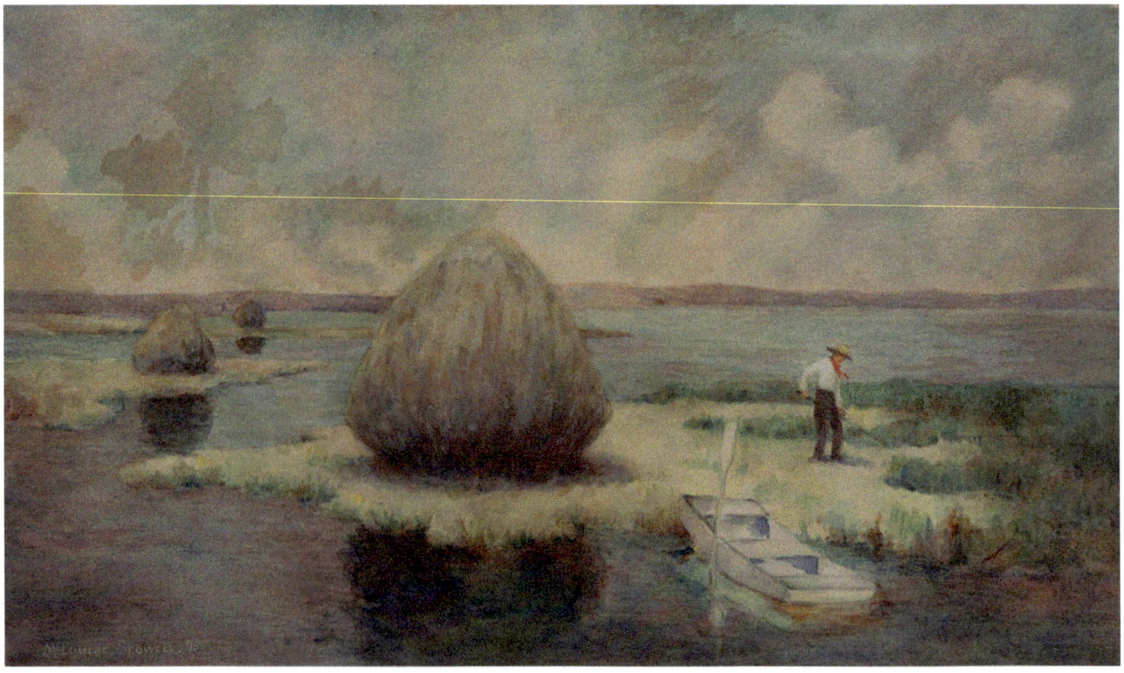

M. Louise Stowell, *On the Marshes*, 1895. Watercolor on paper. Bequest of Miss Gertrude Chappell, 1951.70

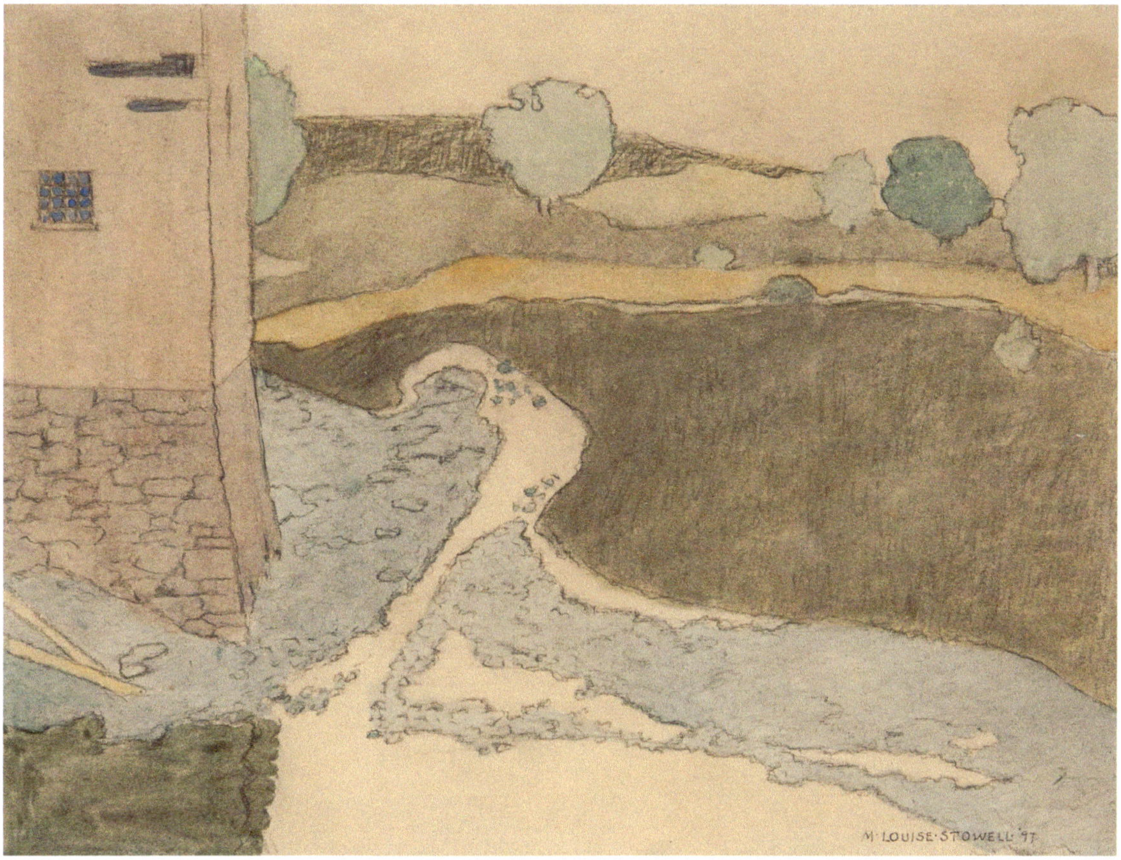


M. Louise Stowell, *Landscape with Mill*, 1897. Watercolor, charcoal, and graphite on paper. 2016.103

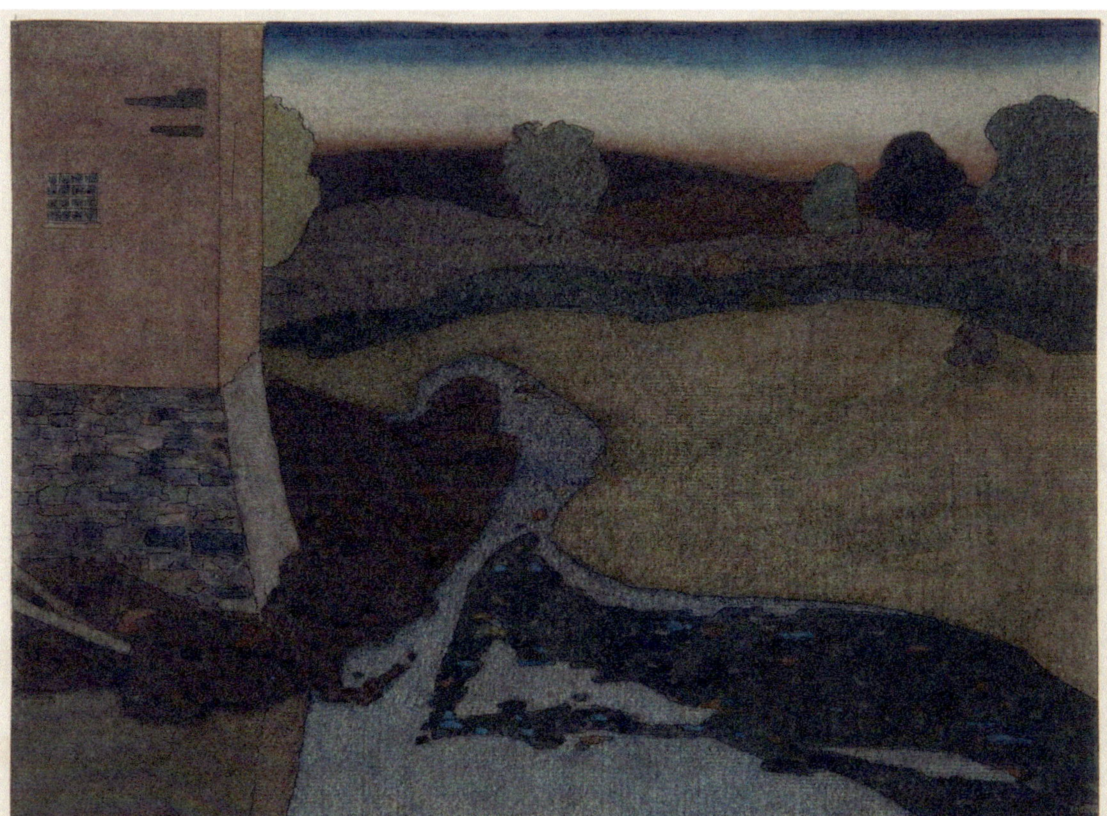

M. Louise Stowell, *Landscape with Mill*, 1901. Watercolor, pastel, charcoal, and black ink on laid paper. 2016.163

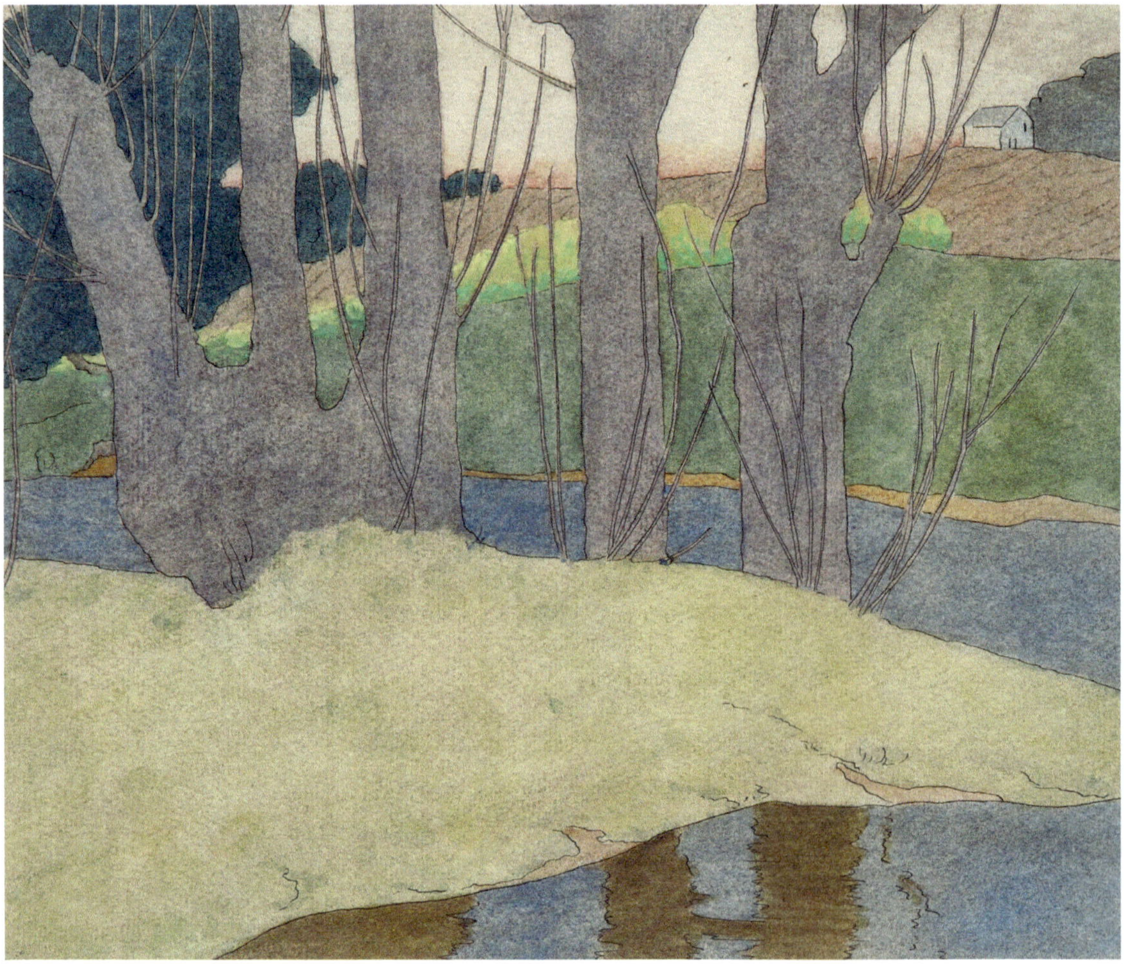

M. Louise Stowell, *The Screen of Willows, Brighton*, 1899. Watercolor, charcoal, gouache, and black ink on paper. 2016.89
*See related work on page 7.*

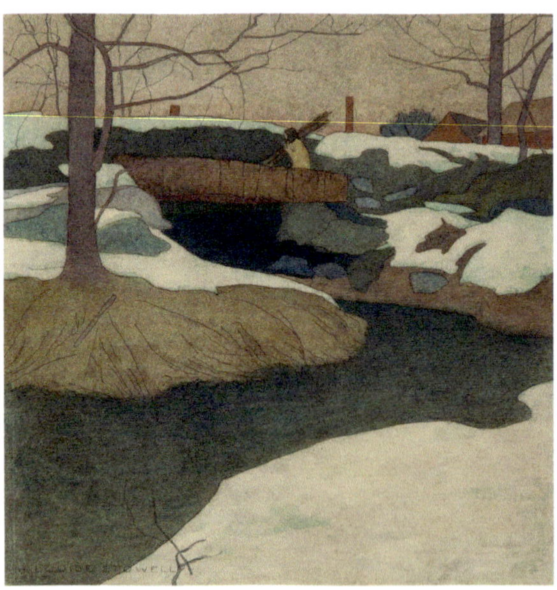

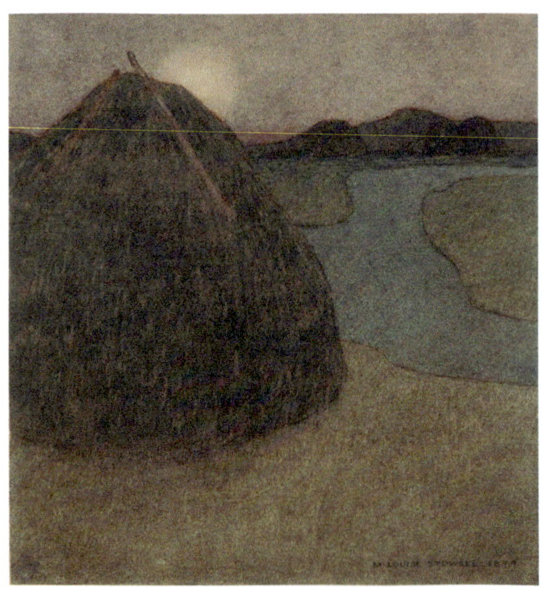

Left: M. Louise Stowell, *Winter Landscape with Stream*, 1900. Watercolor and charcoal on laid paper. 2016.126

Right: M. Louise Stowell, *Haystack, Moonlight*, 1899. Watercolor and charcoal on paper. 2016.124

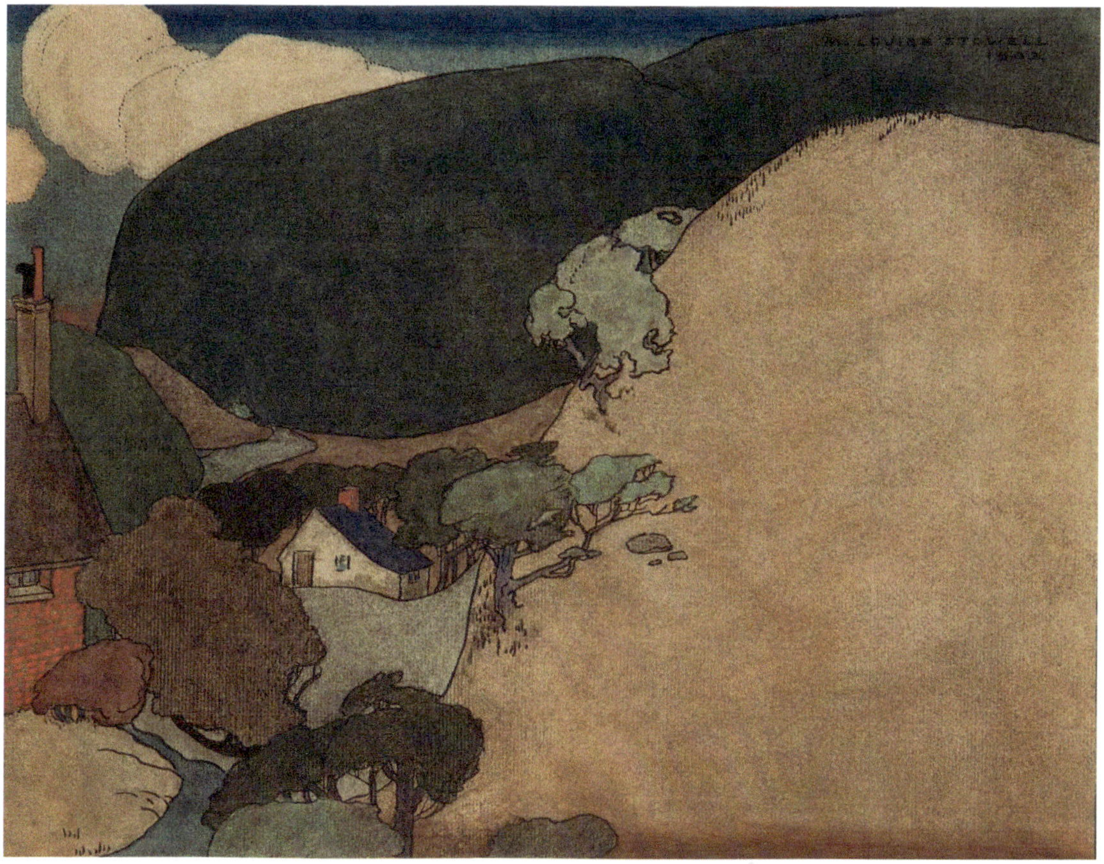

M. Louise Stowell, *Houses in a Valley*, 1902. Watercolor, pastel, charcoal, gouache, and black ink on laid paper. 2016.135

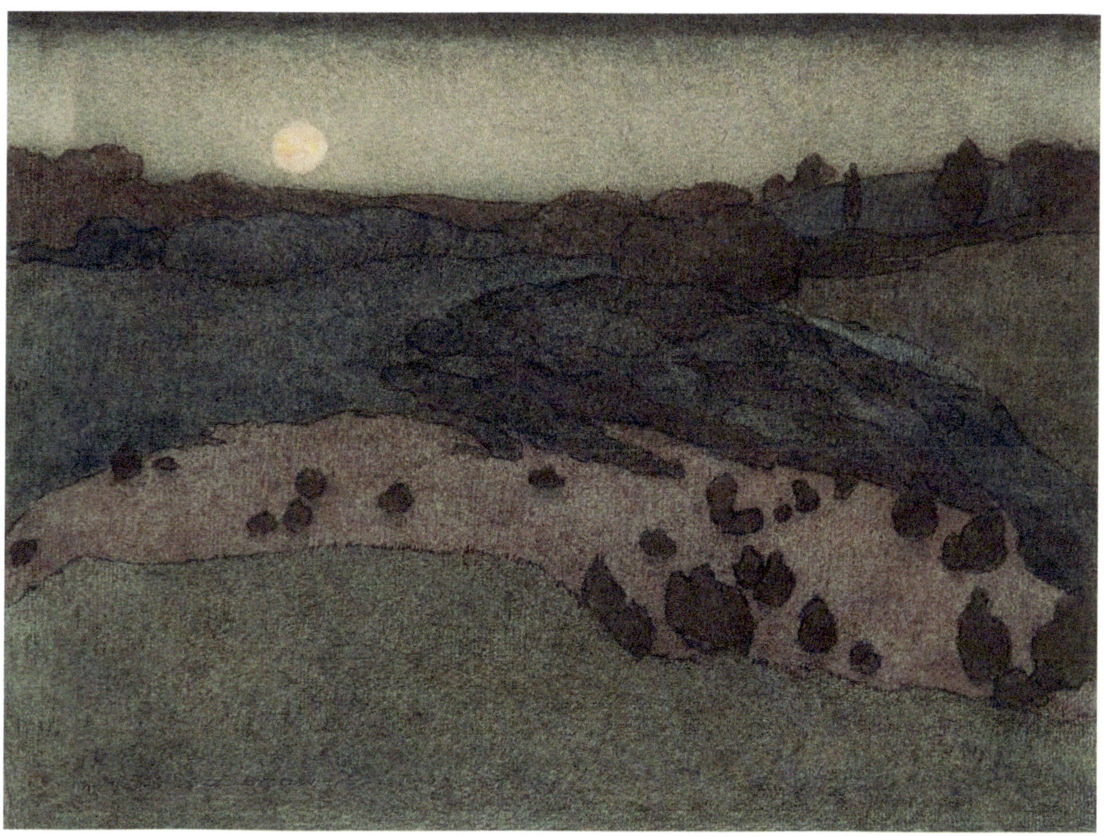

M. Louise Stowell, *Landscape with Moon*, 1903. Watercolor, charcoal, and black ink on paper. 2016.92

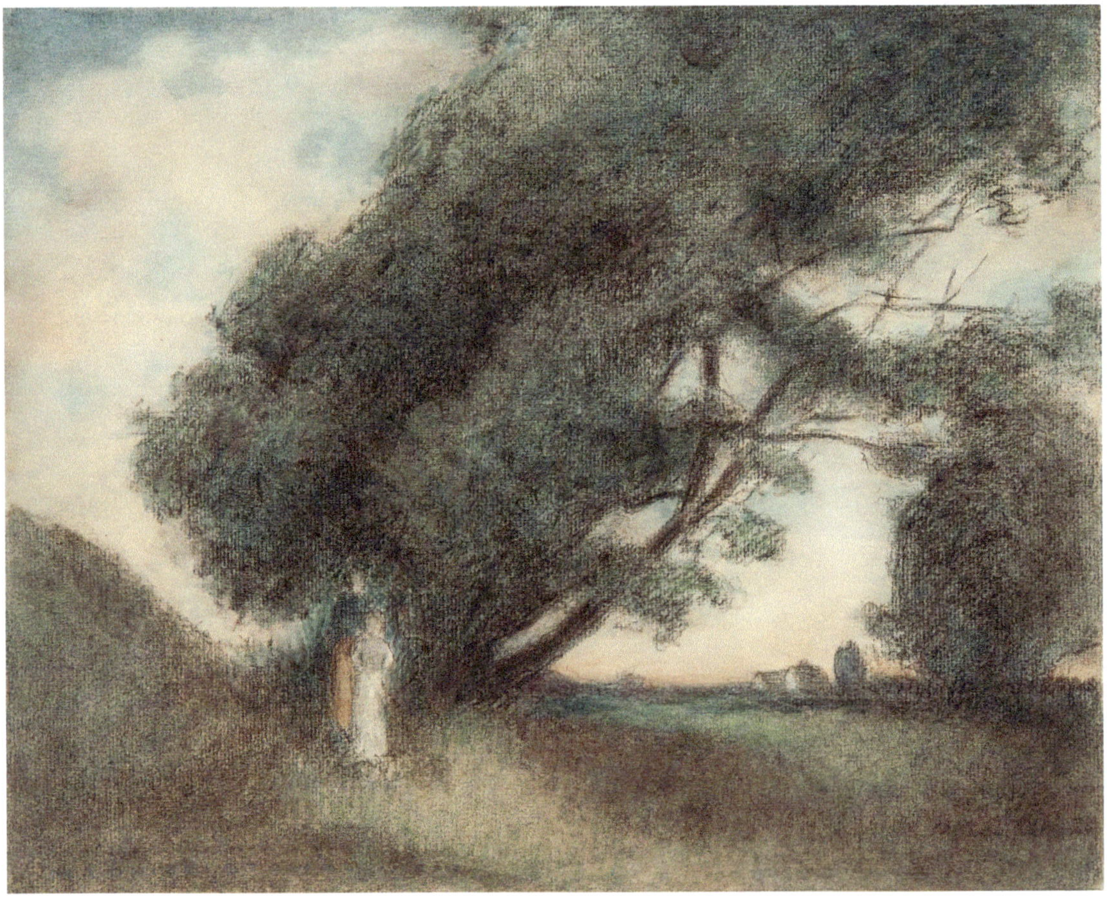

M. Louise Stowell, *Windblown Tree*, 1903. Charcoal and watercolor on laid paper. 2016.127

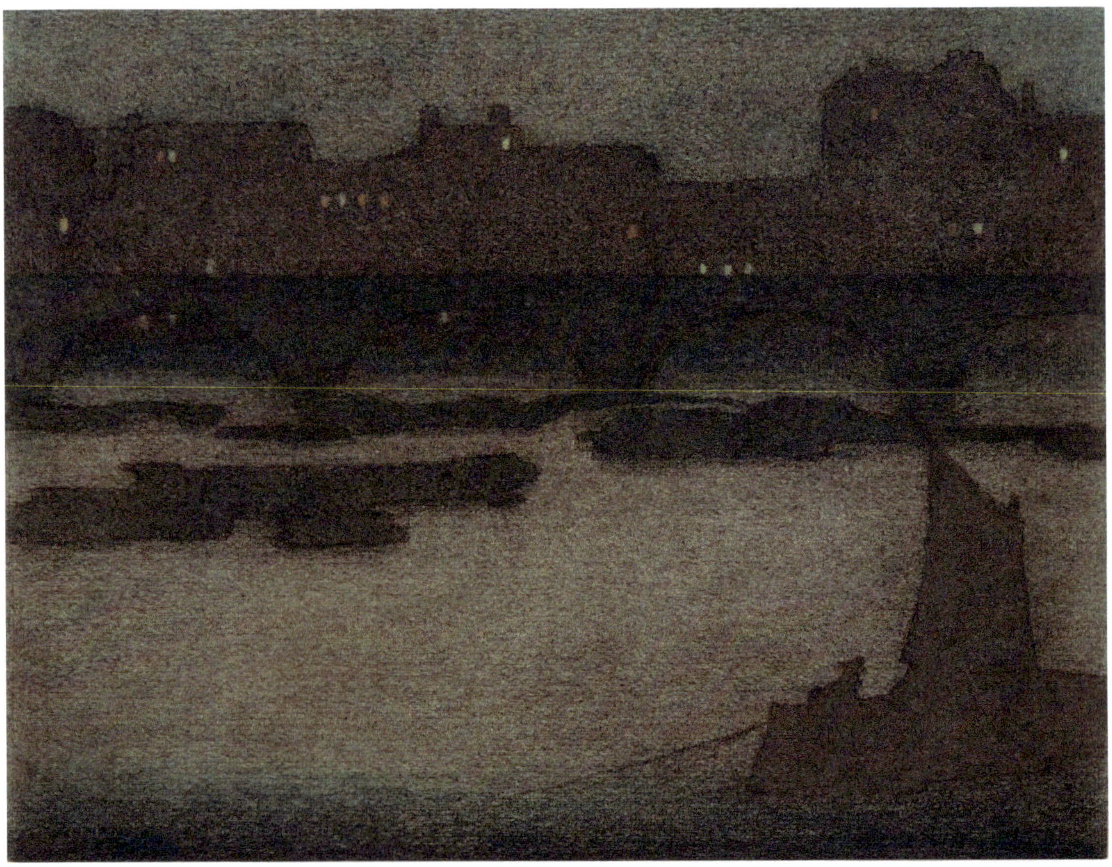

M. Louise Stowell, *The Aqueduct over the Genesee*, Rochester, 1903. Watercolor and charcoal on paper. 2016.94

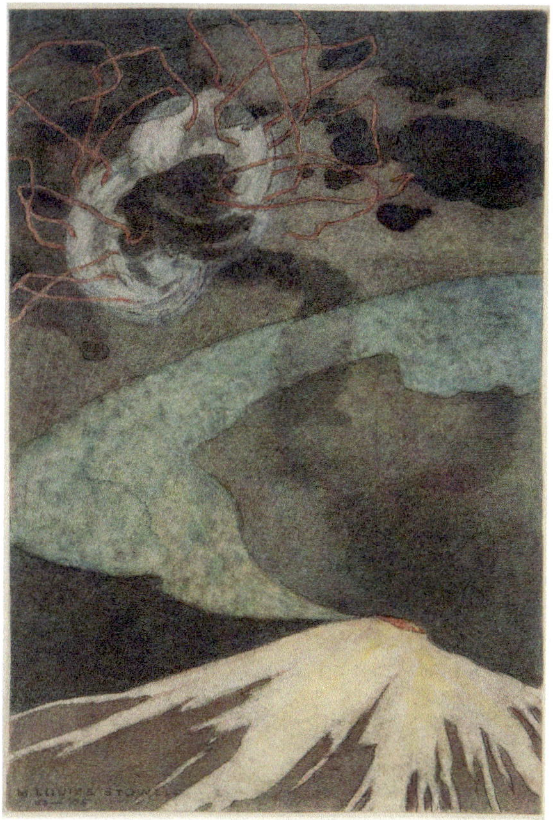

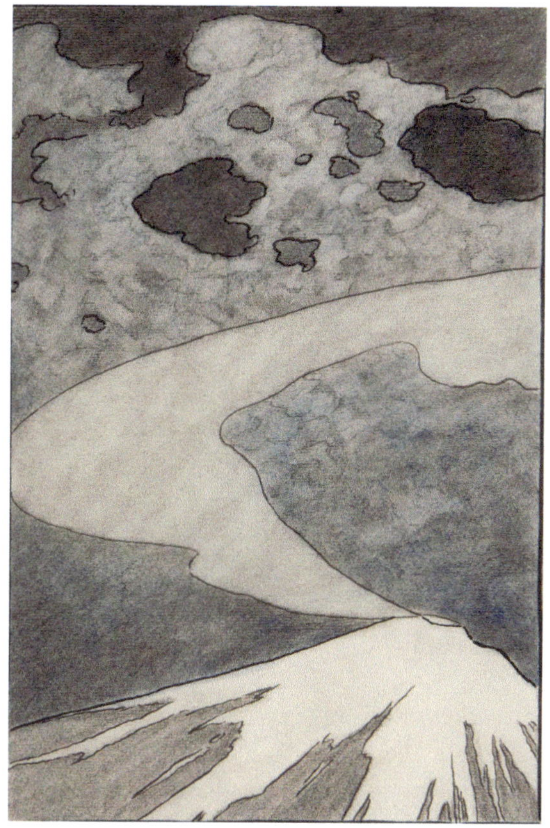

Left: M. Louise Stowell, *Smoke Rising from Mountaintop*, 1903–1905. Watercolor and charcoal on paper. 2016.121

Right: M. Louise Stowell, *Smoke Rising from Mountaintop*, 1903–1905. Charcoal, black ink, and blue watercolor on laid paper. 2016.149

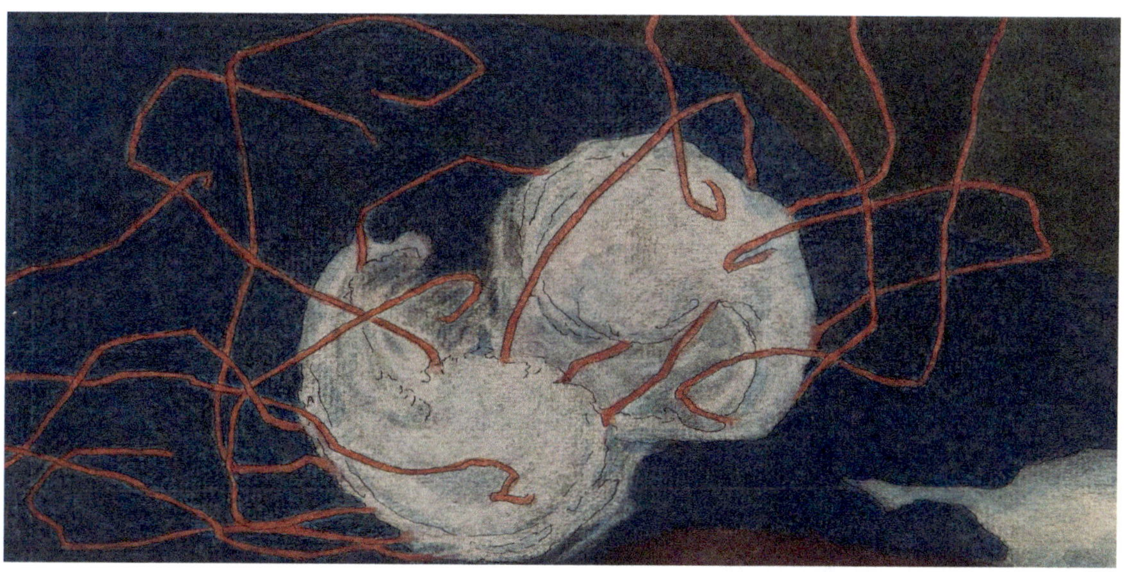

M. Louise Stowell, *Study for "Smoke Rising from Mountaintop,"* 1903–1905. Watercolor, pastel, charcoal, and black ink on paper. 2016.120

Left: M. Louise Stowell, *Drawing for "For Service,"* 1905. Charcoal and graphite on paper. 2016.143

Right: M. Louise Stowell, *For Service*, 1905. Watercolor, charcoal, and black ink on laid paper. 2016.90

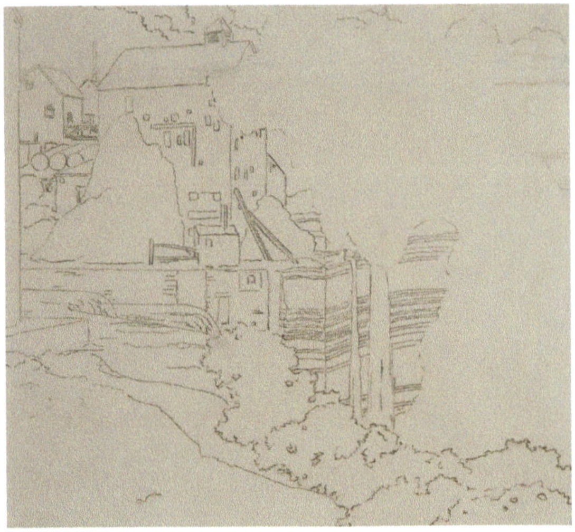

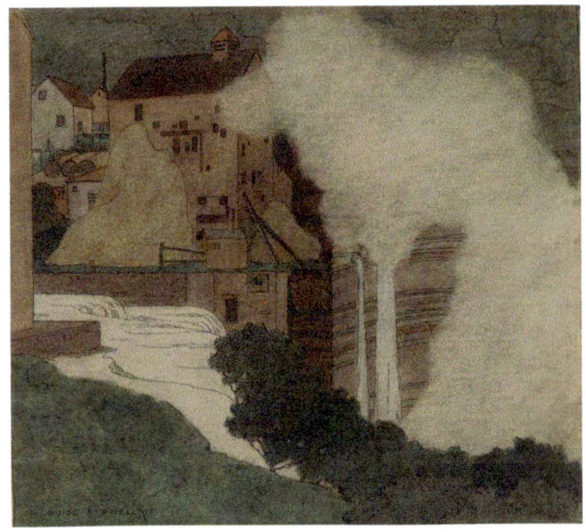

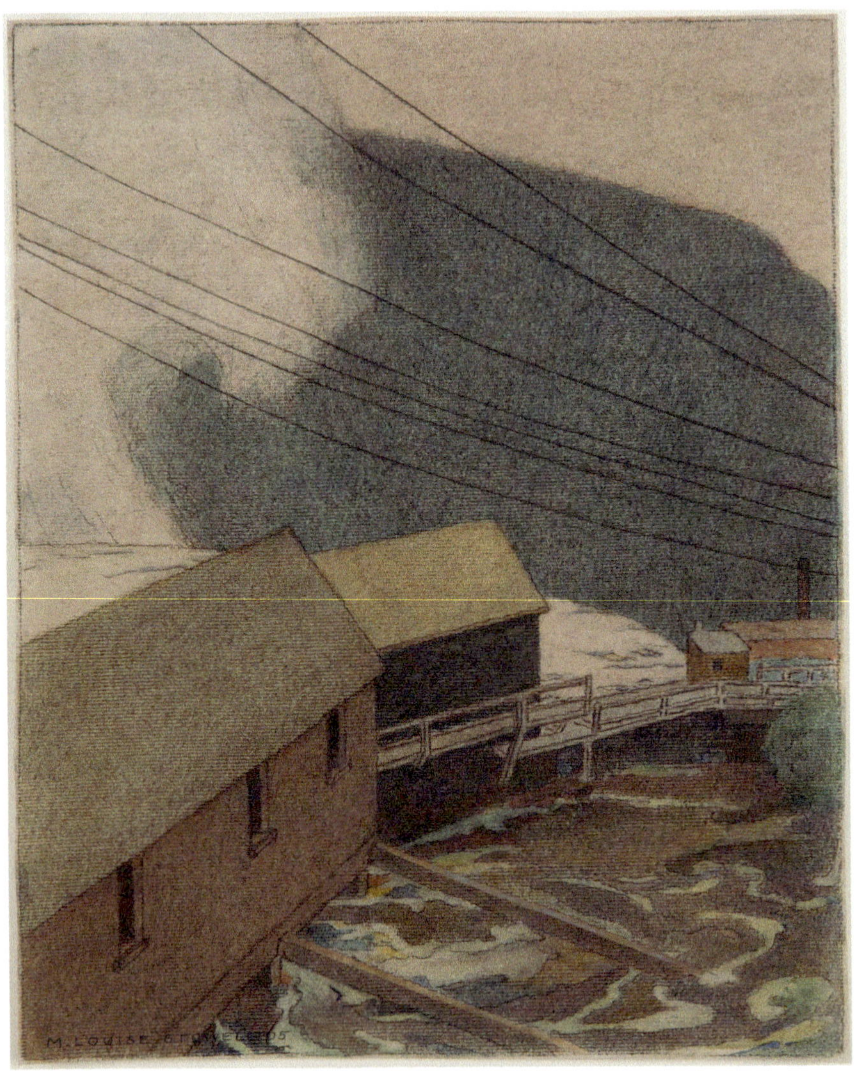

M. Louise Stowell, *The Mill by the Falls, Rochester*, 1905. Pastel, watercolor, charcoal, ink, and graphite on laid paper. 2016.117
*See related work on page 5.*

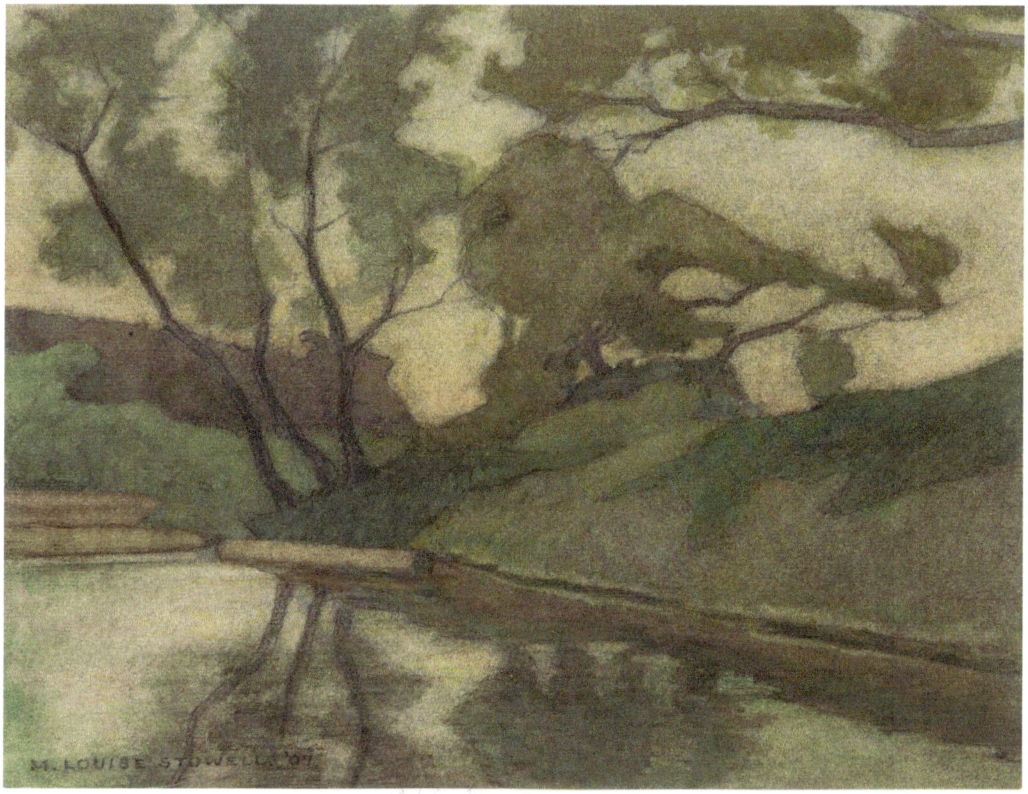

M. Louise Stowell, *Pond with Trees,* 1907. Pastel, watercolor, and charcoal on paper. 2016.119

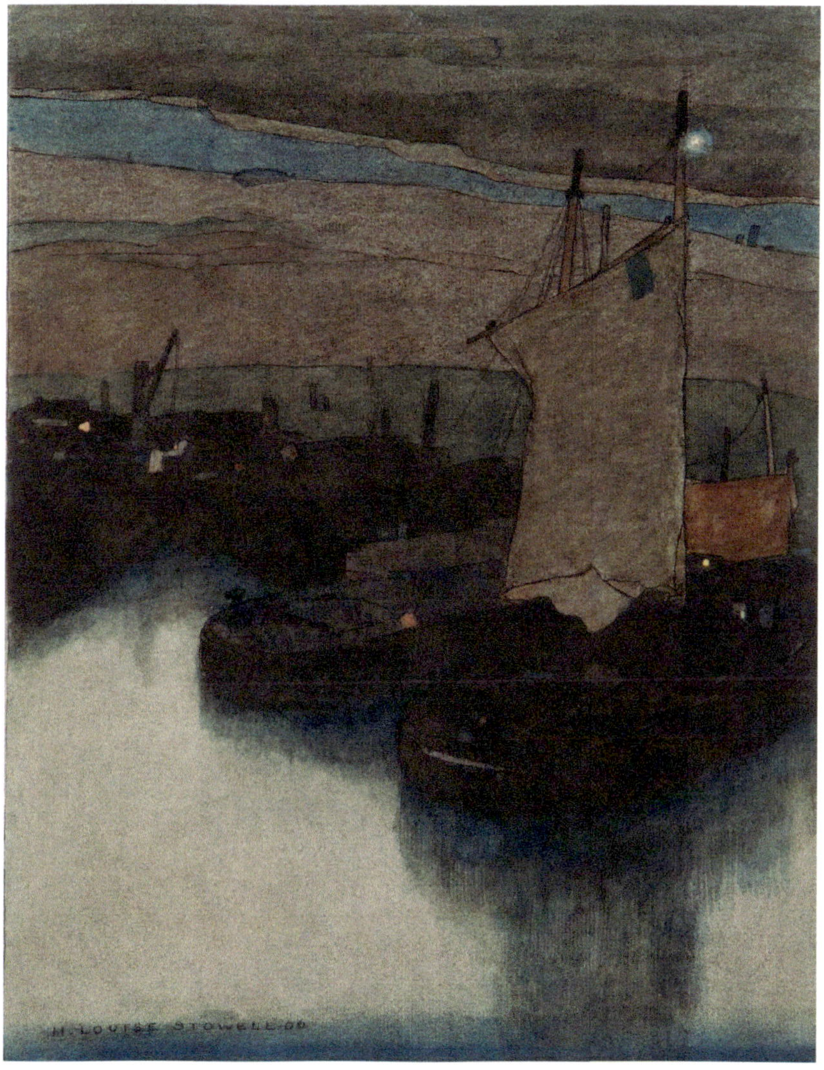

M. Louise Stowell, *Remembered*, 1906. Watercolor, pastel, charcoal, and black ink on board. 2016.91

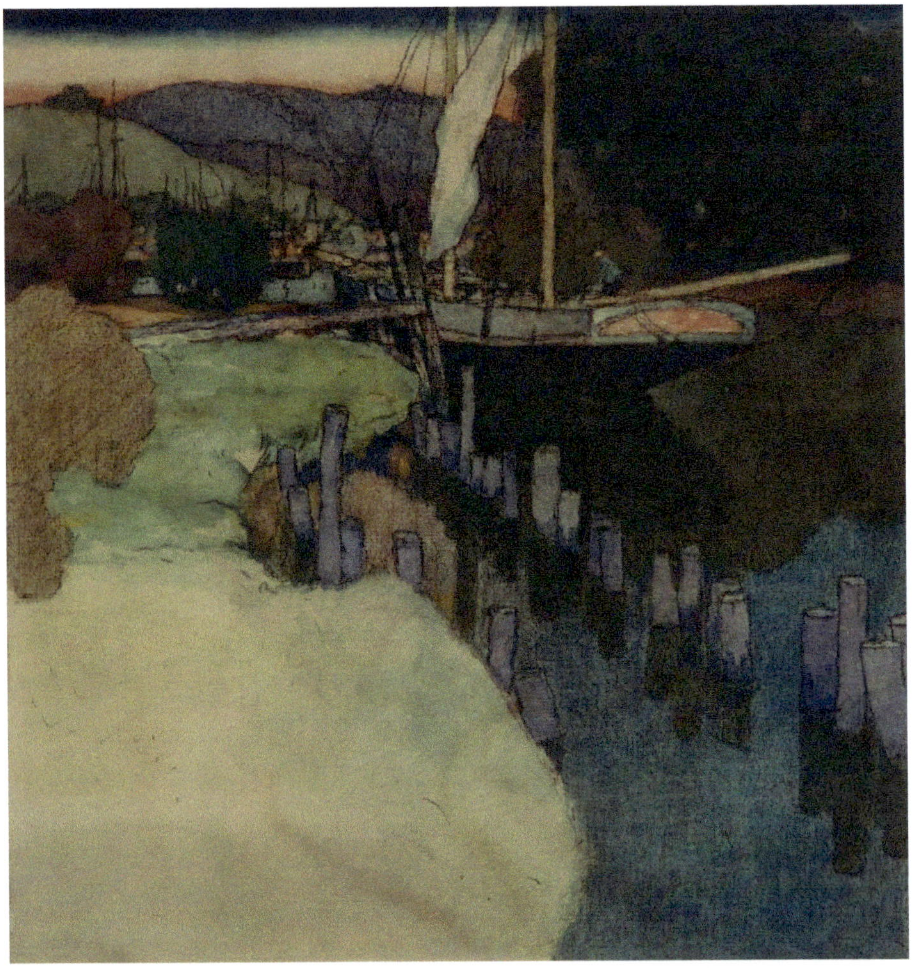

Attributed to M. Louise Stowell, *River Scene with Boats and Pilings*, 19th Century. Watercolor and charcoal on laid paper. 2016.164

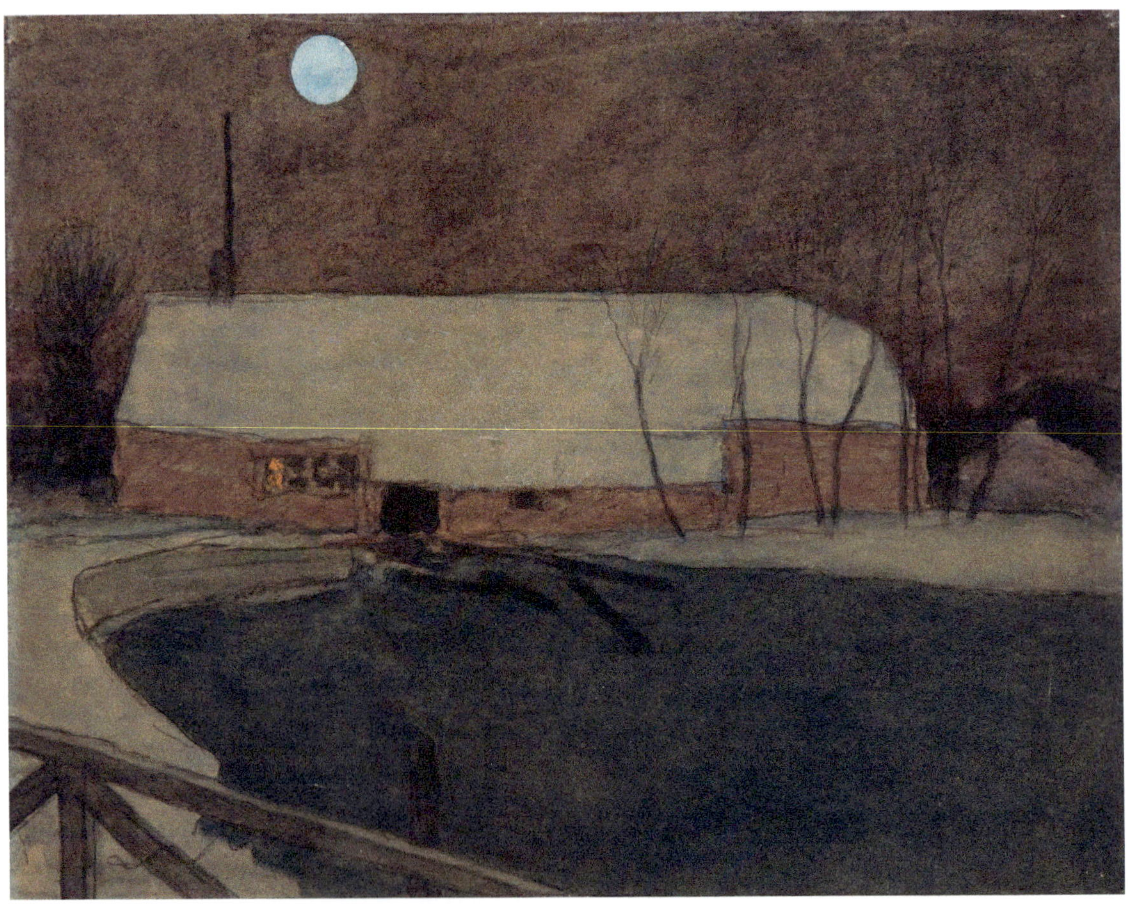

Attributed to M. Louise Stowell, *Cottage with Blue Moon*, 19th–20th centuries. Watercolor, charcoal, gouache, pastel, and paper applique on paper. 2016.172

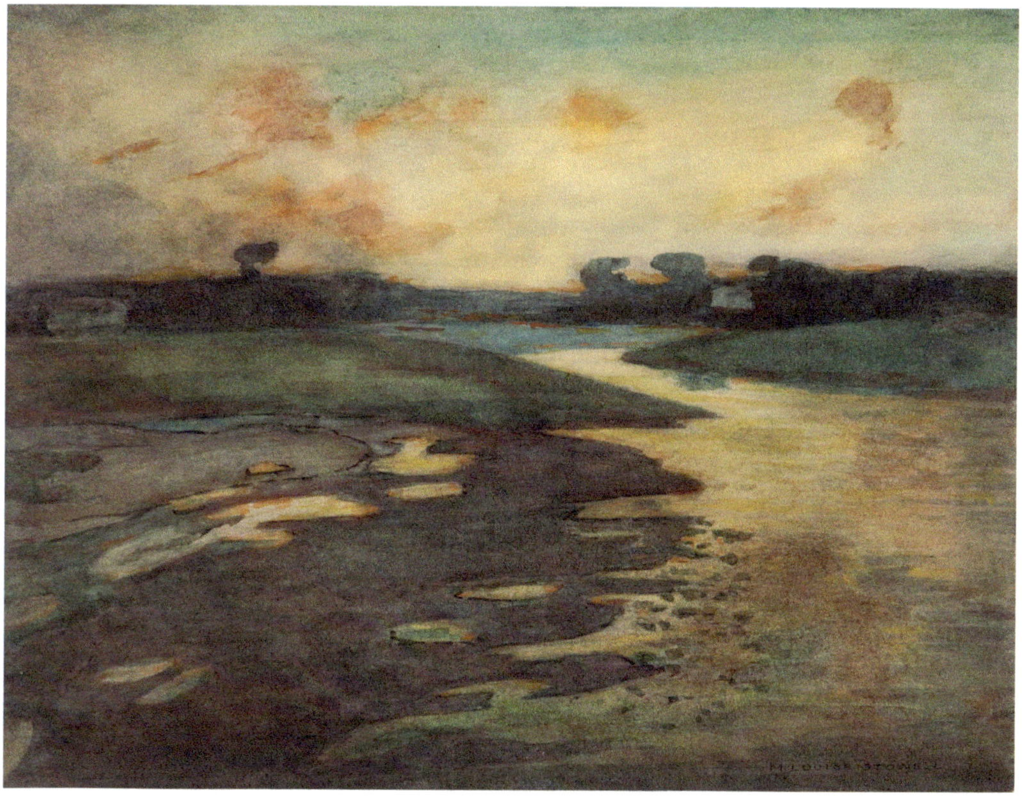


M. Louise Stowell, *Landscape with River*, 19th century. Watercolor, black ink, and gouache on board. 2016.101

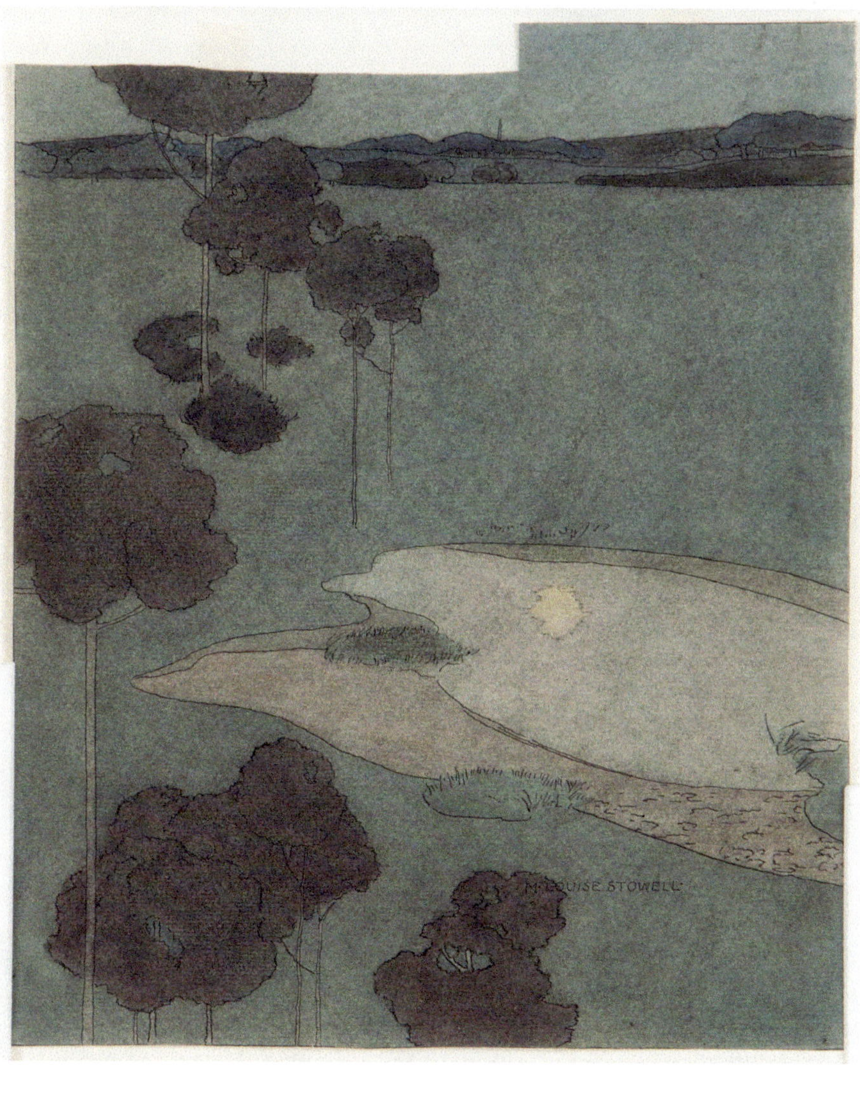


M. Louise Stowell, *Meadow with Pond*, 19th century. Watercolor, pastel, charcoal, and ink on paper. 2016.115

M. Louise Stowell, *Studies for Stained Glass Window: Angel with Ship and Angel with Sacred Heart*, circa 1901. Watercolor, charcoal, and black ink with touches of gouache on laid paper. 2016.139.1, .3
*See related work on page 8.*

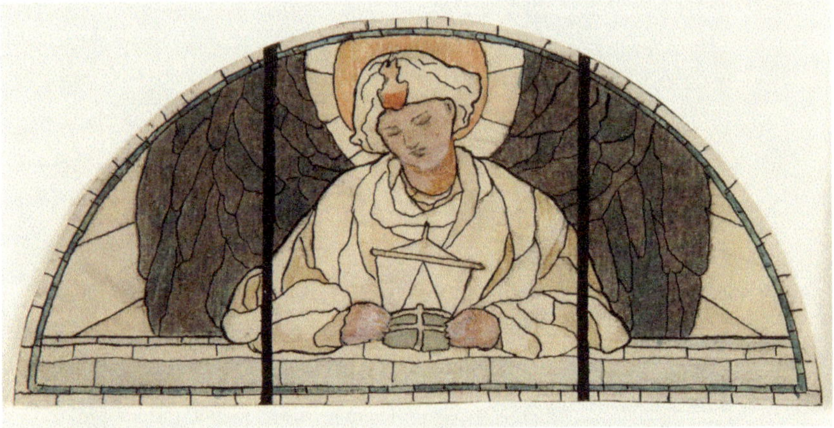

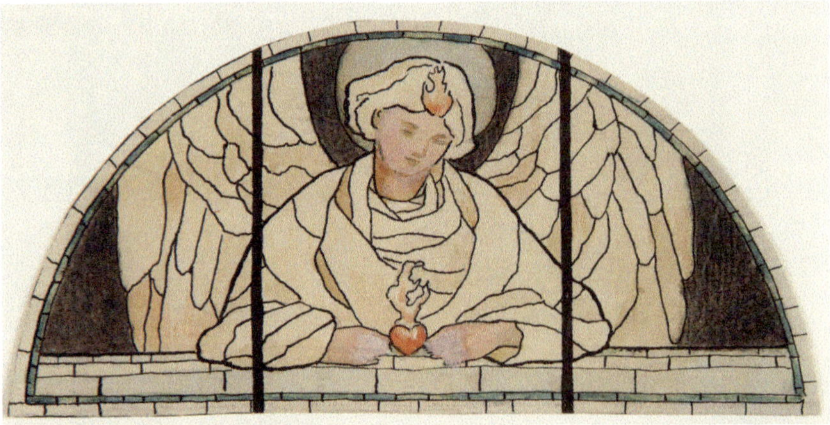

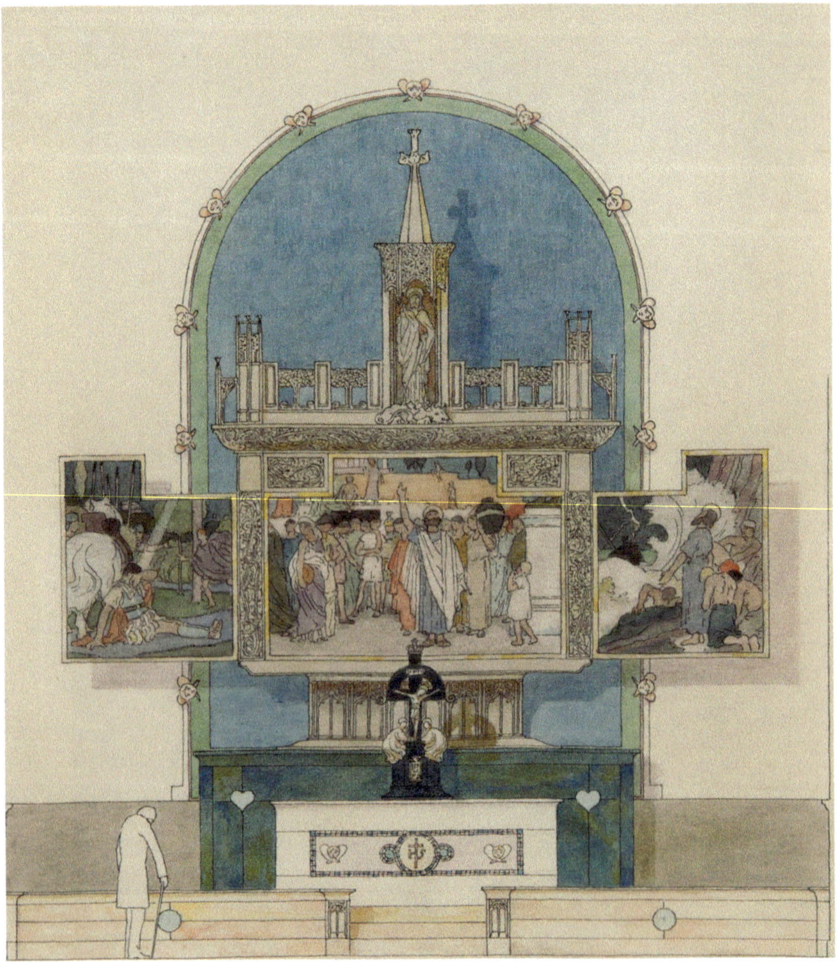

M. Louise Stowell, *Sketch for a Mural for St. Paul's Church*, 19th century. Watercolor, ink, and charcoal on textured paper. 2016.99

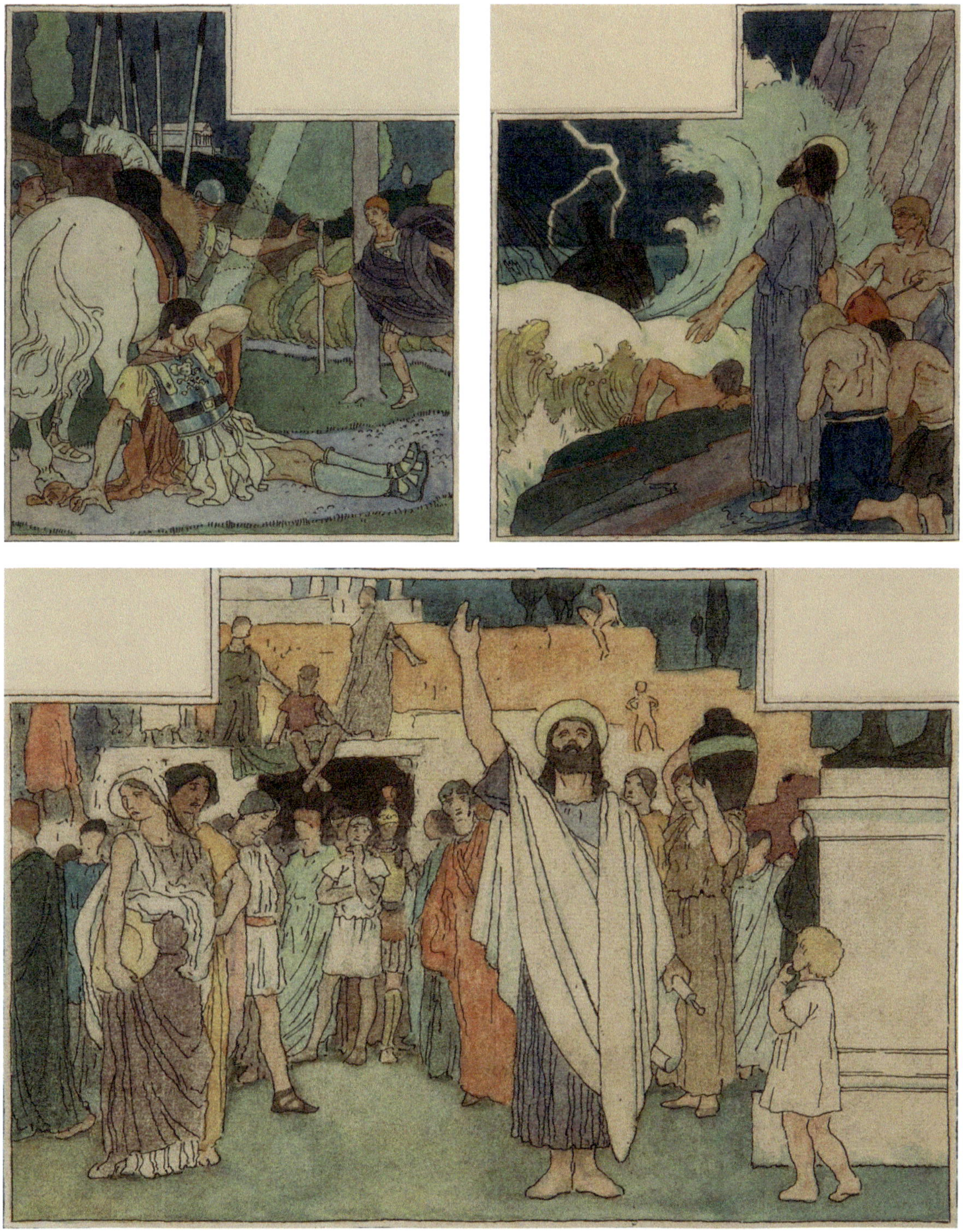

M. Louise Stowell, *Three Sketches for Murals: The Conversion of St. Paul, St. Paul Preaching in Athens,* and *St. Paul Shipwrecked*, 19th century. Watercolor and charcoal on paper. 2016.100.1-.3

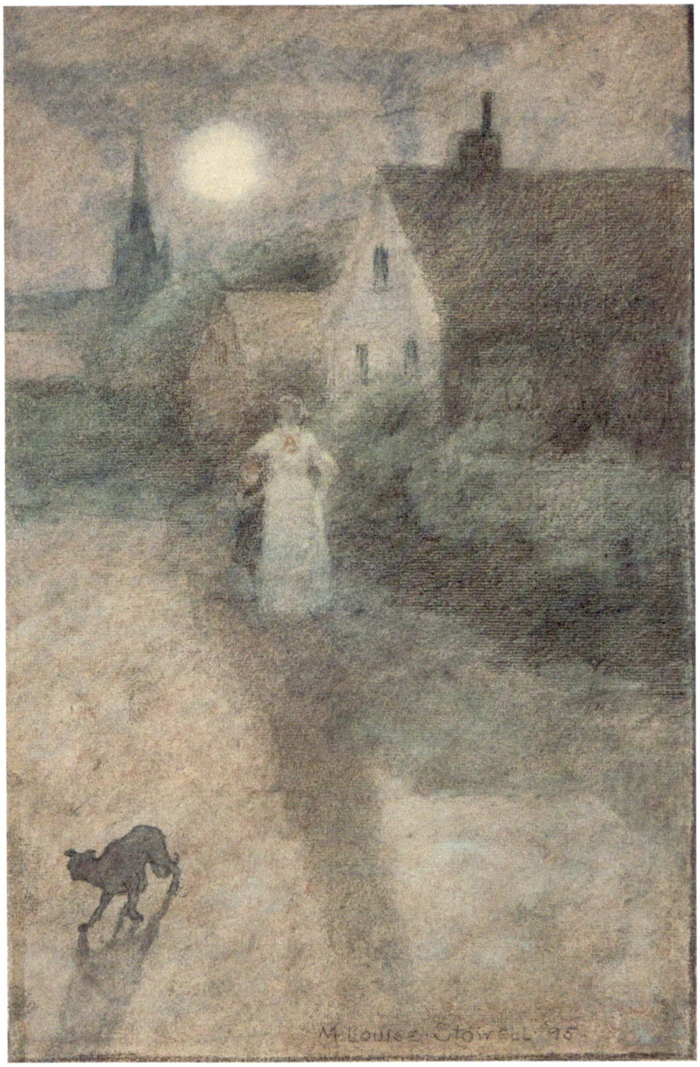


M. Louise Stowell, *Illustration for "The Scarlet Letter,"* 1895. Watercolor, pastel, and charcoal on paper. 2016.136

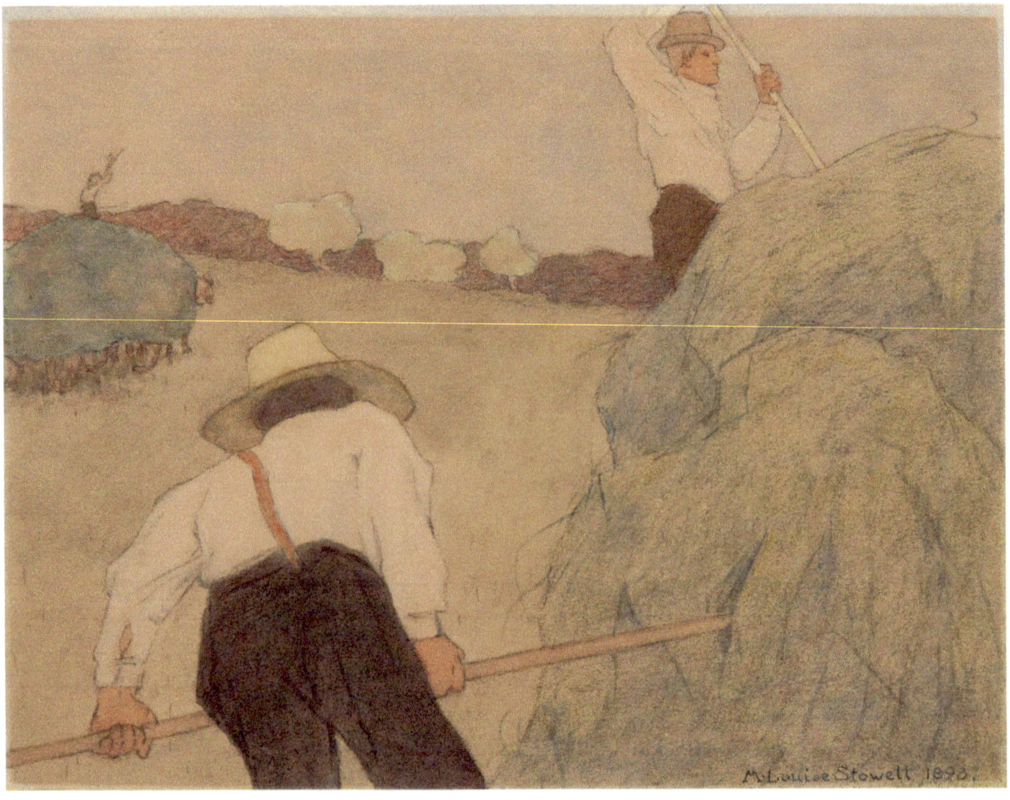


M. Louise Stowell, *Hay Gatherers*, 1898. Watercolor and charcoal on paper. 2016.95

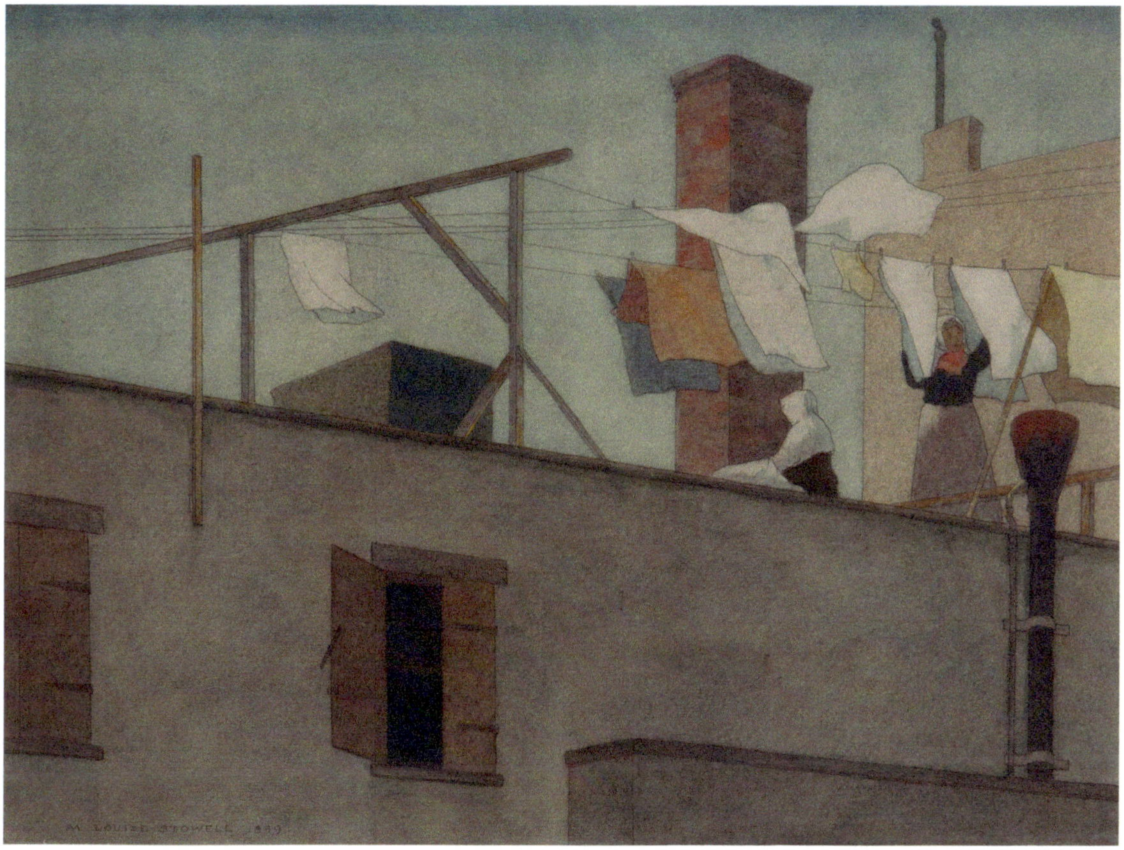

M. Louise Stowell, *The Washline on the Roof*, 1899. Watercolor, charcoal, and black ink with touches of gouache on laid paper. 2016.133

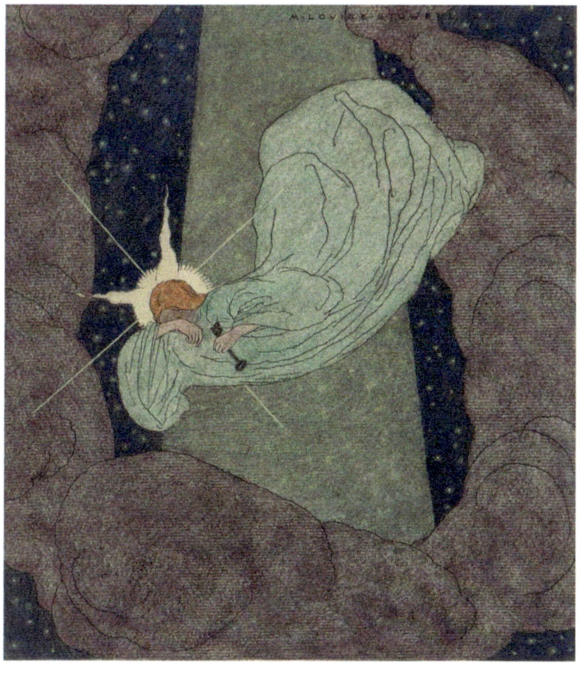

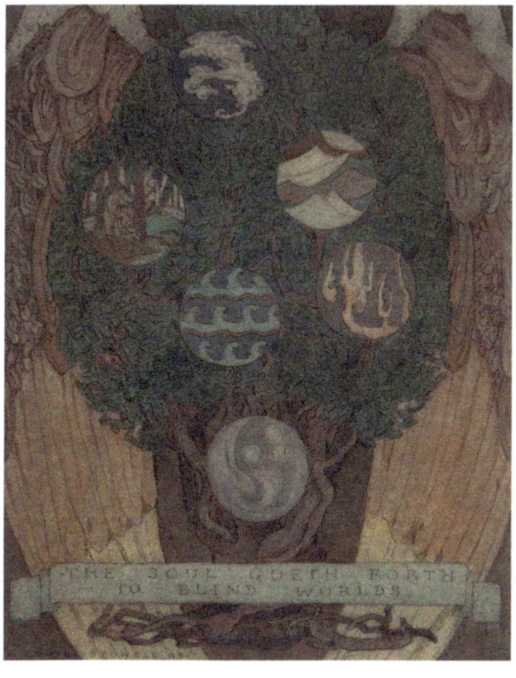


Left: M. Louise Stowell, *The Fall of Lucifer*, 1899. Watercolor, pastel, and black ink on laid paper. 2016.113

Right: M. Louise Stowell, *The Soul Goeth Forth to Blind Worlds*, 1905. Watercolor, charcoal, and watercolor on laid paper. 2016.114

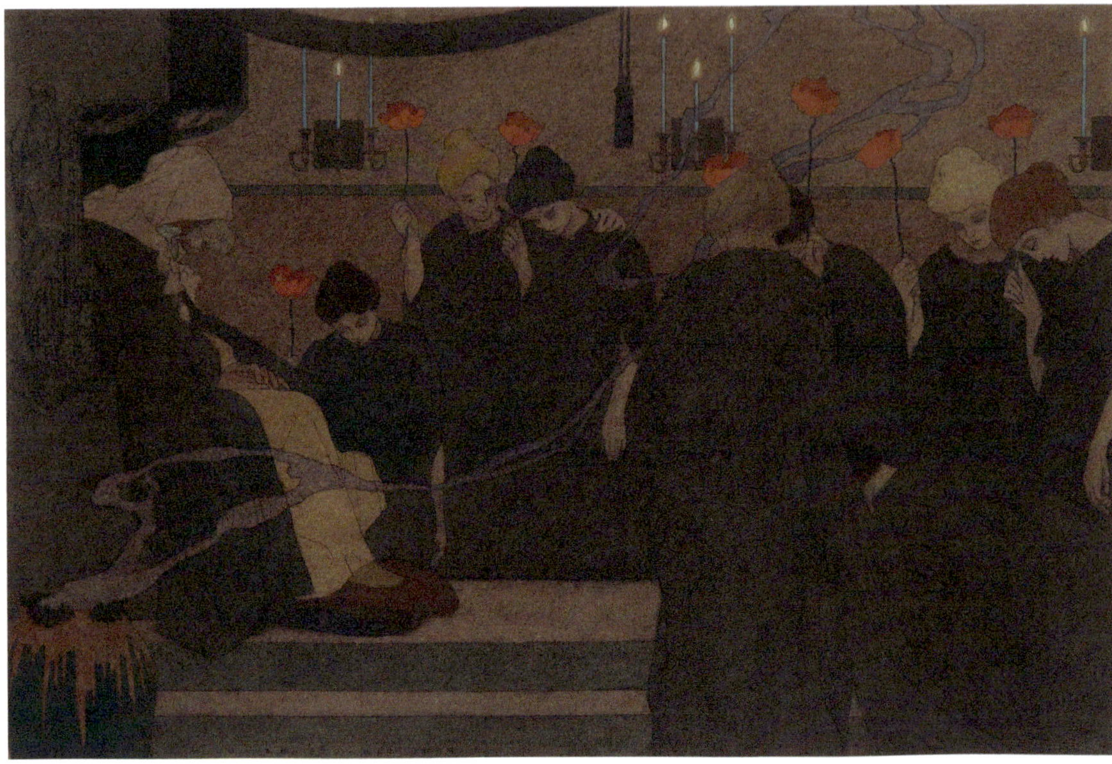

M. Louise Stowell, *The Court of Dreams*, 1899. Watercolor, charcoal, gouache, and black ink on laid paper. 2016.87
*See related work on page 9.*

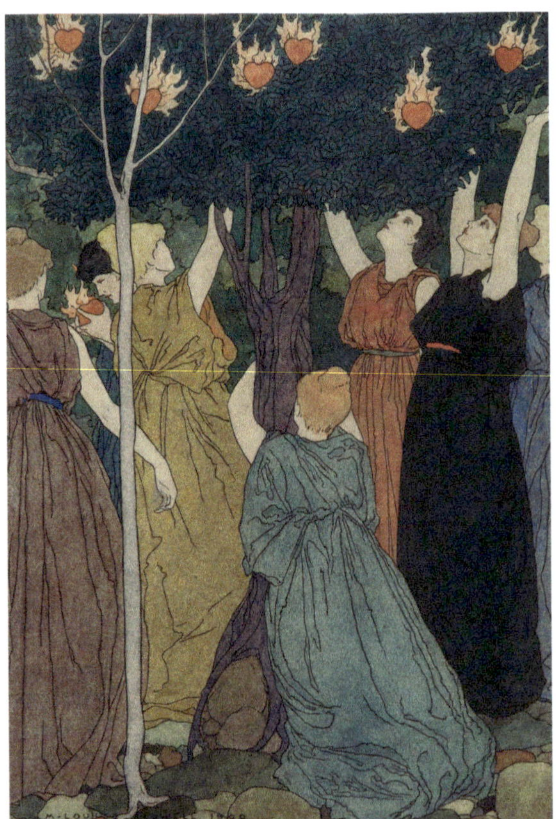

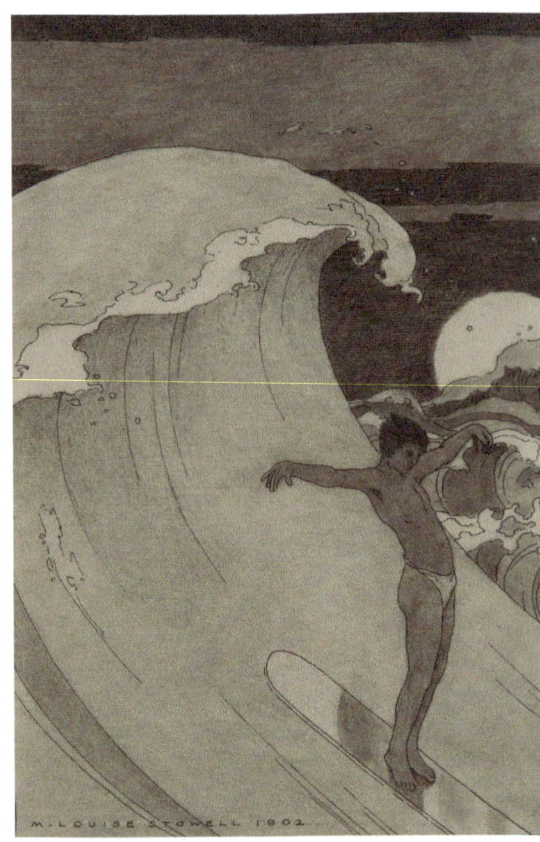


Left: M. Louise Stowell, *The Garden of the Hesperides*, 1900. Watercolor, pastel, charcoal, and ink on laid paper. 2016.122.

Right: M. Louise Stowell, *An Hawaiian, or Kanaka, Surf-Rider*, 1902. Charcoal and black ink on laid paper. 2016.141

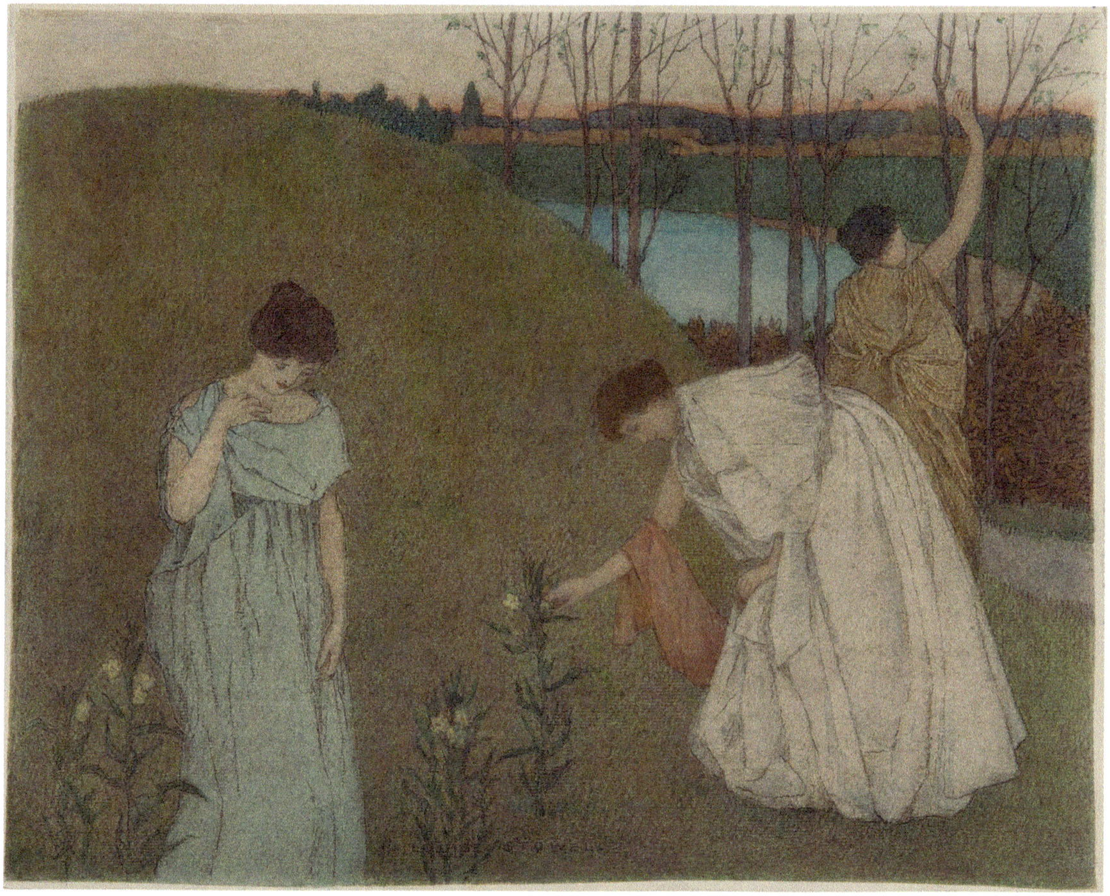

M. Louise Stowell, *Evening Primroses*, 1905. Pastel, watercolor, and charcoal on laid paper. 2016.118

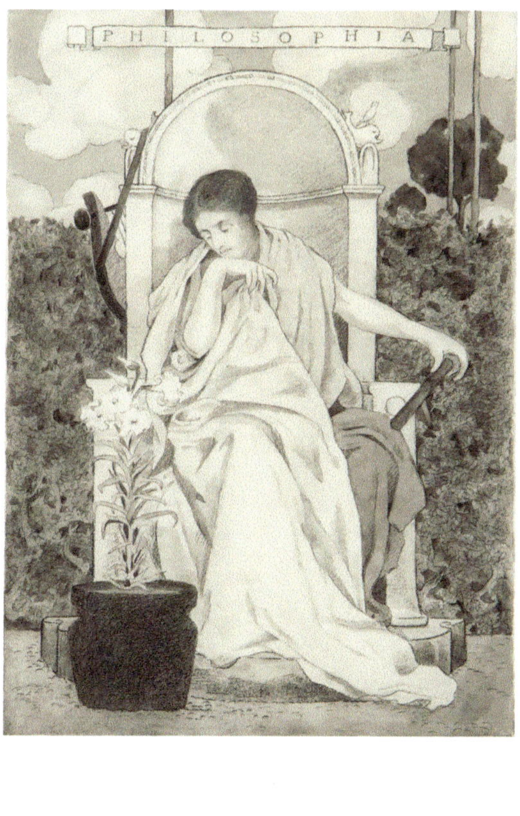


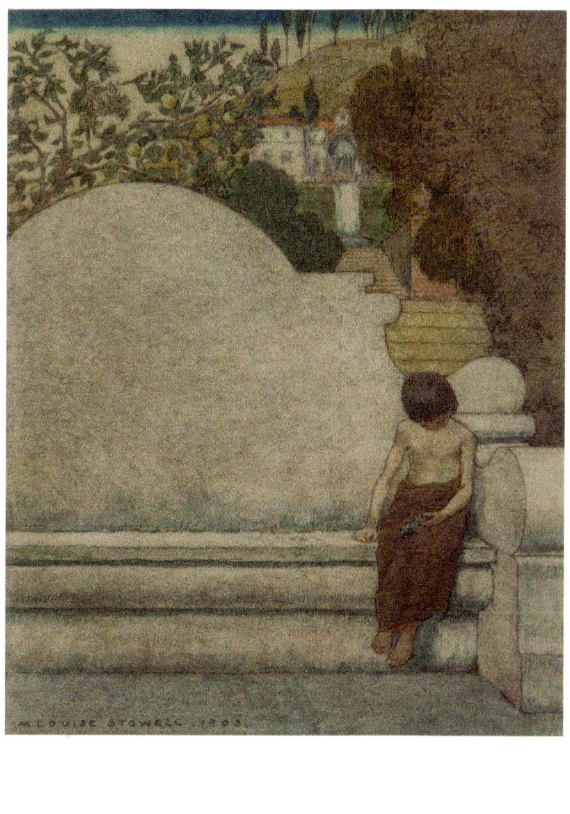

Left: M. Louise Stowell, *Study for "Philosophia,"* 1902. Ink wash and black chalk or charcoal on paper. 2016.138
*See related work on page 8.*

Right: M. Louise Stowell, *The Villa*, 1903. Watercolor, charcoal, and pastel on paper. 2016.110

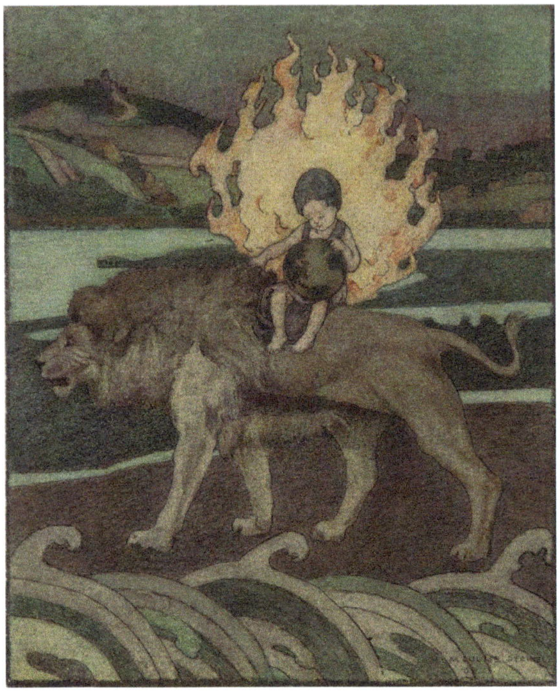

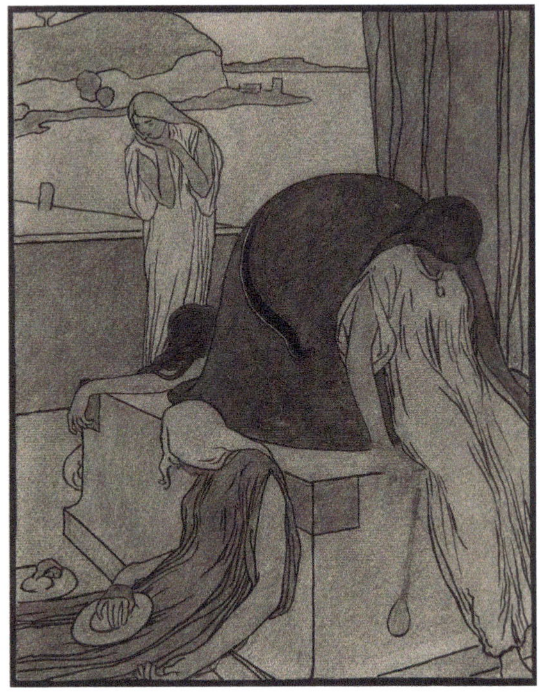

Left: M. Louise Stowell, *Child Riding Lion*, 1908. Watercolor, charcoal, and black ink on paper. 2016.161

Right: M. Louise Stowell, *Four Swooning Female Musicians*, 19th century. Charcoal and black ink on laid paper. 2016.162

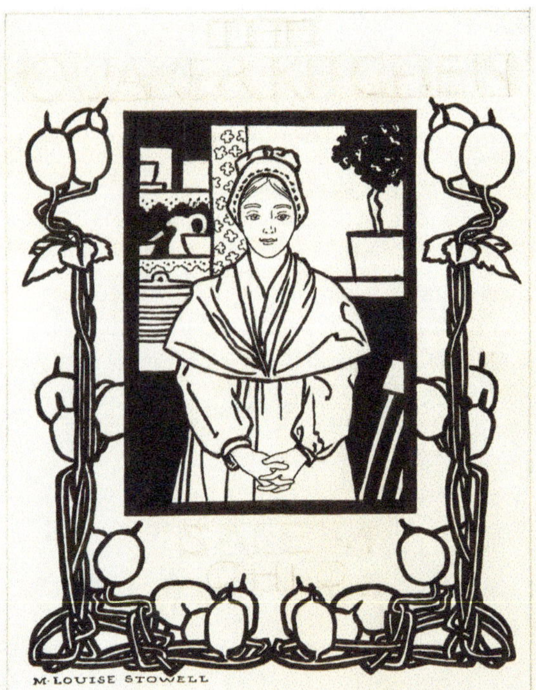


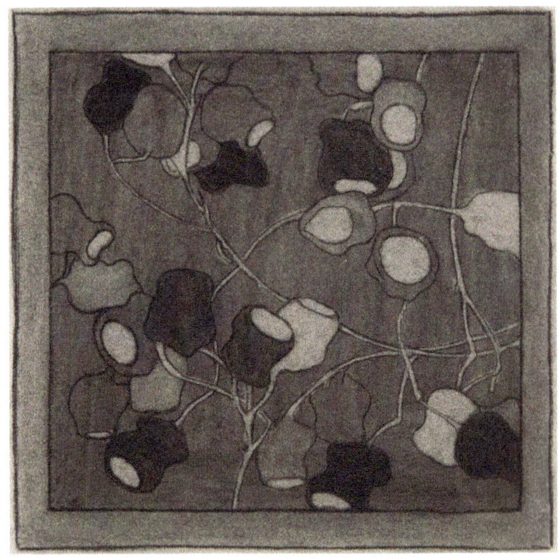

Left: M. Louise Stowell, *The Quaker Kitchen*, 19th–20th centuries. India ink and graphite on paper. 2016.174

Right: M. Louise Stowell, *Pods on Trailing Vine*, 19th century. Charcoal on laid paper. 2016.148

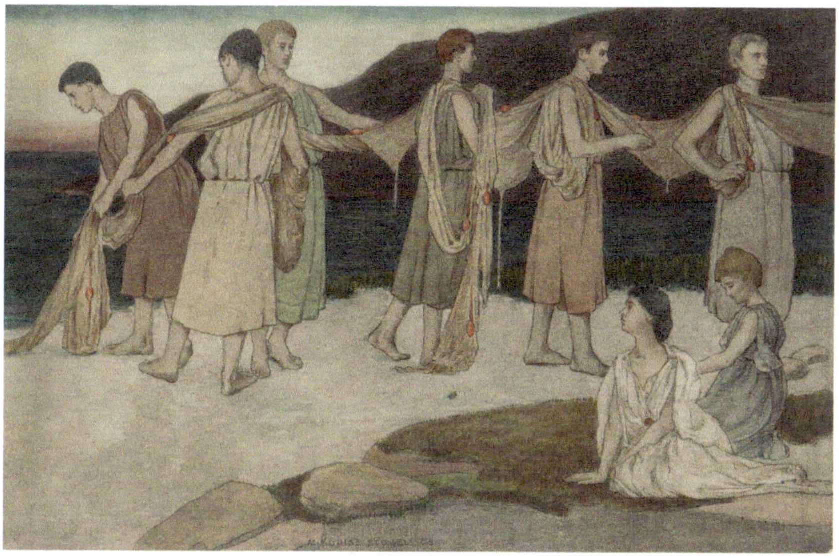

M. Louise Stowell, *An Interlude*, 1905. Watercolor, pastel, and charcoal on board. 2016.123

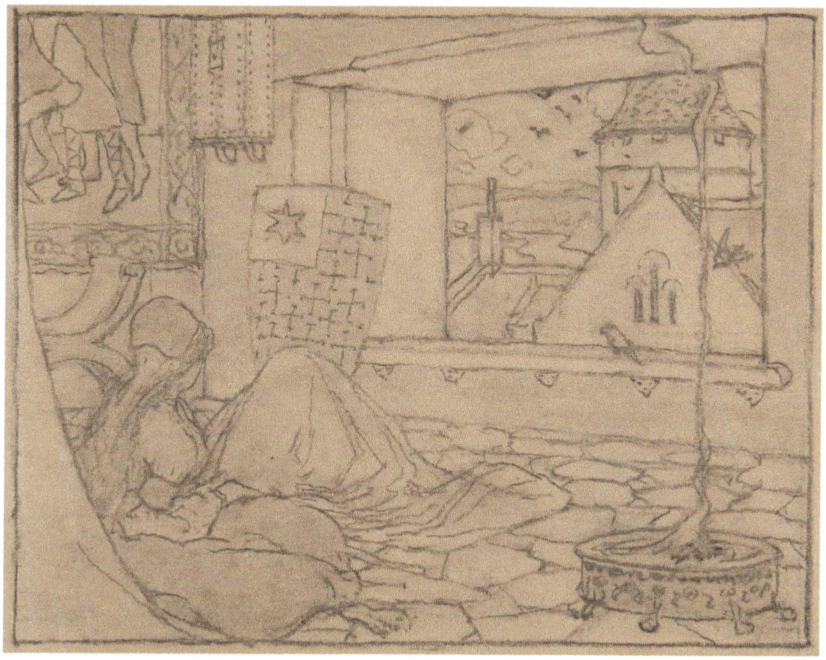

M. Louise Stowell, *Medieval Interior Scene*, 19th–20th centuries. Charcoal on paper. 2016.144

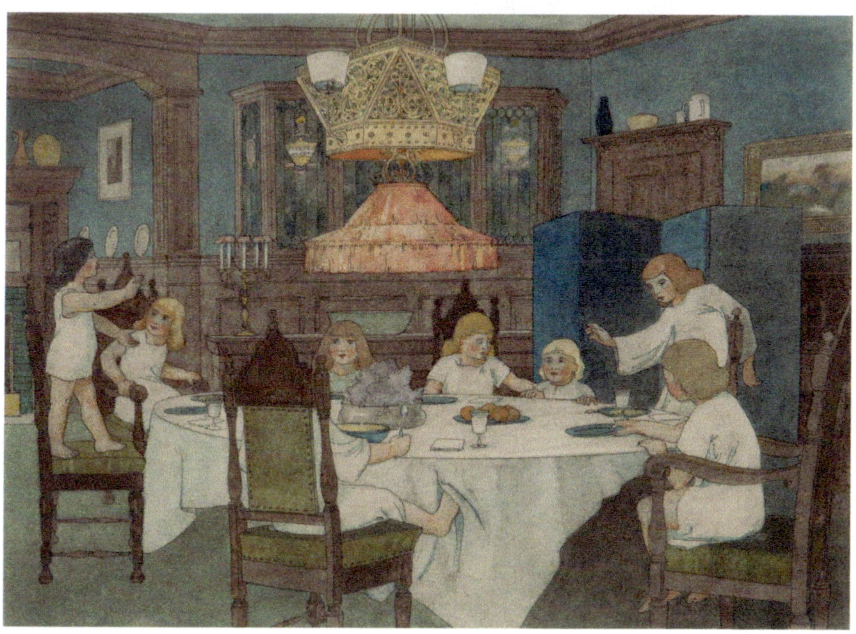

Attributed to M. Louise Stowell, *Children in Nightclothes at a Table*, 19th century. Watercolor, charcoal, and black ink on laid paper. 2016.155

Almost every one of these illustrations exists in two forms: an ink and charcoal drawing, with margins carefully notated as to color schemes, and a version in watercolor. The rhymes in the titles are written onto many of the works. These rhymes were compiled in *The New England Primer*, the first reader for children printed in America.

In the late 1600s, these little rhymes were used to teach children Biblical lessons in an easy-to-remember alphabetical format. The *Primer* was used well into the nineteenth century, but Stowell's illustrations do not seem to have been included in any published version.

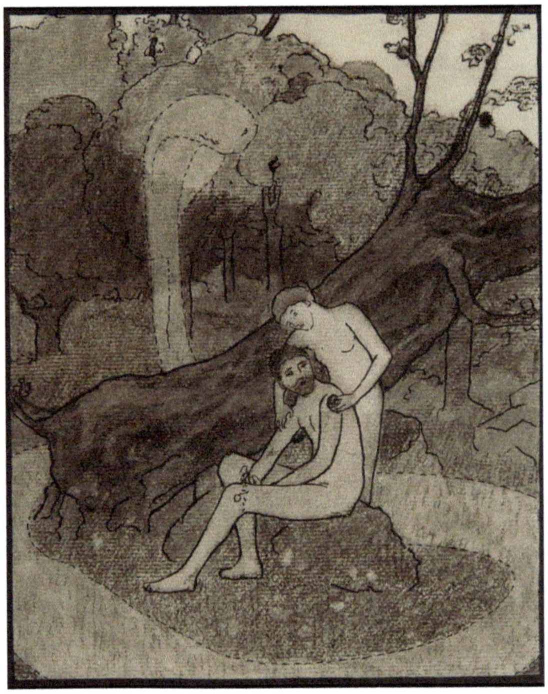

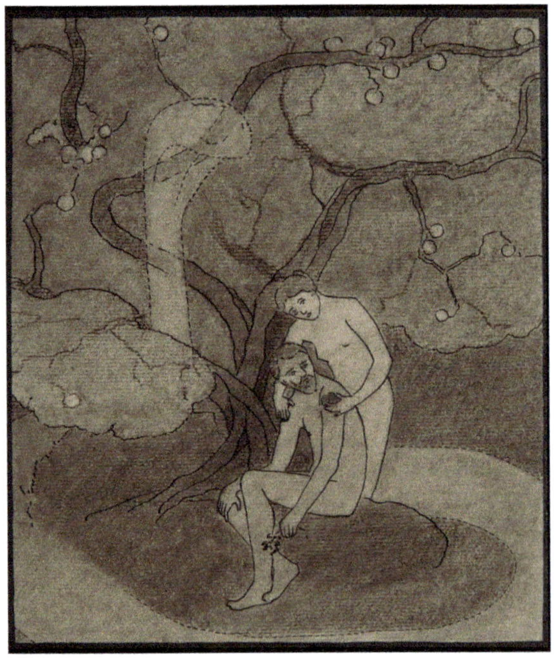

Left: M. Louise Stowell, *In Adam's Fall We Sinned All*, 19th century. Charcoal and black ink on laid paper. 2016.130.3

Right: M. Louise Stowell, *In Adam's Fall We Sinned All*, 19th century. Charcoal and black ink on laid paper. 2016.130.2

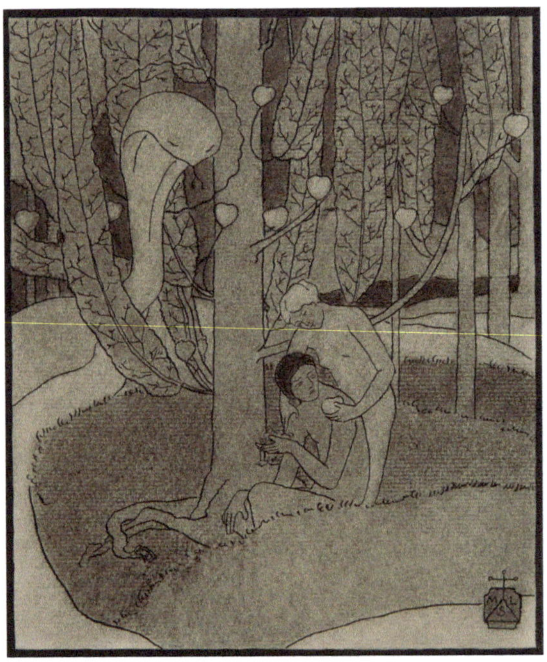

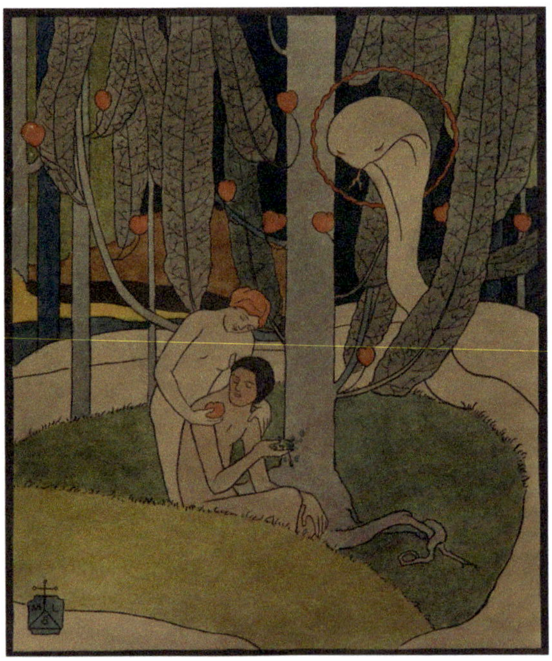

Left: M. Louise Stowell, *In Adam's Fall We Sinned All*, 19th century. Charcoal and black ink on laid paper. 2016.130.1

Right: M. Louise Stowell, *In Adam's Fall We Sinned All*, 19th century. Watercolor and black ink on paper. 2016.129.1

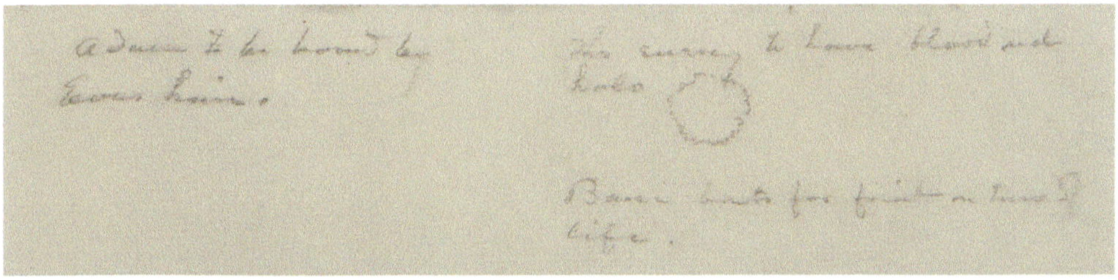

Detail of: M. Louise Stowell, *In Adam's Fall We Sinned All*, 19th century. Charcoal and black ink on laid paper. 2016.130.2

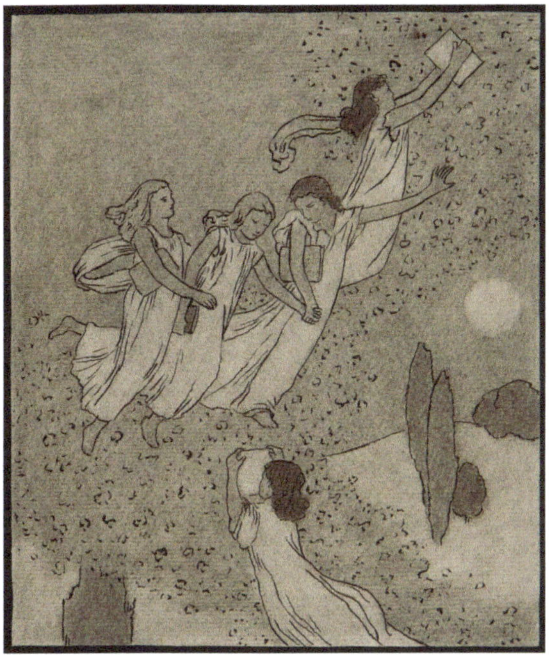

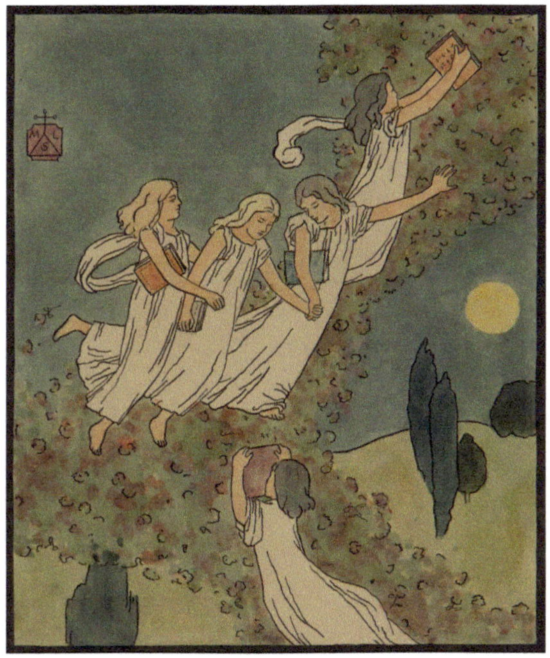

Left: M. Louise Stowell, *Heaven to Find the Bible Mind*, 19th century. Charcoal and black ink on laid paper. 2016.130.4

Right: M. Louise Stowell, *Heaven to find the Bible mind*, 19th century. Watercolor and black ink on paper. 2016.129.2

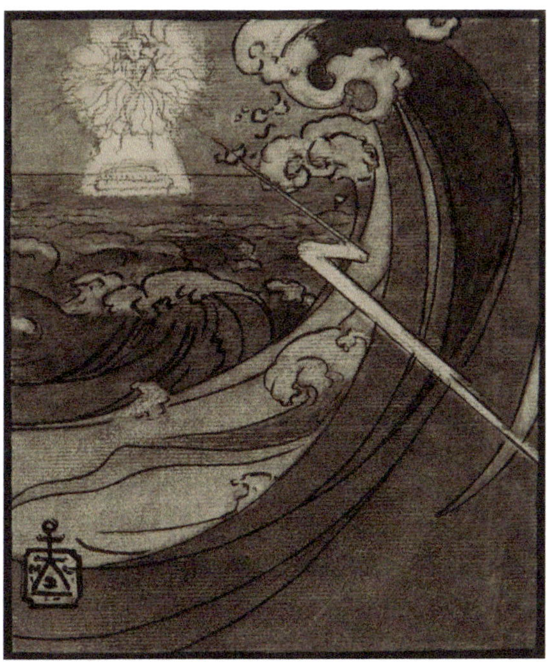

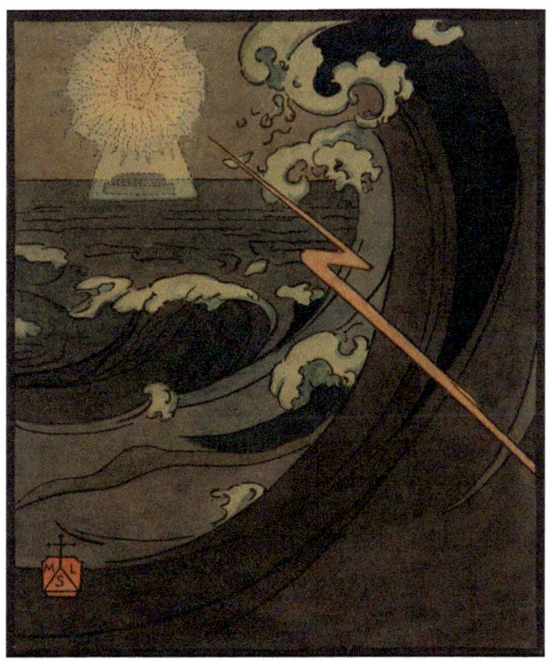

Left: M. Louise Stowell, *The Deluge Drowned the Earth Around*, 19th century. Charcoal and black ink on laid paper. 2016.130.6

Right: M. Louise Stowell, *The Deluge Drowned the Earth Around*, 19th century. Watercolor and black ink on paper. 2016.129.3

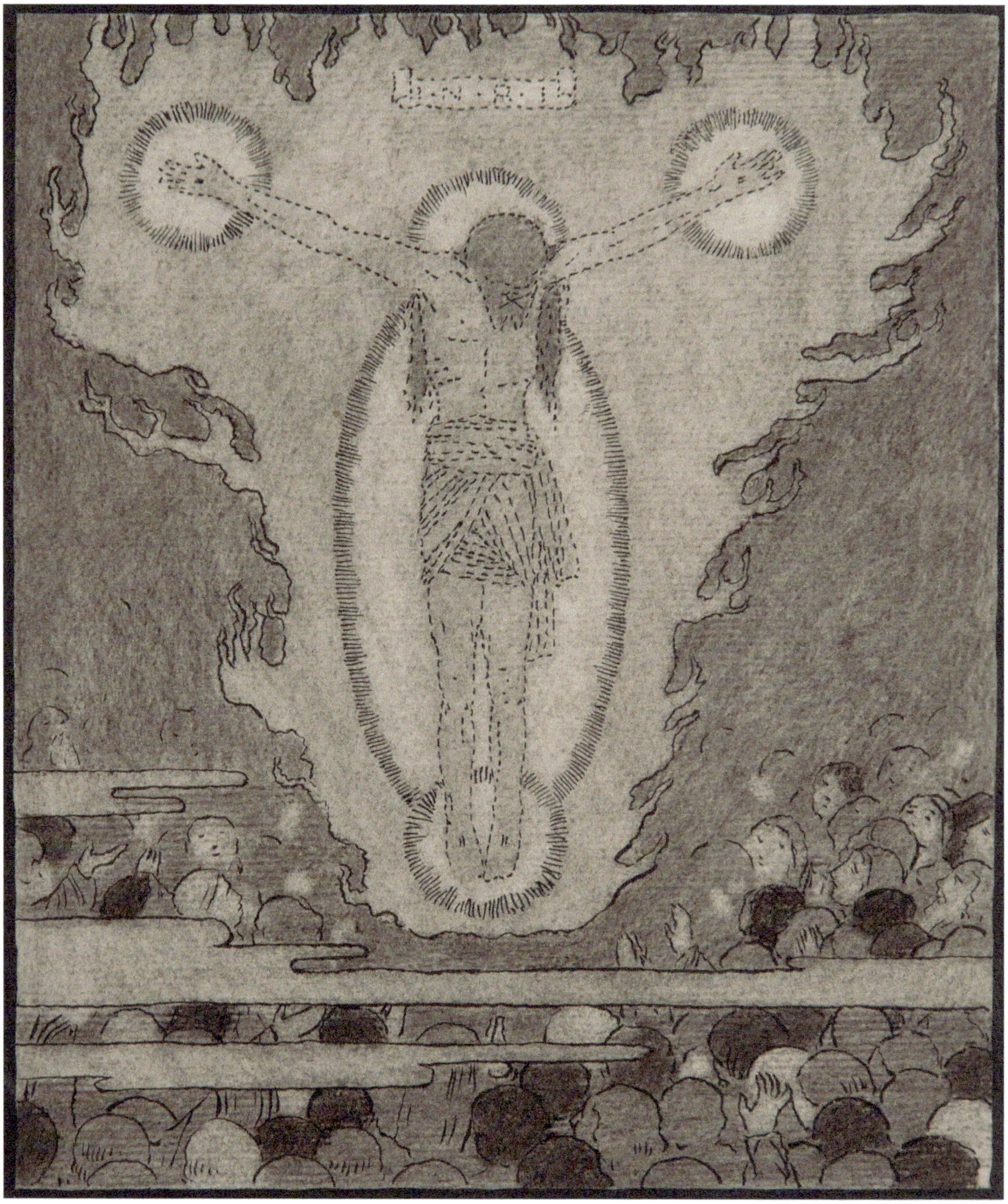

M. Louise Stowell, *Christ Crucified, For Sinners Died*, 19th century. Charcoal and black ink on laid paper. 2016.130.5

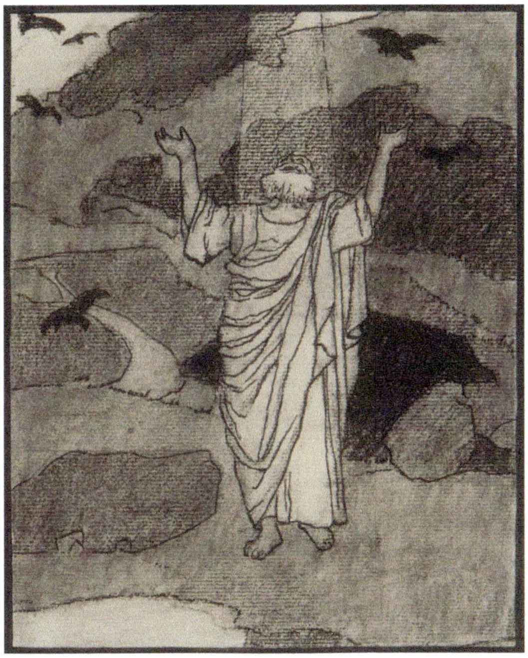

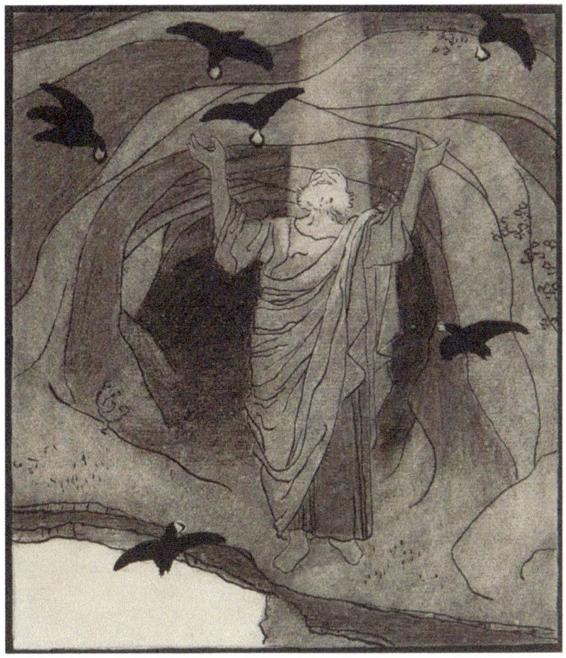

Left: M. Louise Stowell, *Elijah Hid, By Ravens Fed*, 19th century. Charcoal and black ink on laid paper. 2016.130.8

Right: M. Louise Stowell, *Elijah Hid, by Ravens Fed*, 19th century. Charcoal and black ink on laid paper. 2016.130.7

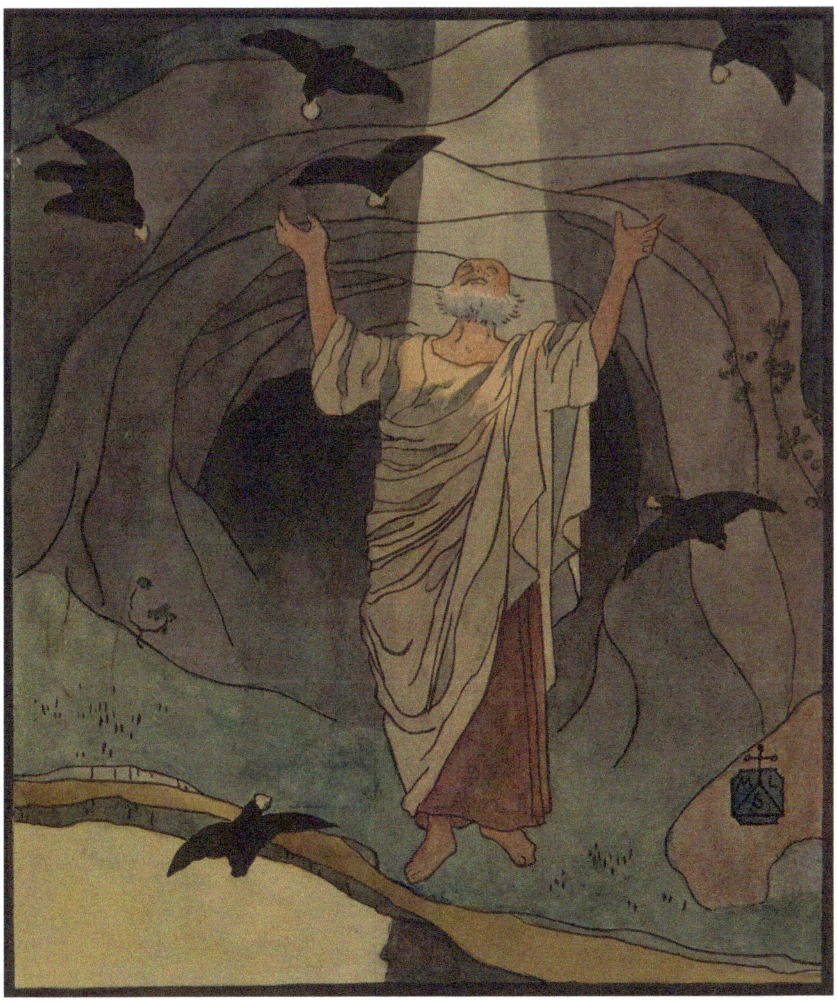

M. Louise Stowell, *Elijah Hid, by Ravens Fed*, 19th century. Watercolor and black ink on paper. 2016.129.4

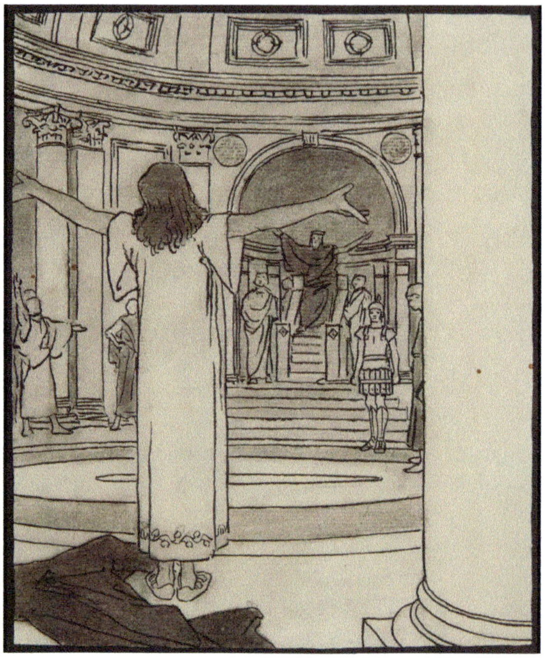

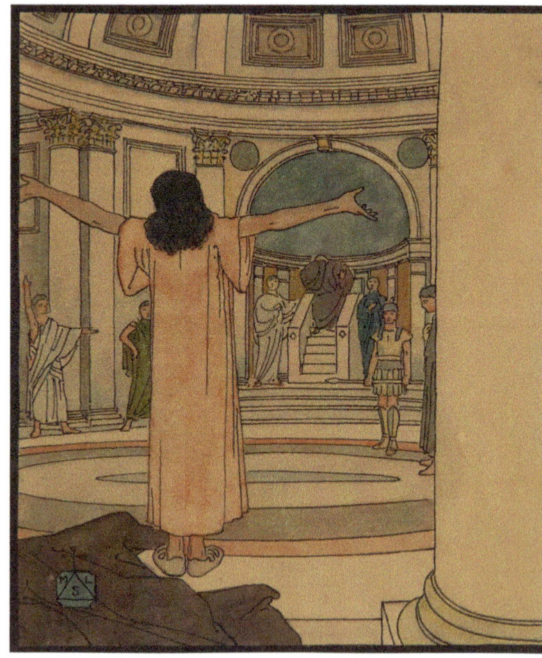

Left: M. Louise Stowell, *The Judgment Made Felix Afraid*, 19th century. Charcoal and black ink on laid paper. 2016.130.9

Right: M. Louise Stowell, *The Judgment Made Felix Afraid*, 19th century. Watercolor and black ink on paper. 2016.129.5

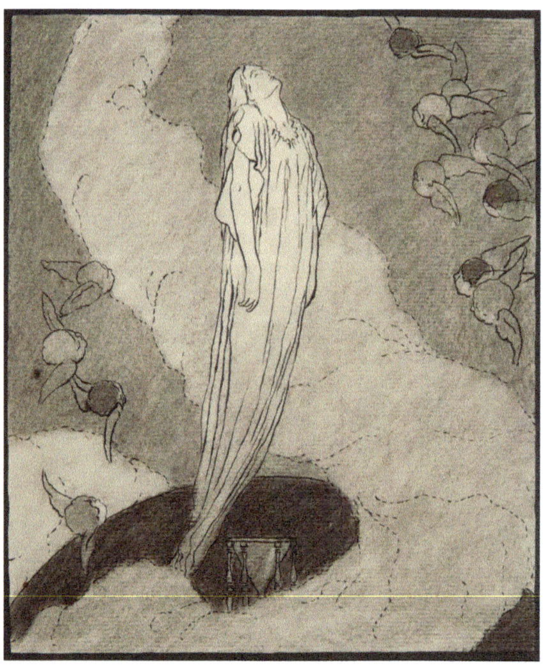

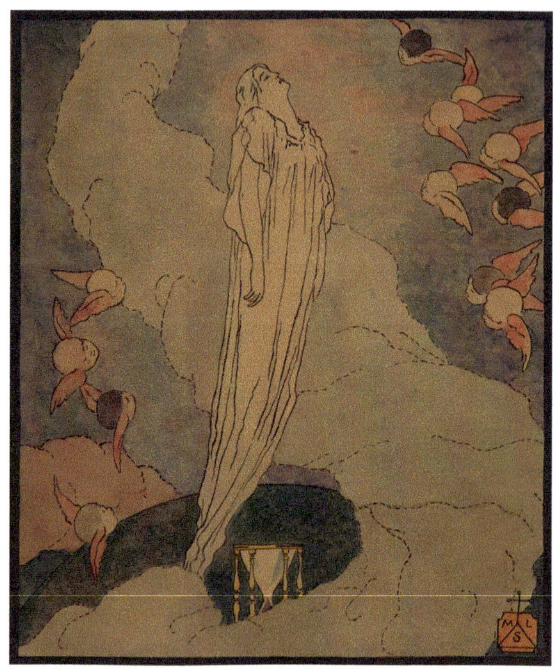

Left: M. Louise Stowell, *As Runs the Glass, our Life Doth Pass*, 19th century. Charcoal and black ink on laid paper. 2016.130.10

Right: M. Louise Stowell, *As Runs the Glass, our Life Doth Pass*, 19th century. Watercolor and black ink on paper. 2016.129.6

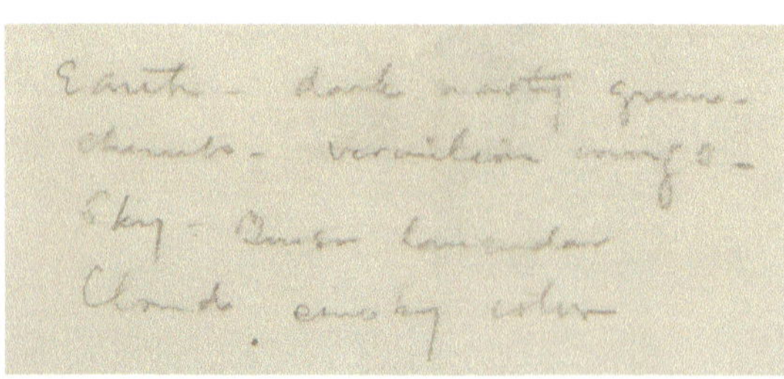

Detail of: M. Louise Stowell, *As Runs the Glass, our Life Doth Pass*, 19th century. Charcoal and black ink on laid paper. 2016.130.10

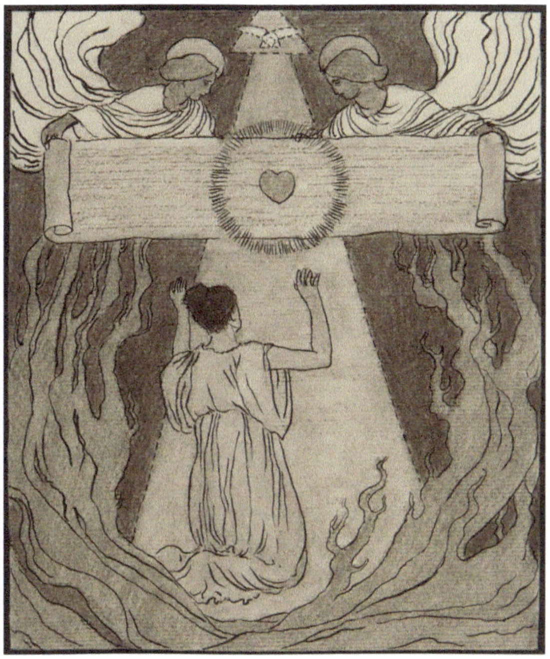

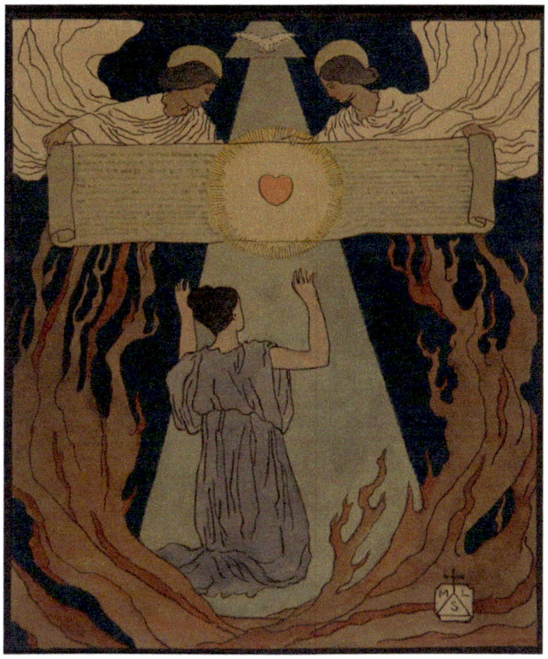

Left: M. Louise Stowell, *My Book and Heart Must Never Part*, 19th century. Charcoal and black ink on laid paper. 2016.130.11

Right: M. Louise Stowell, *My Book and Heart Must Never Part*, 19th century. Watercolor and black ink on paper. 2016.129.7

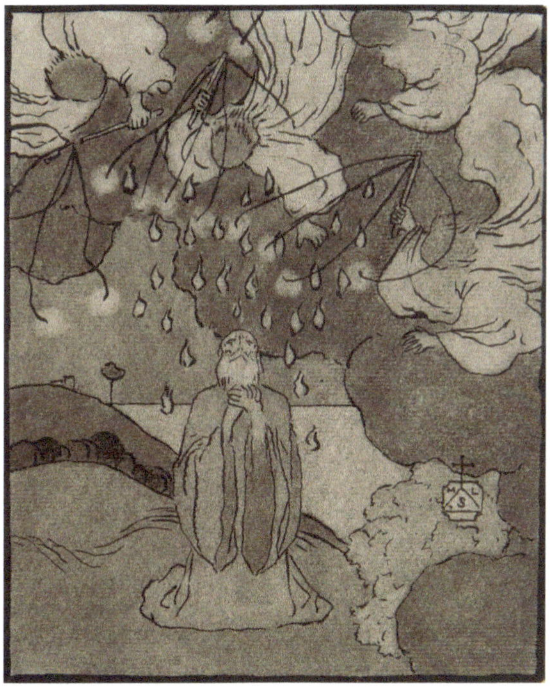

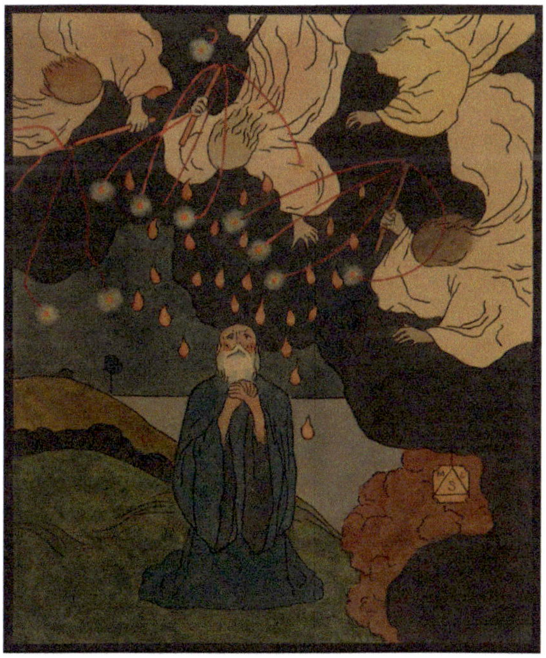

Left: M. Louise Stowell, *Job Feels the Rod Yet Blesses God*, 19th century. Charcoal and black ink on laid paper. 2016.130.12

Right: M. Louise Stowell, *Job Feels the Rod Yet Blesses God*, 19th century. Watercolor and black ink on paper. 2016.129.8

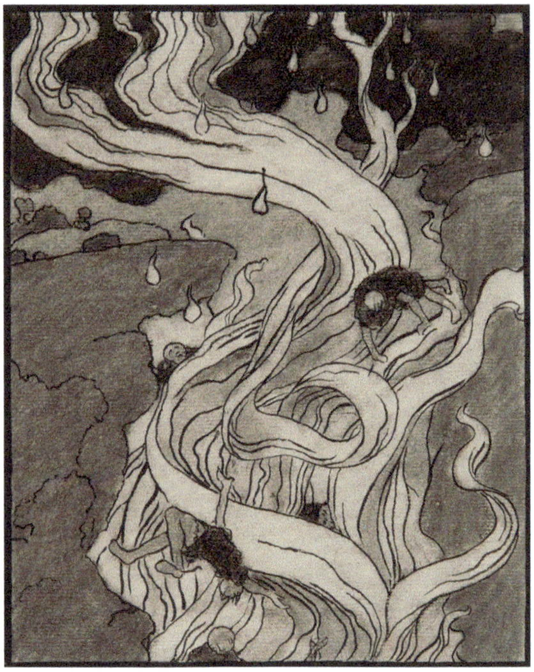

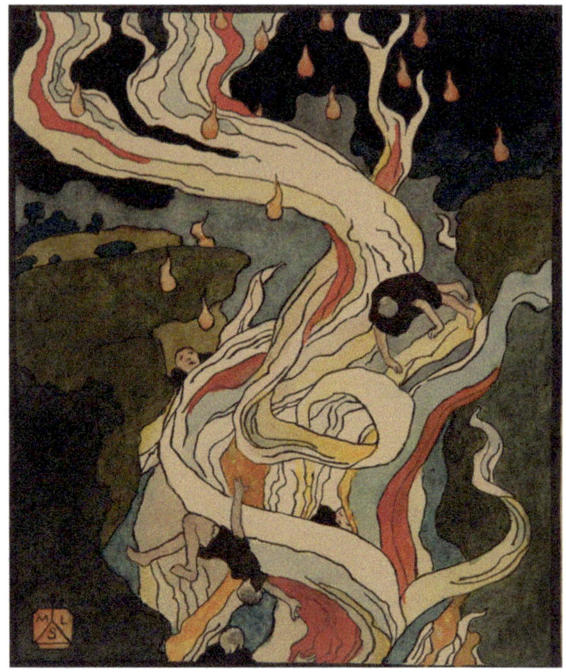

Left: M. Louise Stowell, *Proud Korah's Troop was Swallowed Up*, 19th century. Charcoal and black ink on laid paper. 2016.130.13

Right: M. Louise Stowell, *Proud Korah's Troop was Swallowed Up*, 19th century. Watercolor and black ink on paper. 2016.129.9

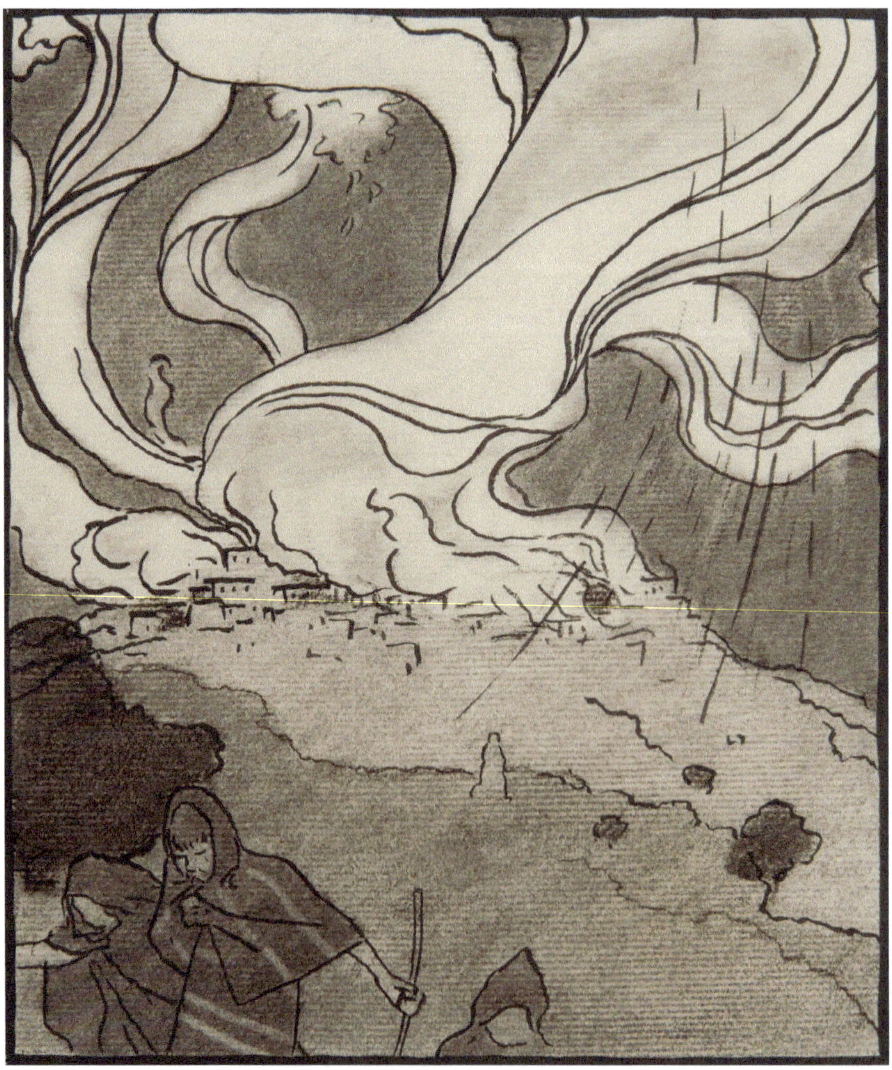

M. Louise Stowell, *Lot Fled to Zoar, Saw Fiery Shower on Sodom Pour*, 19th century. Charcoal and black ink on laid paper. 2016.130.14

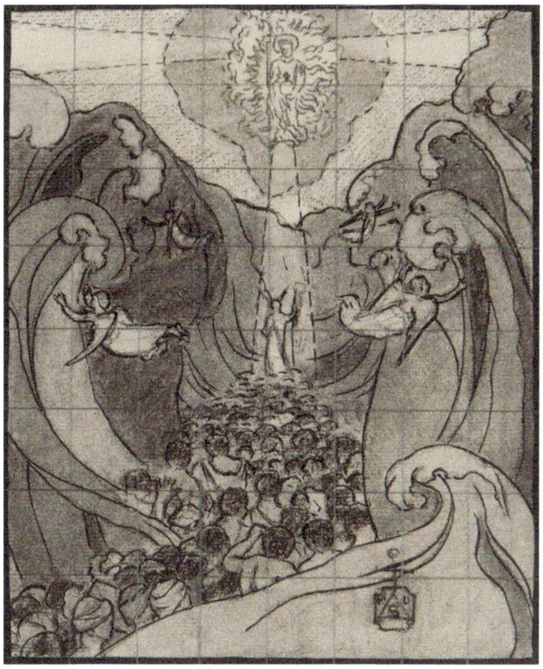

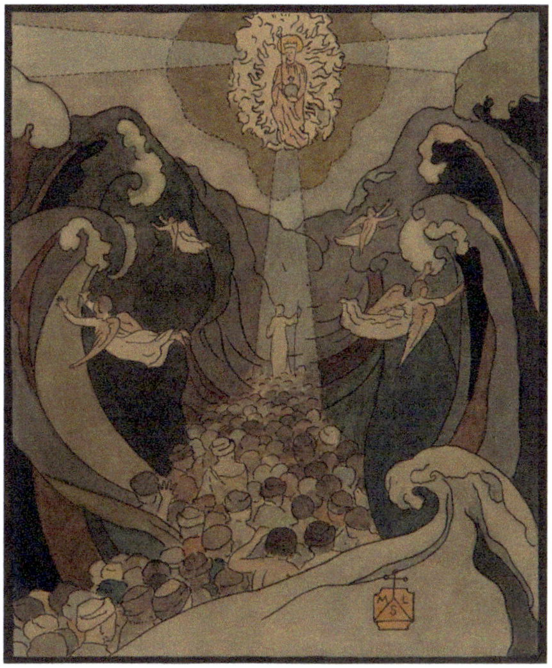

Left: M. Louise Stowell, *Moses Was He who Israel's Host Led Through the Sea*, 19th century. Charcoal and black ink on laid paper. 2016.130.15

Right: M. Louise Stowell, *Moses Was He who Israel's Host Led Through the Sea*, 19th century. Watercolor and black ink on paper. 2016.129.10

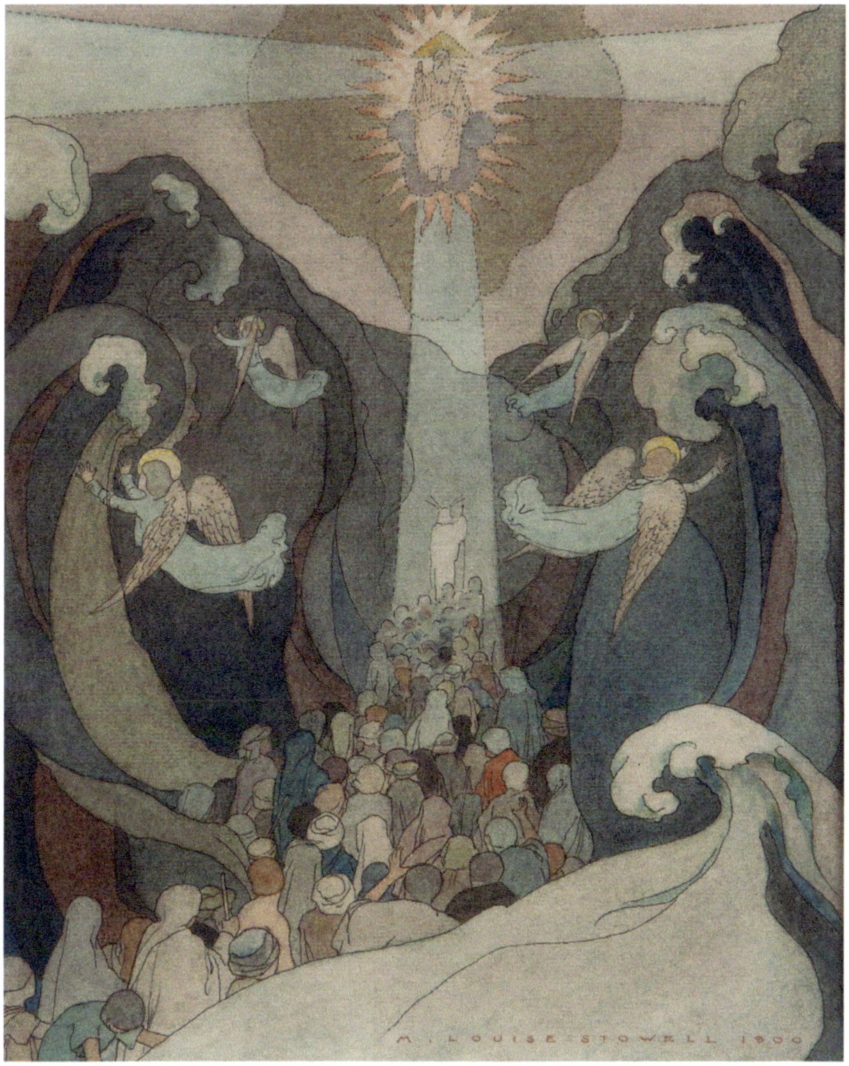


M. Louise Stowell, *Moses was he who Israel's host led through the sea*, 1900. Watercolor, charcoal, and black ink on paper. 2016.128

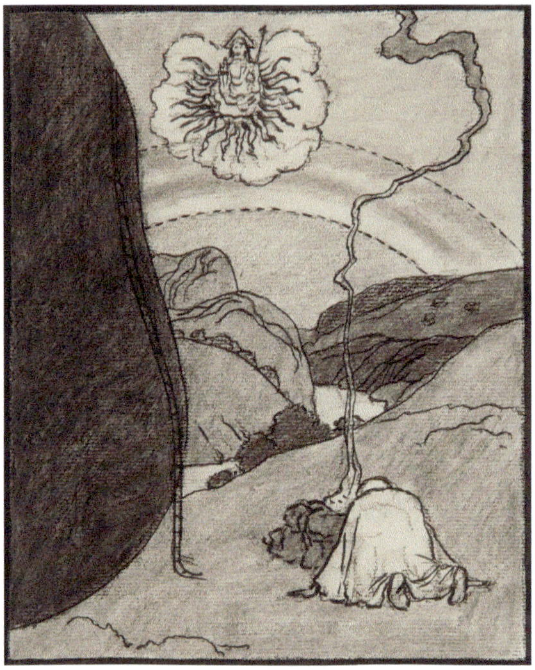

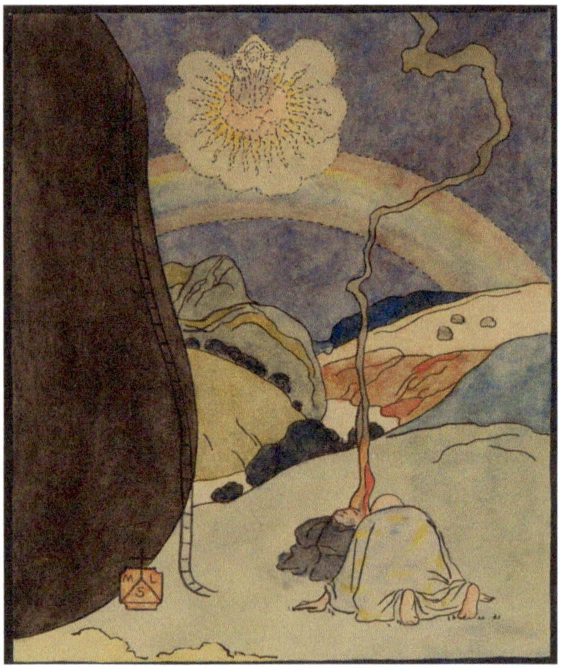

Left: M. Louise Stowell, *Noah Did View the Old World and New*, 19th century. Charcoal and black ink on laid paper. 2016.130.16

Right: M. Louise Stowell, *Noah Did View the Old World and New*, 19th century. Watercolor and black ink on paper. 2016.129.11

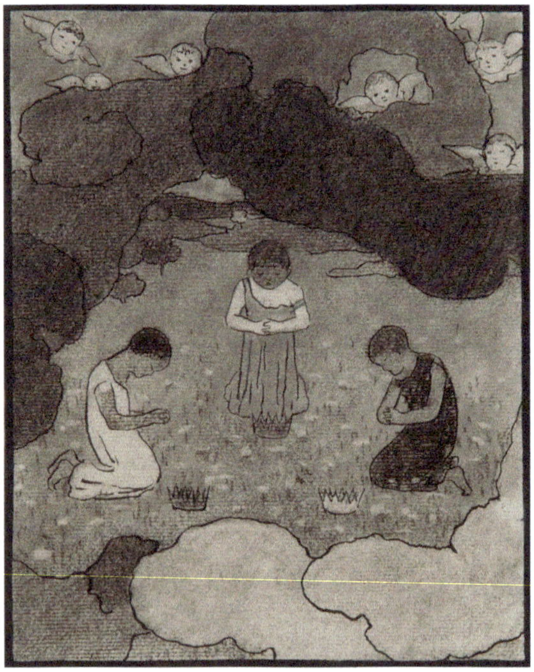

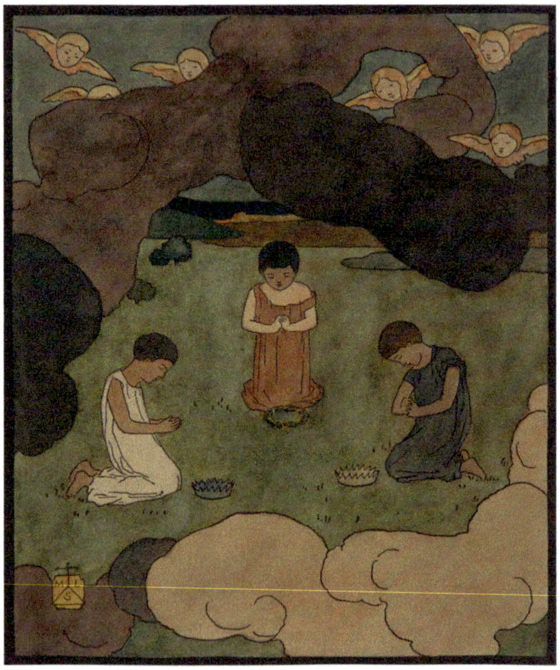

Left: M. Louise Stowell, *Young Obadias, David, Josias, All Were Pious*, 19th century. Charcoal and black ink on laid paper. 2016.130.17

Right: M. Louise Stowell, *Young Obadias, David, Josias, All Were Pious*, 19th century. Watercolor and black ink on paper. 2016.129.12

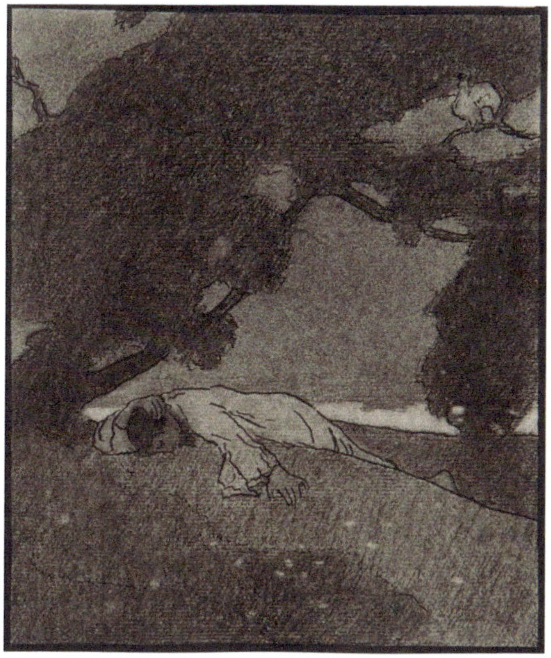

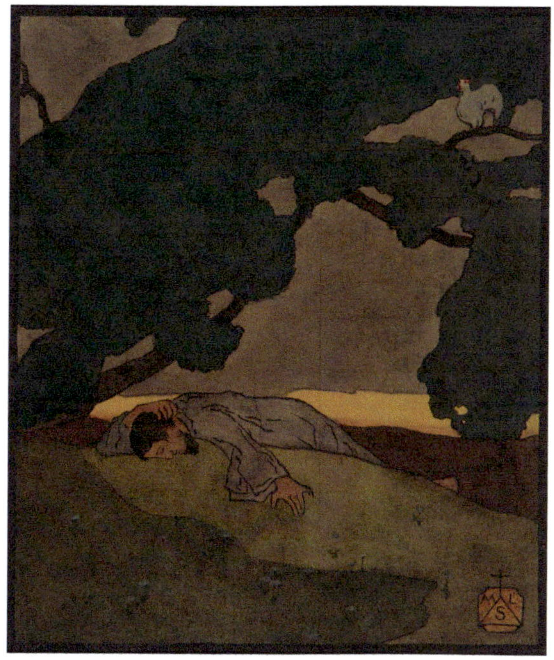

Left: M. Louise Stowell, *Peter Denied His Lord and Cried*, 19th century. Charcoal and black ink on laid paper. 2016.130.18

Right: M. Louise Stowell, *Peter Denied His Lord and Cried*, 19th century. Watercolor and black ink on paper. 2016.129.13

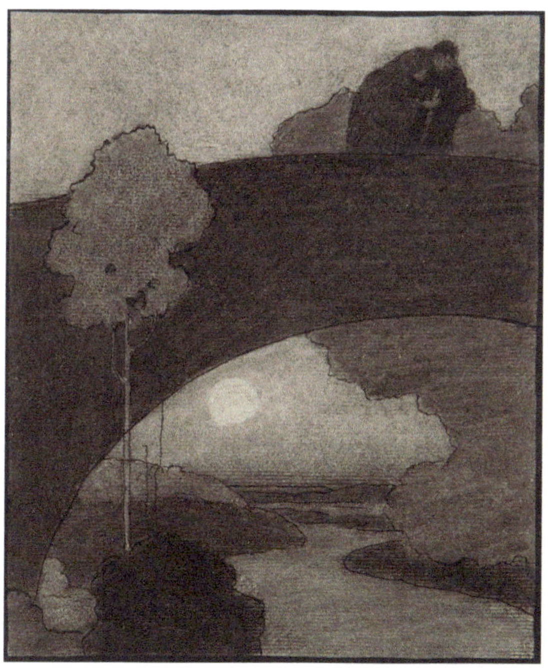

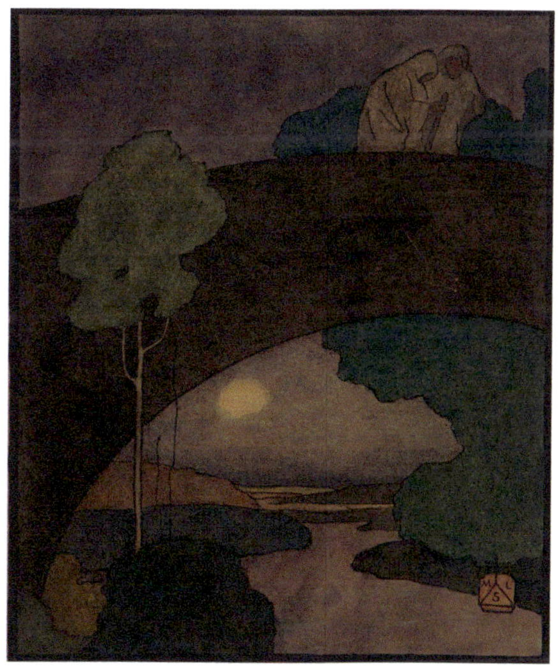

Left: M. Louise Stowell, *Young Pious Ruth Left All for Truth*, 19th century. Charcoal and black ink on laid paper. 2016.130.20

Right: M. Louise Stowell, *Young Pious Ruth Left All for Truth*, 19th century. Watercolor and black ink on paper. 2016.129.15

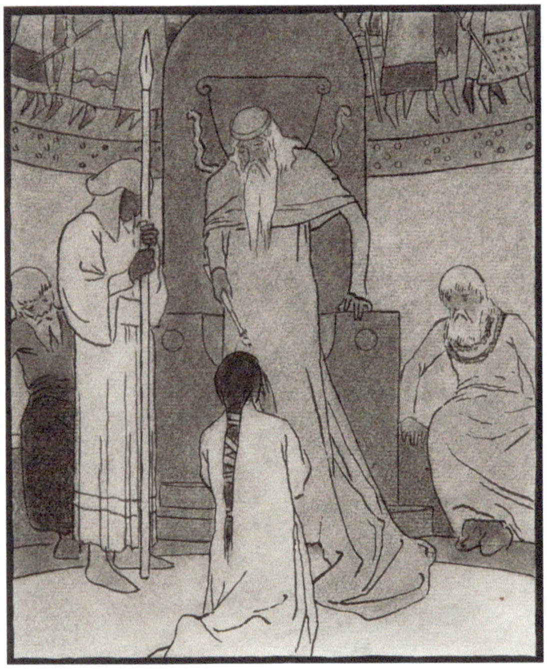

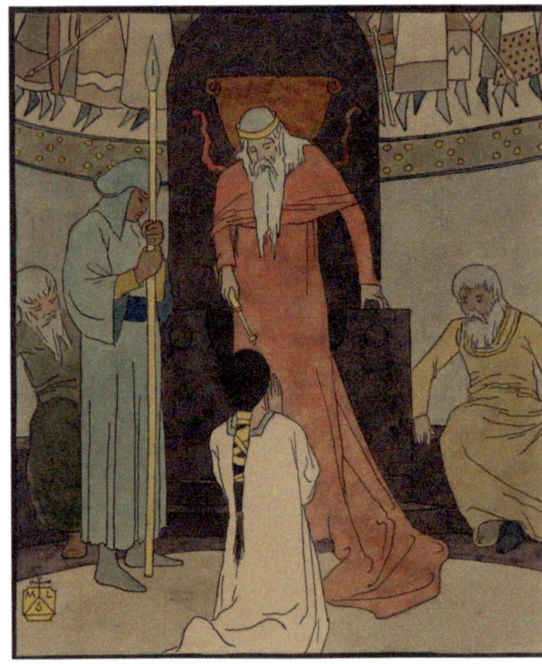

Left: M. Louise Stowell, *Queen Esther Sues and Saves the Jews*, 19th century. Charcoal and black ink on laid paper. 2016.130.19

Right: M. Louise Stowell, *Queen Esther Sues and Saves the Jews*, 19th century. Watercolor and black ink on paper. 2016.129.14

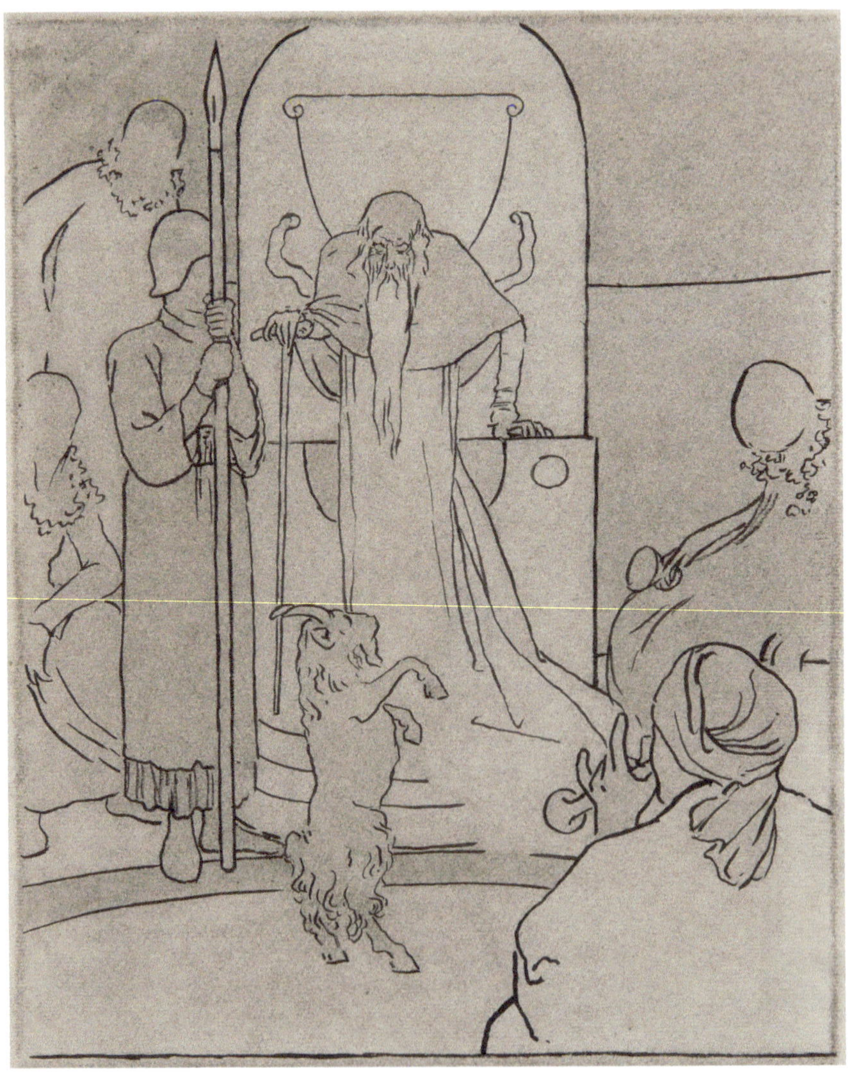

M. Louise Stowell, *Court Figures with Dancing Goat*, 19th century. Charcoal and black ink on laid paper. 2016.147

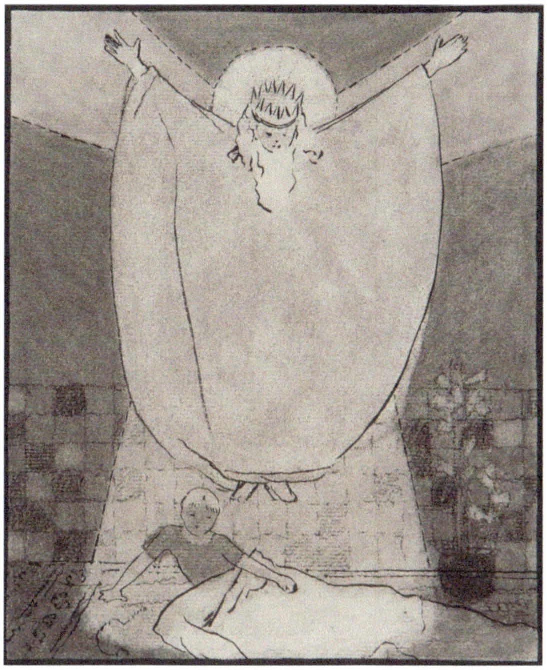

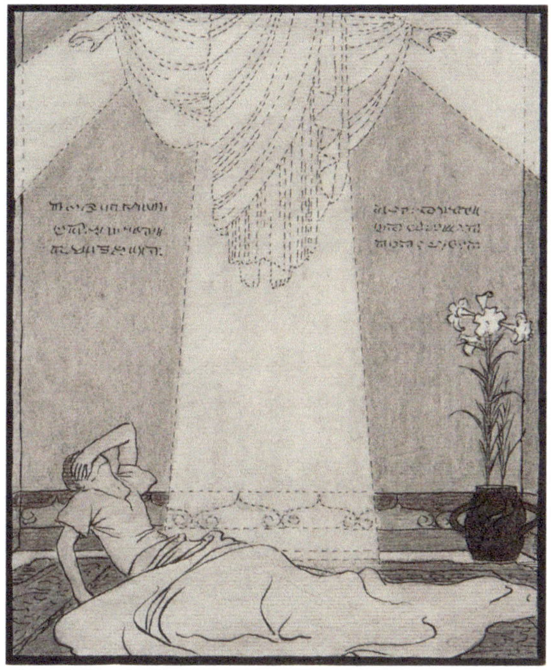

Left: M. Louise Stowell, *Young Samuel Dear the Lord Did Fear*, 19th century. Charcoal and black ink on laid paper. 2016.130.22

Right: M. Louise Stowell, *Young Samuel Dear the Lord Did Fear*, 19th century. Charcoal and black ink on laid paper. 2016.130.21

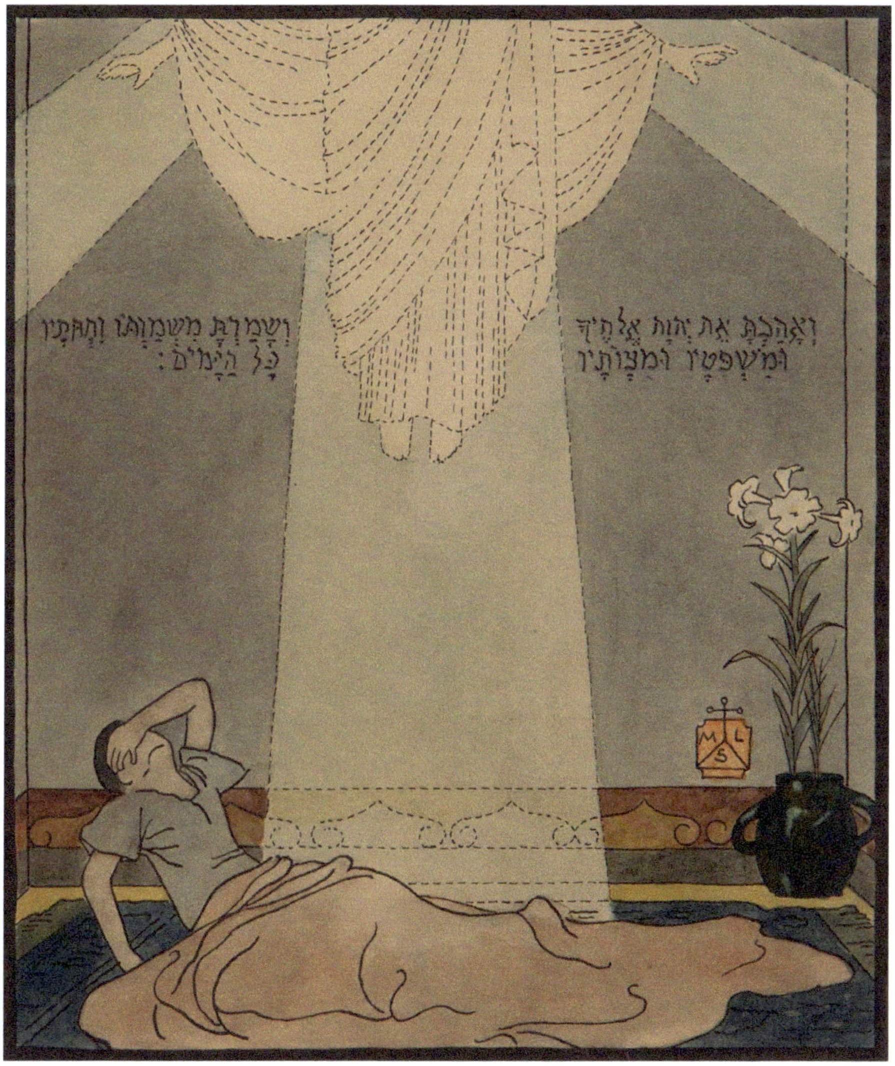

M. Louise Stowell, *Young Samuel Dear the Lord Did Fear*, 19th century. Watercolor and black ink on paper. 2016.129.16

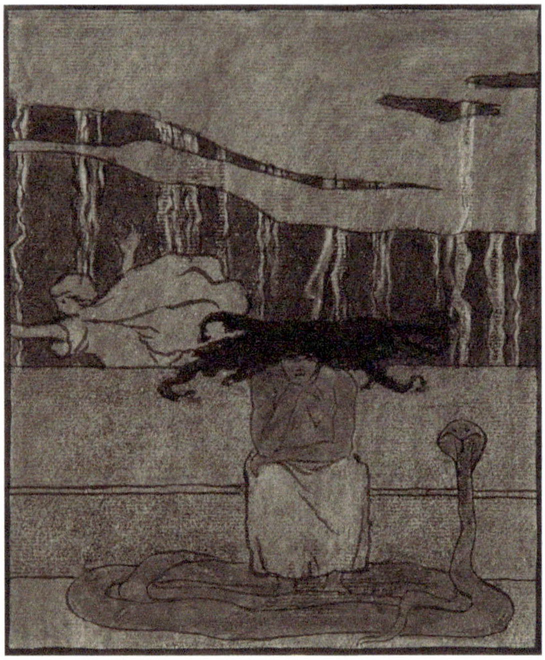

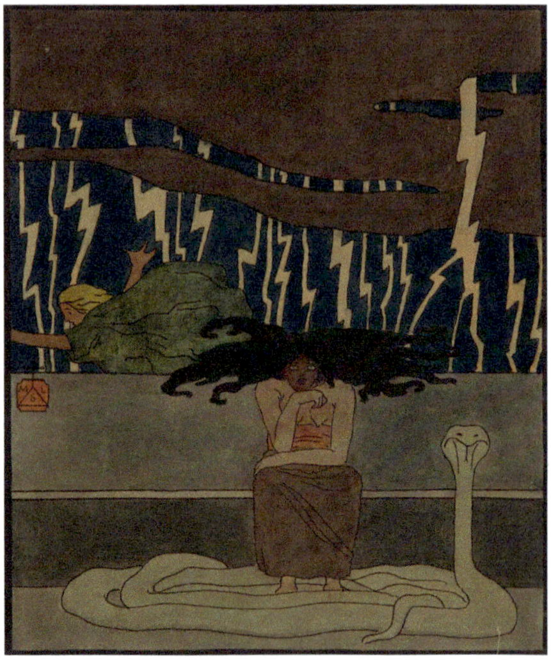

Left: M. Louise Stowell, *Young Timothy Learned Sin to Flee*, 19th century. Charcoal and black ink on laid paper. 2016.130.23

Right: M. Louise Stowell, *Young Timothy Learned Sin to Flee*, 19th century. Watercolor and black ink on paper. 2016.129.17

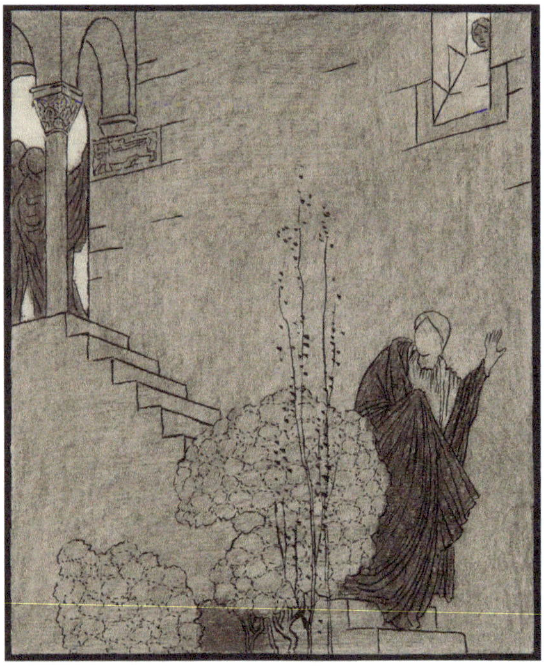

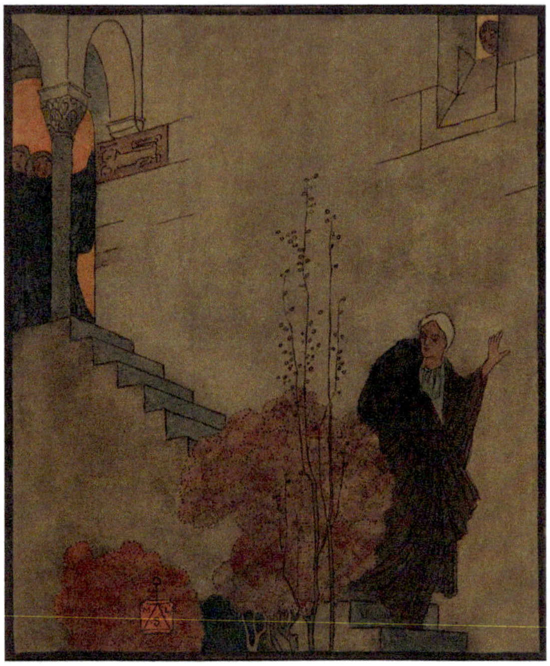

Left: M. Louise Stowell, *Vashti for Pride was Set Aside*, 19th century. Charcoal and black ink on laid paper. 2016.130.24

Right: M. Louise Stowell, *Vashti for Pride was Set Aside*, 19th century. Watercolor and black ink on paper. 2016.129.18

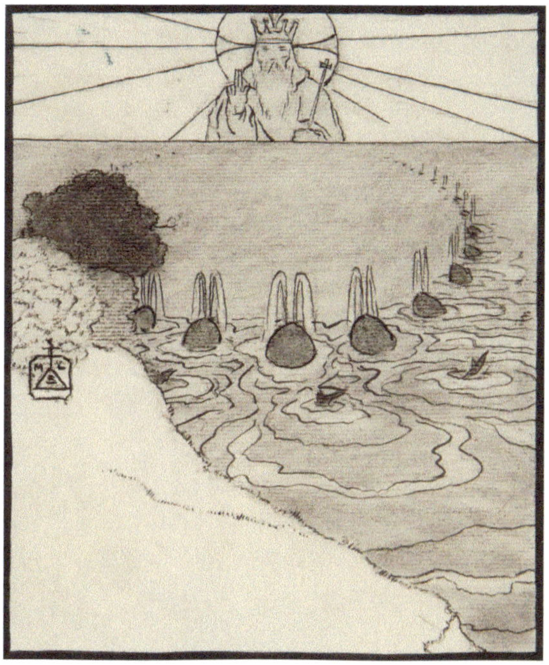

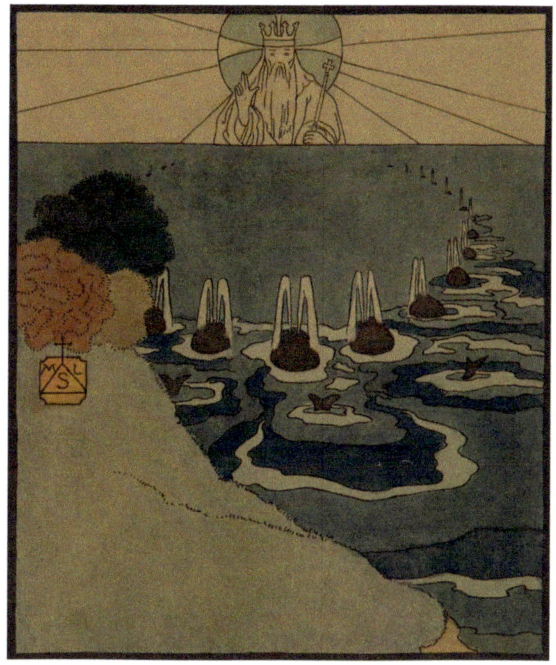

Left: M. Louise Stowell, *Whales in the Sea God's Voice Obey*, 19th century. Charcoal and black ink on laid paper. 2016.130.25

Right: M. Louise Stowell, *Whales in the Sea God's Voice Obey*, 19th century. Watercolor and black ink on paper. 2016.129.19

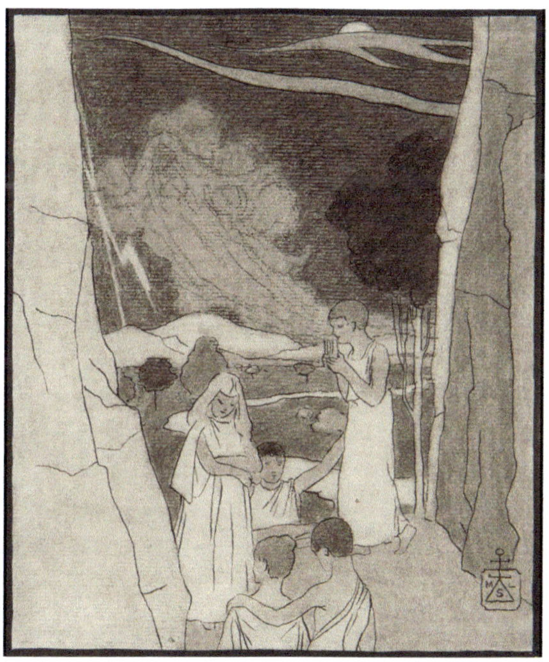

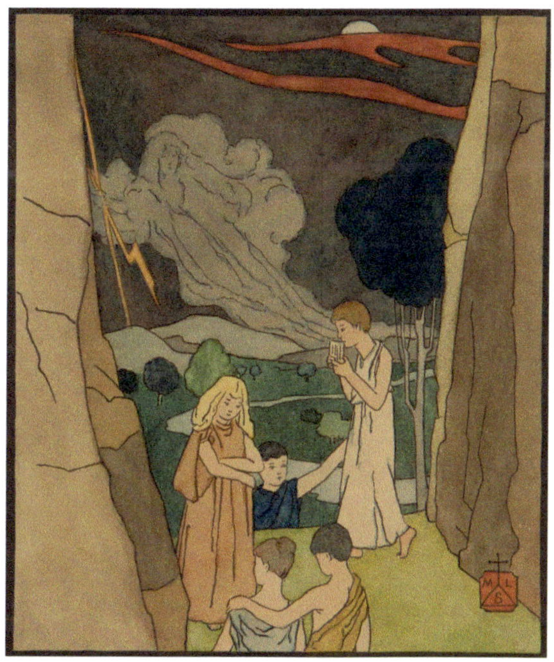

Left: M. Louise Stowell, *While Youth Do Cheer, Death May Be Near*, 19th century. Charcoal and black ink on laid paper. 2016.130.27

Right: M. Louise Stowell, *While Youth Do Cheer, Death May Be Near*, 19th century. Watercolor and black ink on paper. 2016.129.20

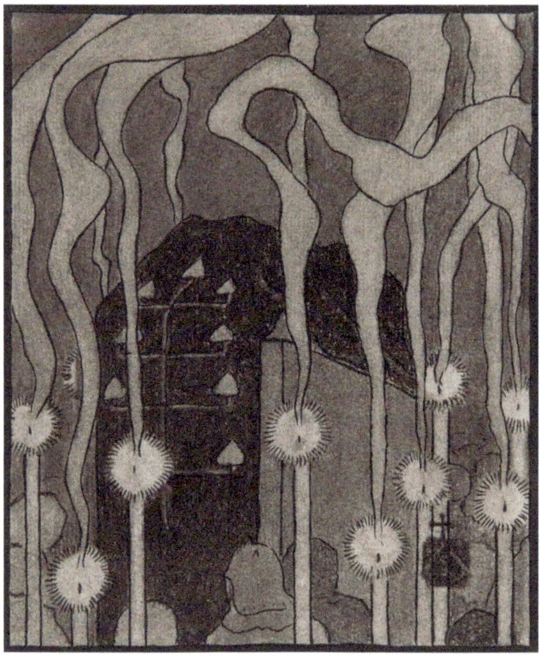

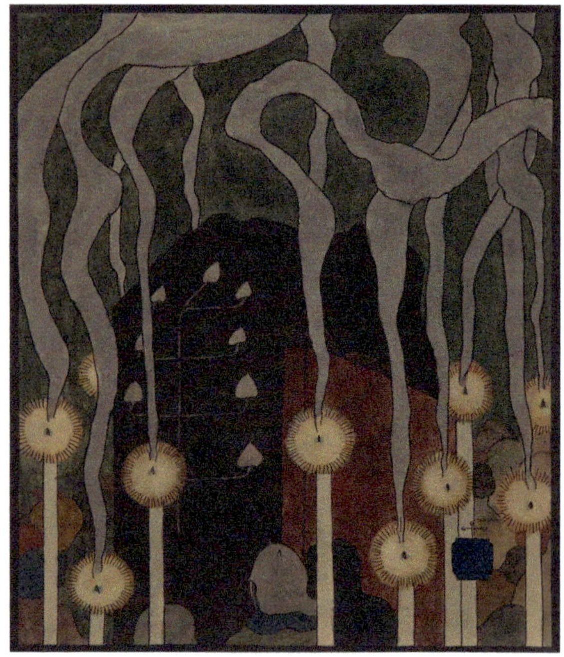

Left: M. Louise Stowell, *Xerxes Did Die, and So Must I*, 19th century. Charcoal and black ink on laid paper. 2016.130.26

Right: M. Louise Stowell, *Xerxes Did Die, and So Must I*, 19th century. Watercolor and black ink on paper. 2016.129.21

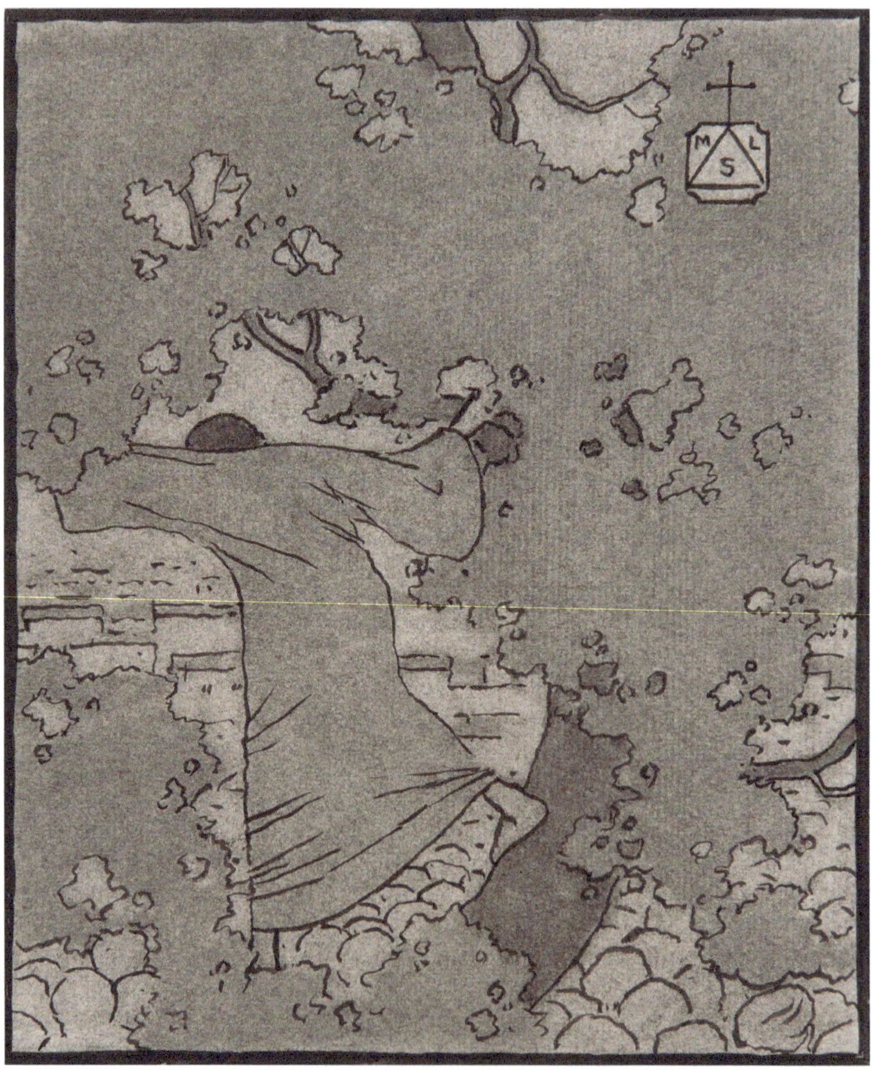

M. Louise Stowell, *Zaccheus He Did Climb the Tree Our Lord to See*, 19th century. Charcoal and black ink on laid paper. 2016.130.28

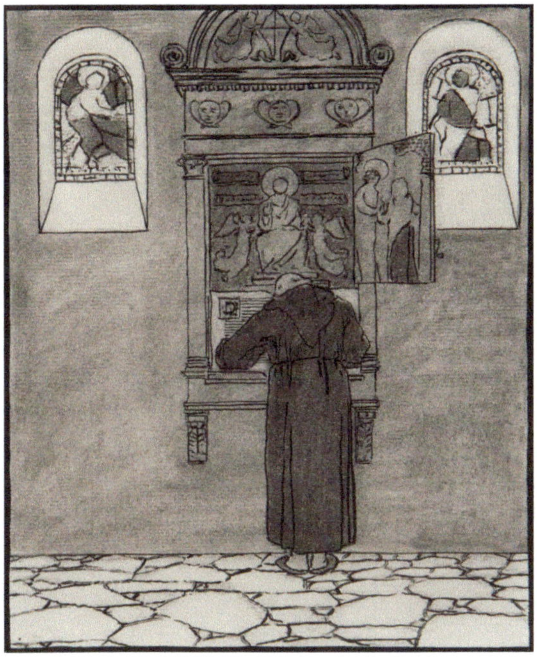

M. Louise Stowell, *Study for a New England Primer*, 19th century. Charcoal and black ink on laid paper. 2016.130.29

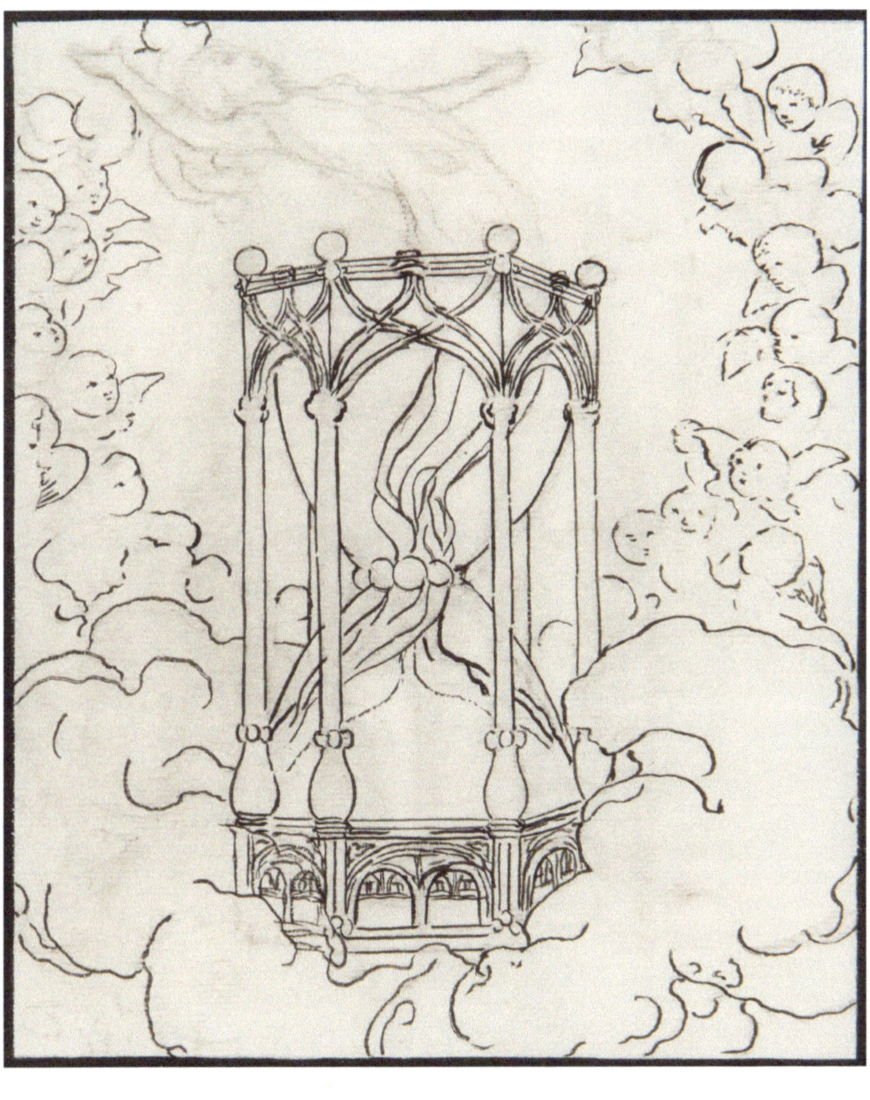

M. Louise Stowell, *As Runs the Glass, Our Life Doth Pass*, 19th century. Black ink and charcoal on laid paper. 2016.130.30

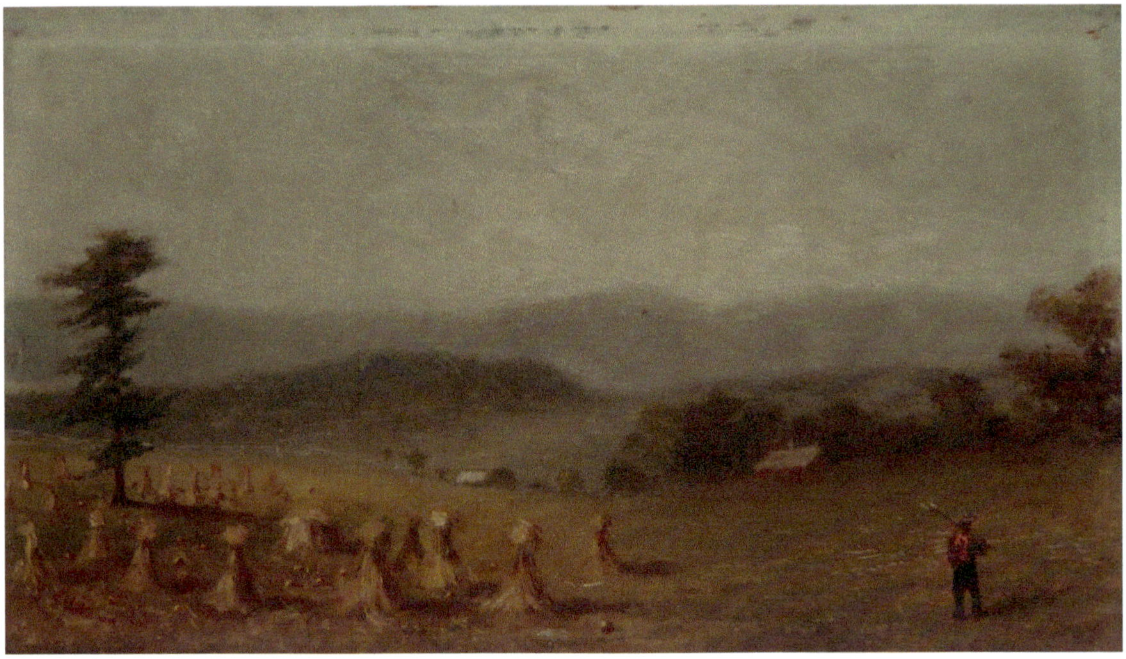

Harvey Ellis, *Farmer and Cornstalks*, 1877. Oil on board. 2016.30

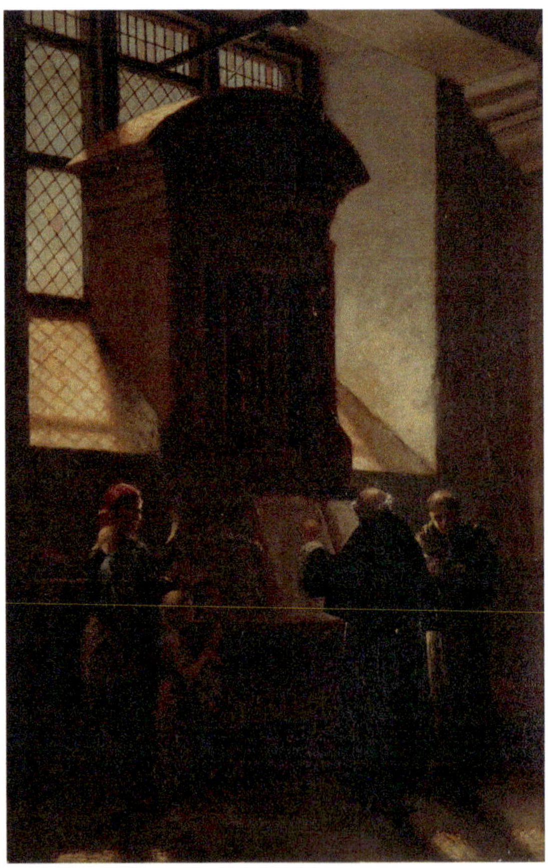

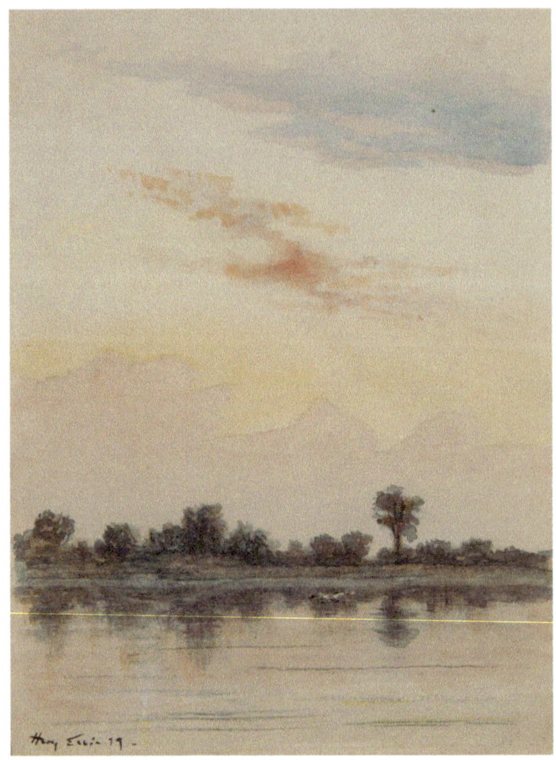

Left: Harvey Ellis, *Reading the Bible, Old Chelsea Church, England, AD 1270*, 1878. Oil on canvas. 2016.38

Right: Harvey Ellis, *Lake, Sky, and Trees*, 1879. Watercolor, white gouache, and graphite on paper. 2016.52

Harvey Ellis, *The Star in the East*, 1877. Oil on canvas. 2016.54

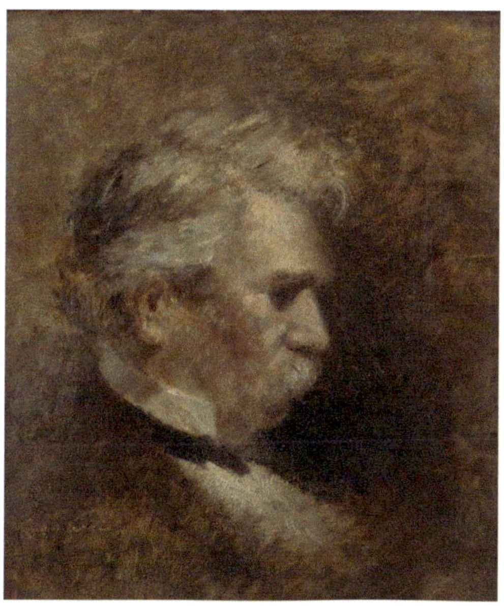

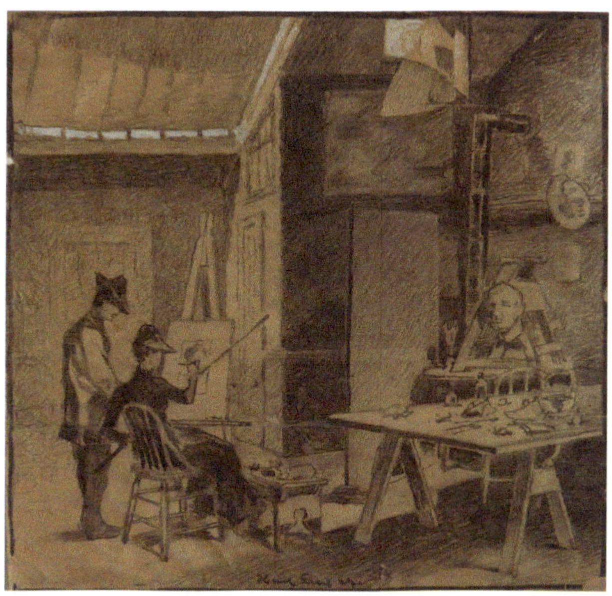

Left: Harvey Ellis, *Portrait of the Artist's Father*, 1879. Oil on canvas. Gift of Mary M. Gazley, 1997.4

Right: Harvey Ellis, *The Old Rochester Art Club Studio in Reynolds Arcade*, 1879. Graphite with charcoal and white gouache on tan wove paper. Anonymous gift, 1972.93

Left: Harvey Ellis, *Study of a Farmer*, 1883. Charcoal on brown laid paper. 2016.39

Right: Harvey Ellis, *The Picnic*, 1871. Ink wash and graphite on paper. 2016.80

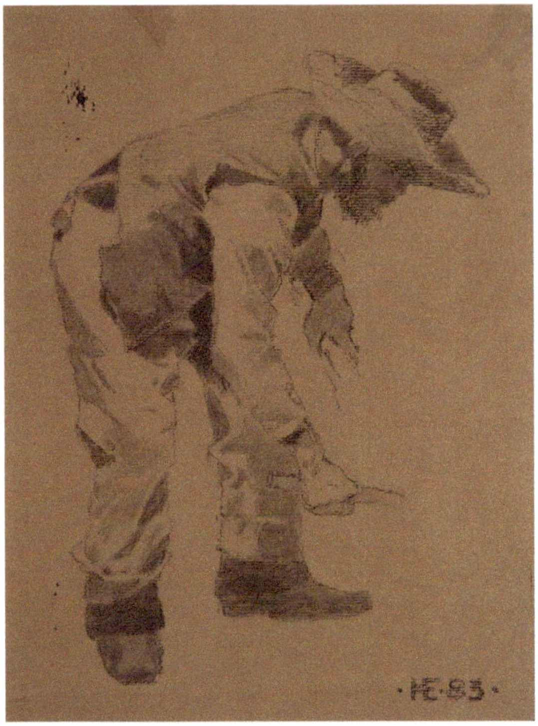

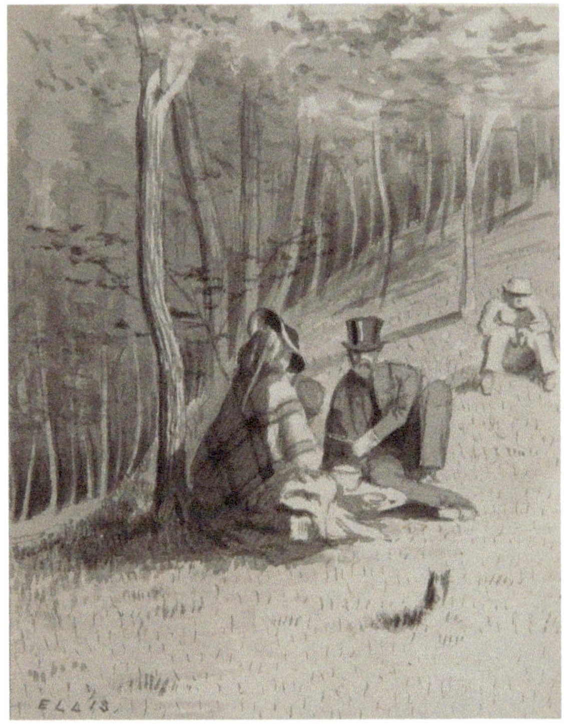

Harvey Ellis, *The Sea Breeze–Lake Ontario*, 1880. Oil on canvas. 2016.29

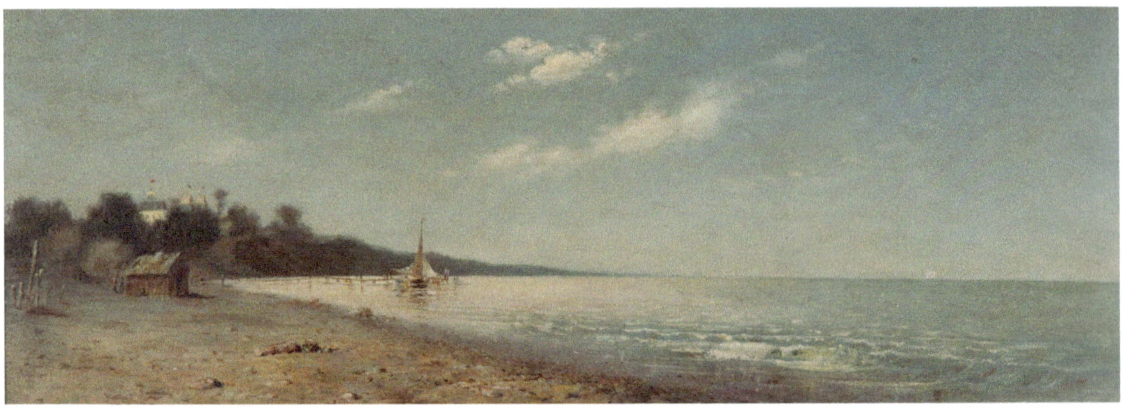

Left: Harvey Ellis, *Seated Girl*, 1879. Charcoal and graphite on paper. 2016.85

Right: Harvey Ellis, *Man with a Scythe*, 1881. Oil on thin board. 2016.83

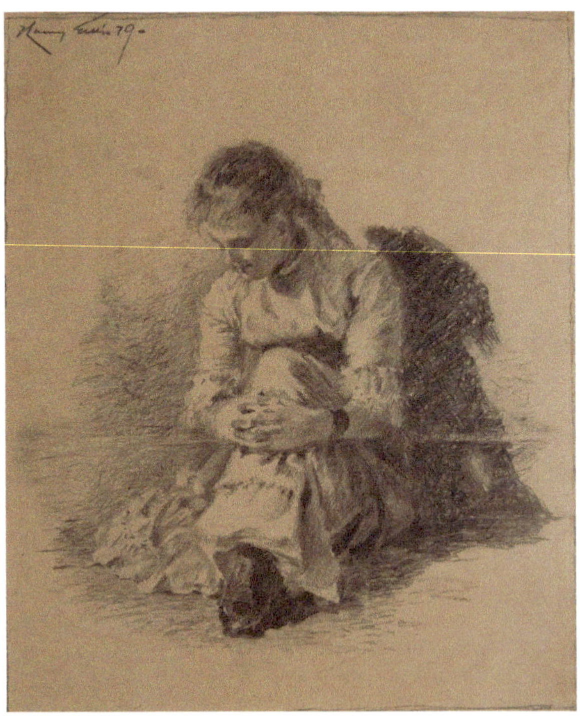

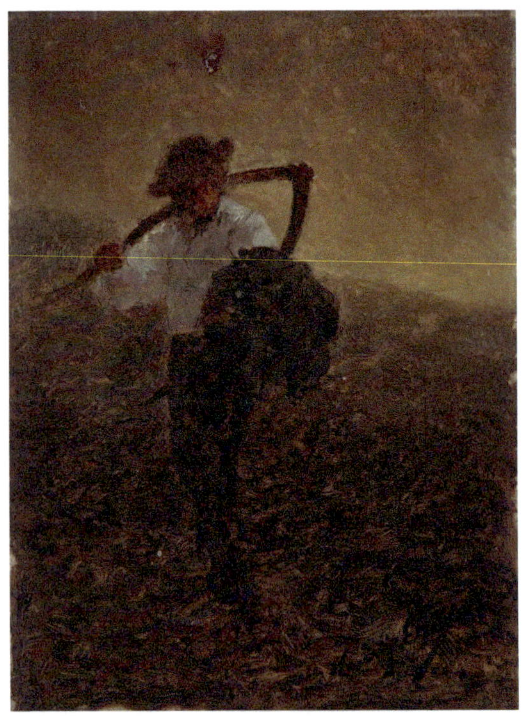

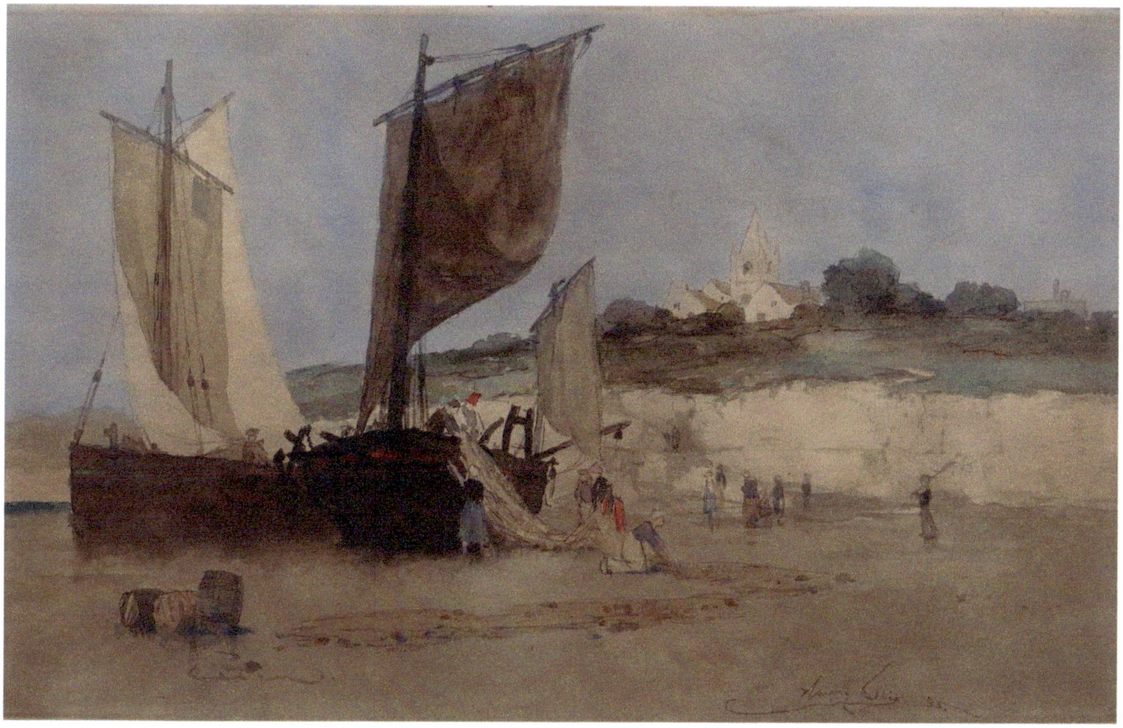

Harvey Ellis, *Fishermen Drying Sails and Nets*, 1885. Watercolor and graphite on paper. Gift of Jean R. France, Architectural Historian, 2022.2

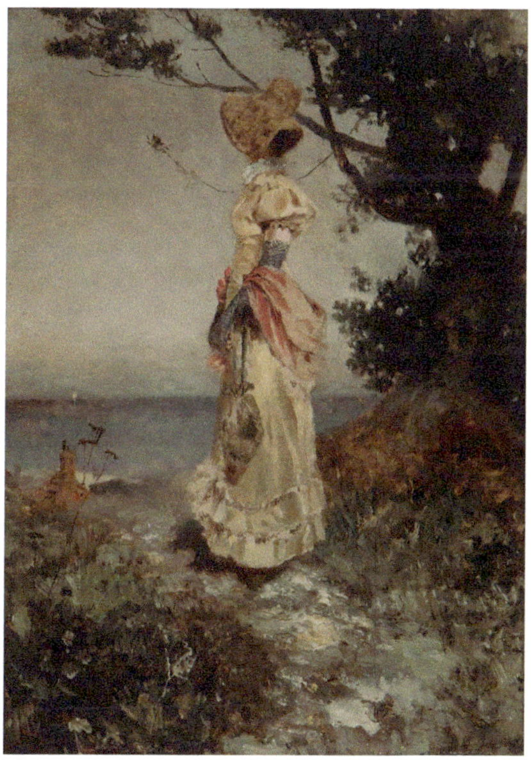

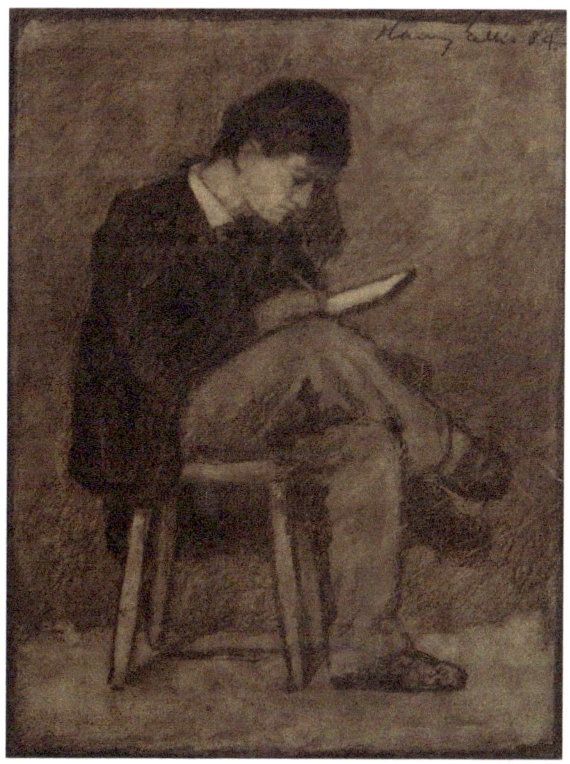

Left: Harvey Ellis, *The Lass that Loved a Sailor*, 1881. Oil on canvas. 2016.37

Right: Harvey Ellis, *Seated Man*, 1884. Charcoal on laid tan paper. Gift of Mr. and Mrs. Robert L. Loveless, 1973.24

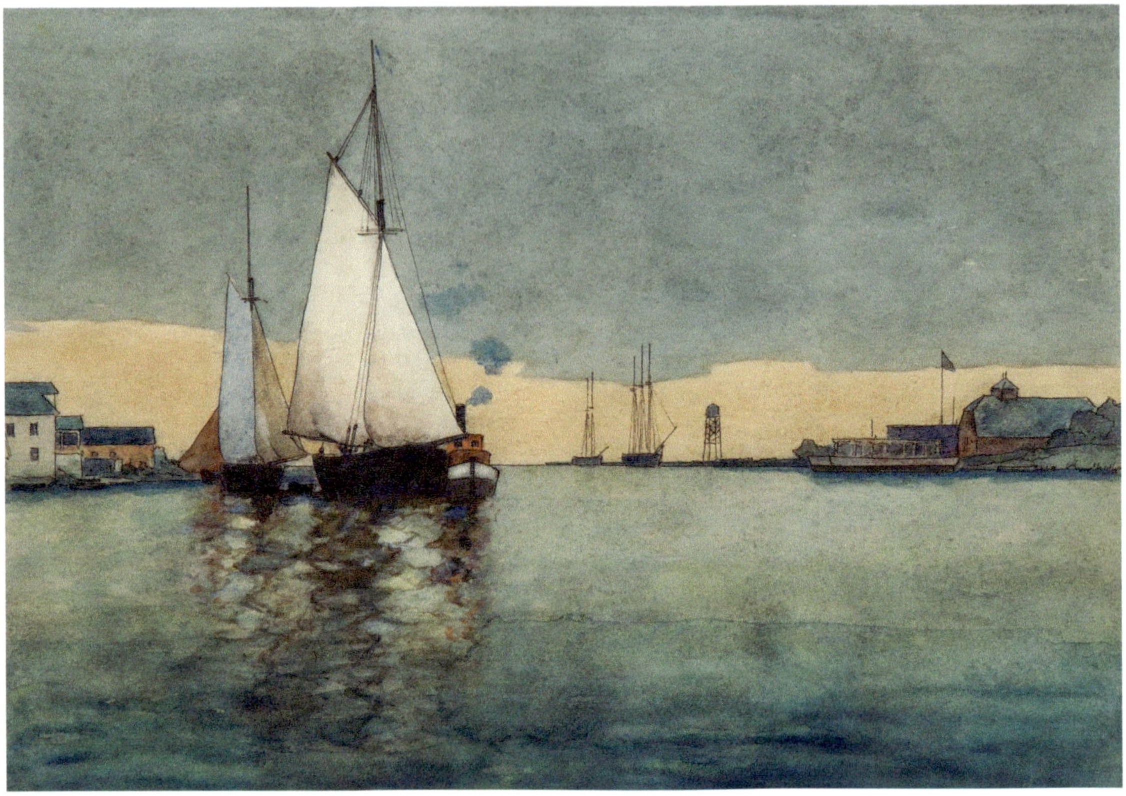

Attributed to Harvey Ellis, *Lake and River Port*, 19th–20th centuries Watercolor and ink on paper. 2016.67

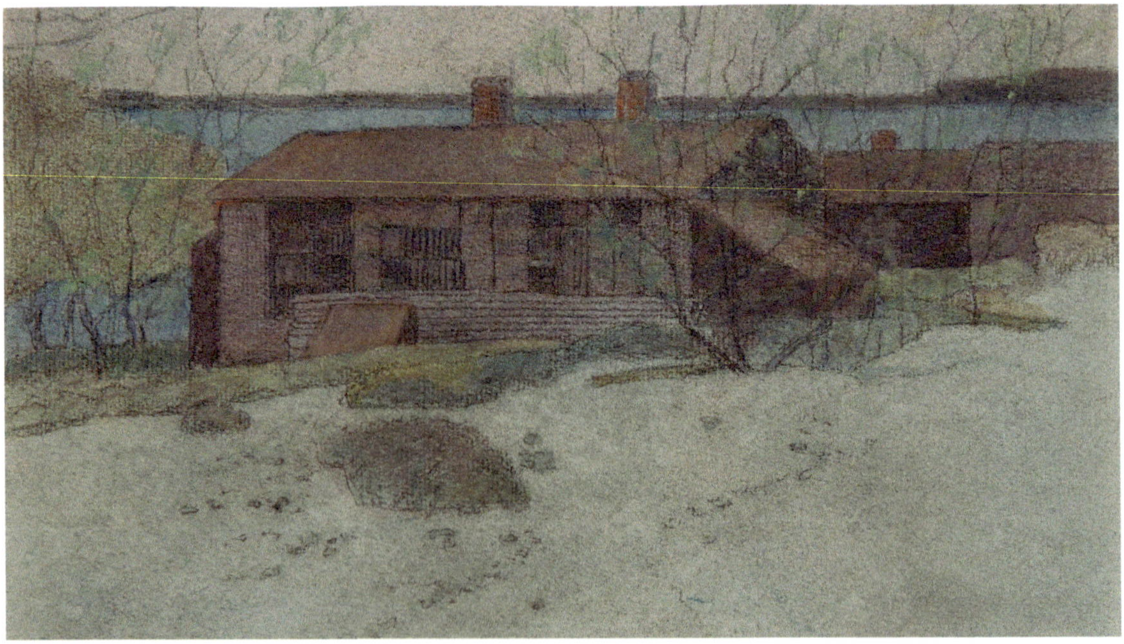

Harvey Ellis, *House on a Lake*, 19th–20th centuries. Pastel, charcoal, and watercolor on laid paper. 2016.75

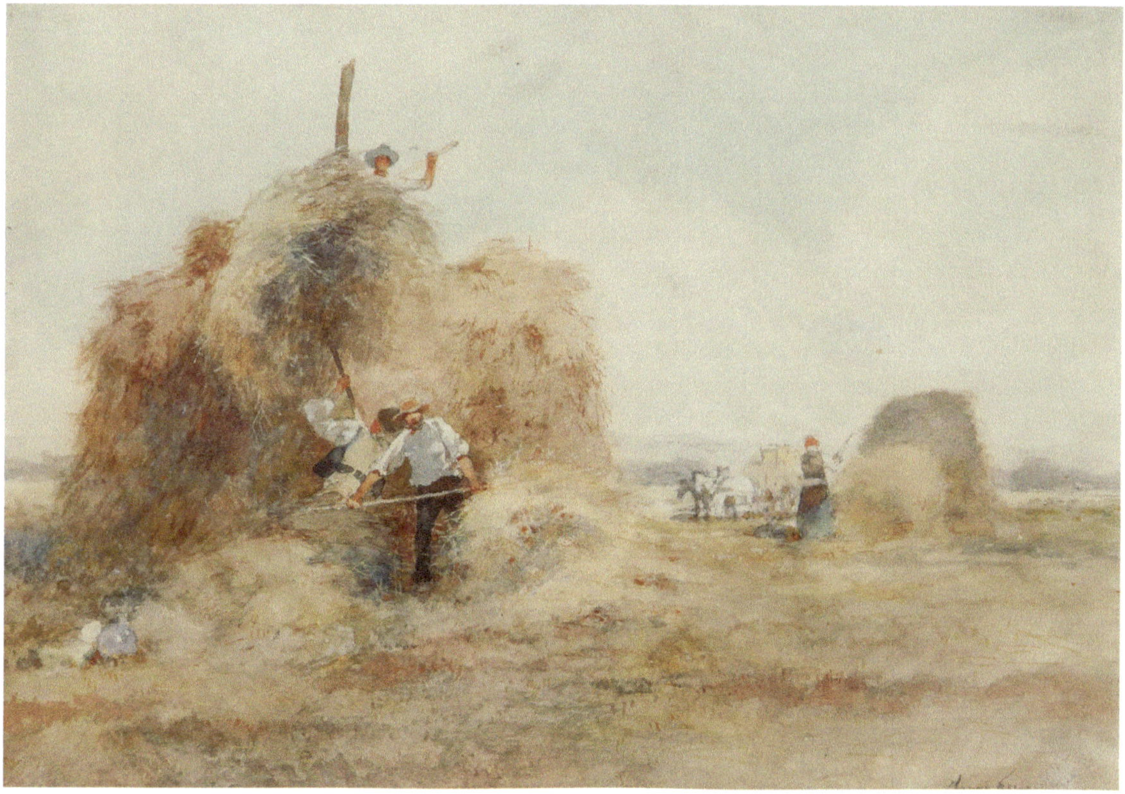

Harvey Ellis, *Pitching Hay*, 19th-20th centuries. Watercolor and graphite on paper. 2016.17

Harvey Ellis, *Night Scene, Erie Canal*, 19th-20th centuries. Oil on Academy board. 2016.14

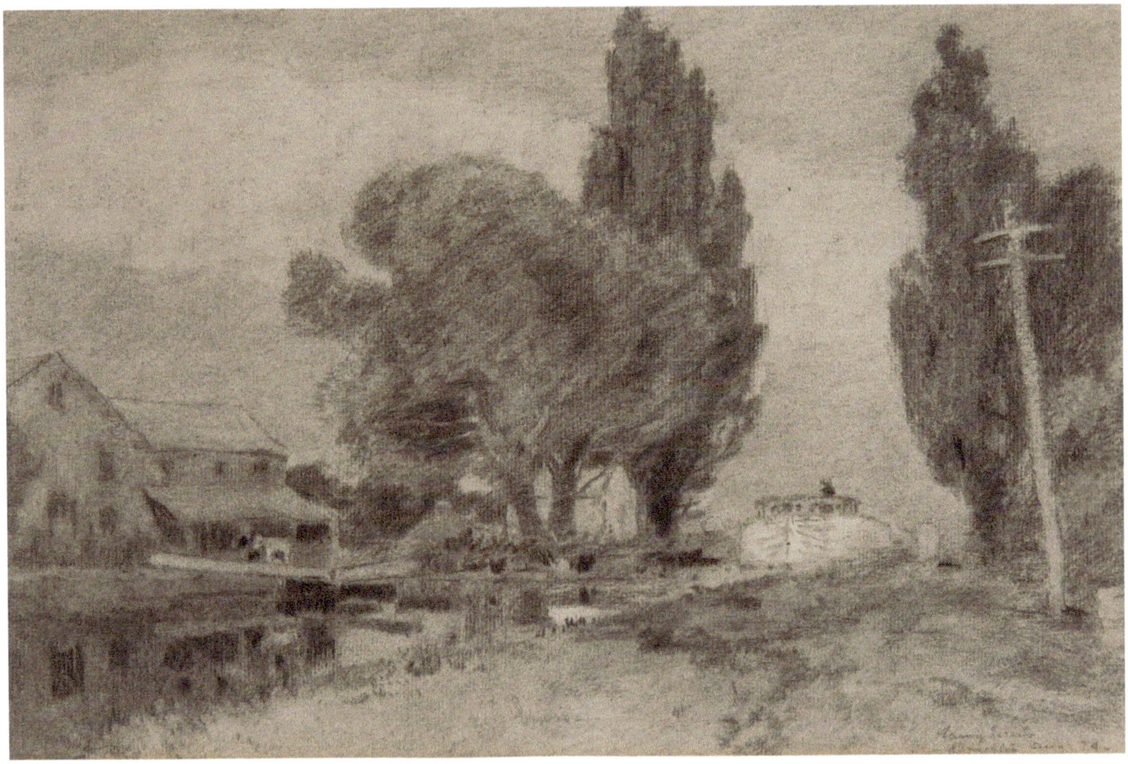

Harvey Ellis, *Landscape with Canal Boat and Farmhouse*, 1894. Charcoal on laid paper. 2016.42

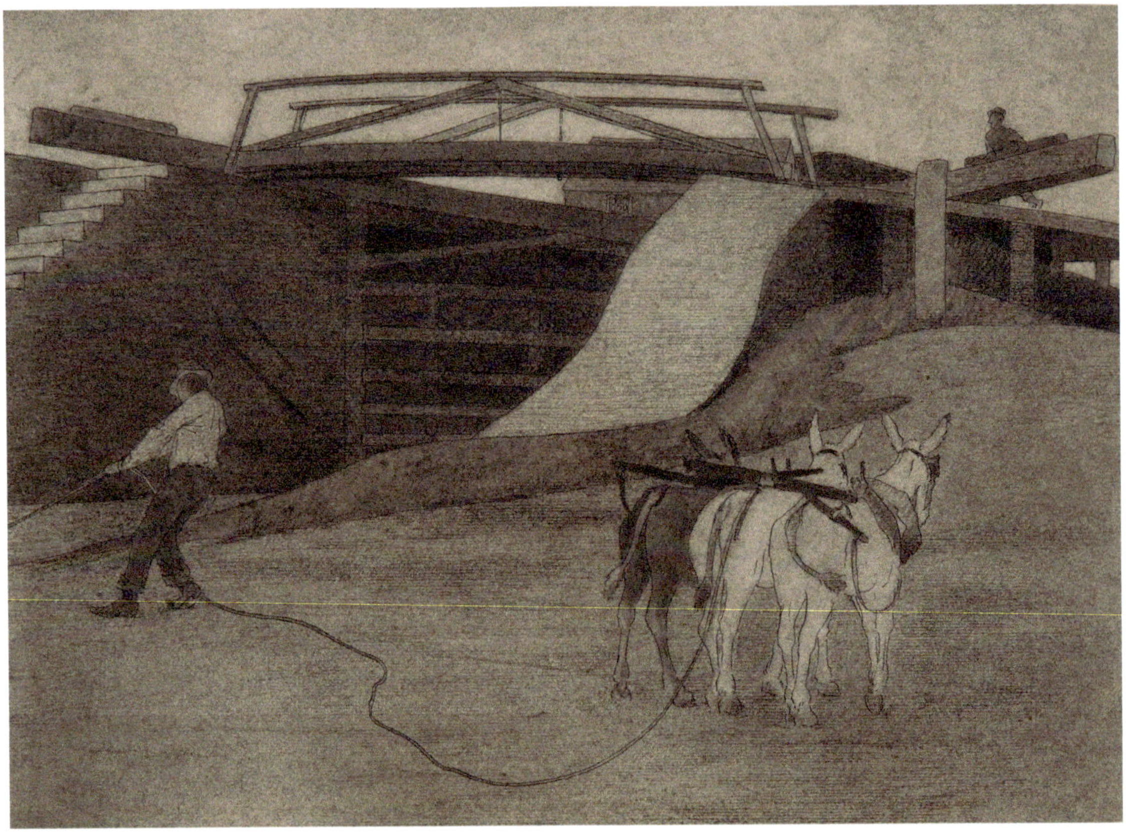

Harvey Ellis, *Mules at the Canal Lock*, circa 1894. Charcoal and black ink on laid paper. 2016.43

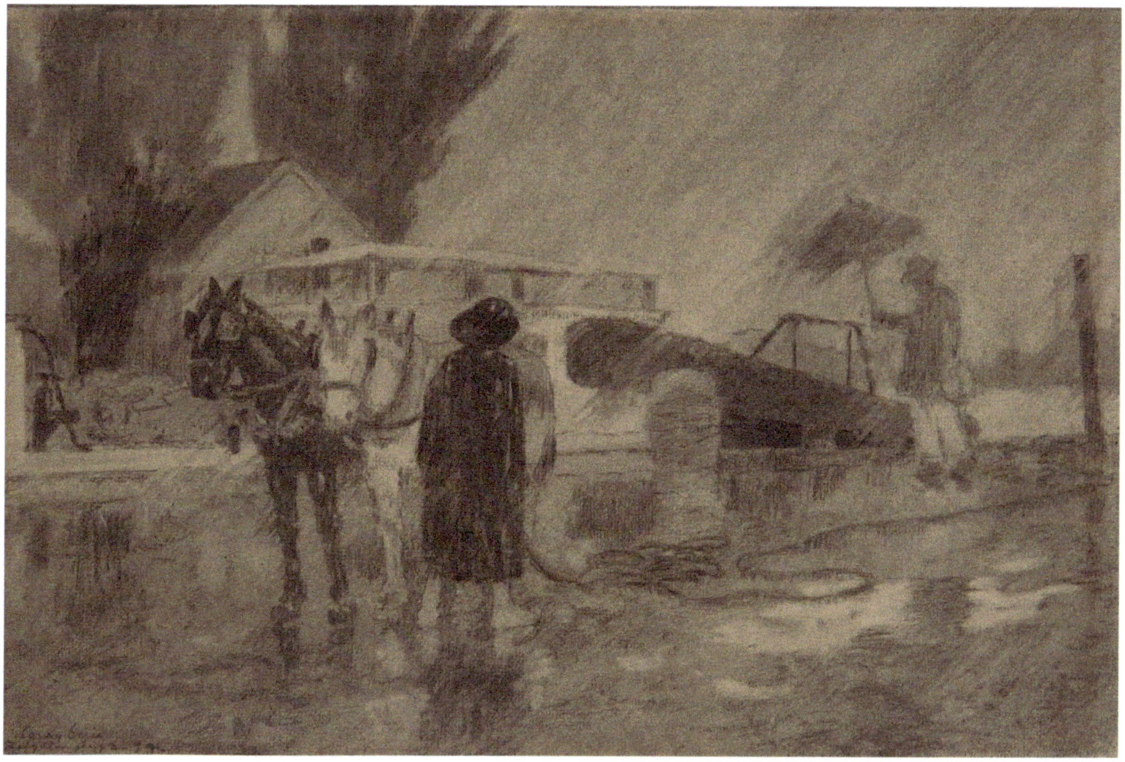

Harvey Ellis, *At the Eastern Wide Waters in a Rain Storm*, 1894. Charcoal on laid paper. 2016.45

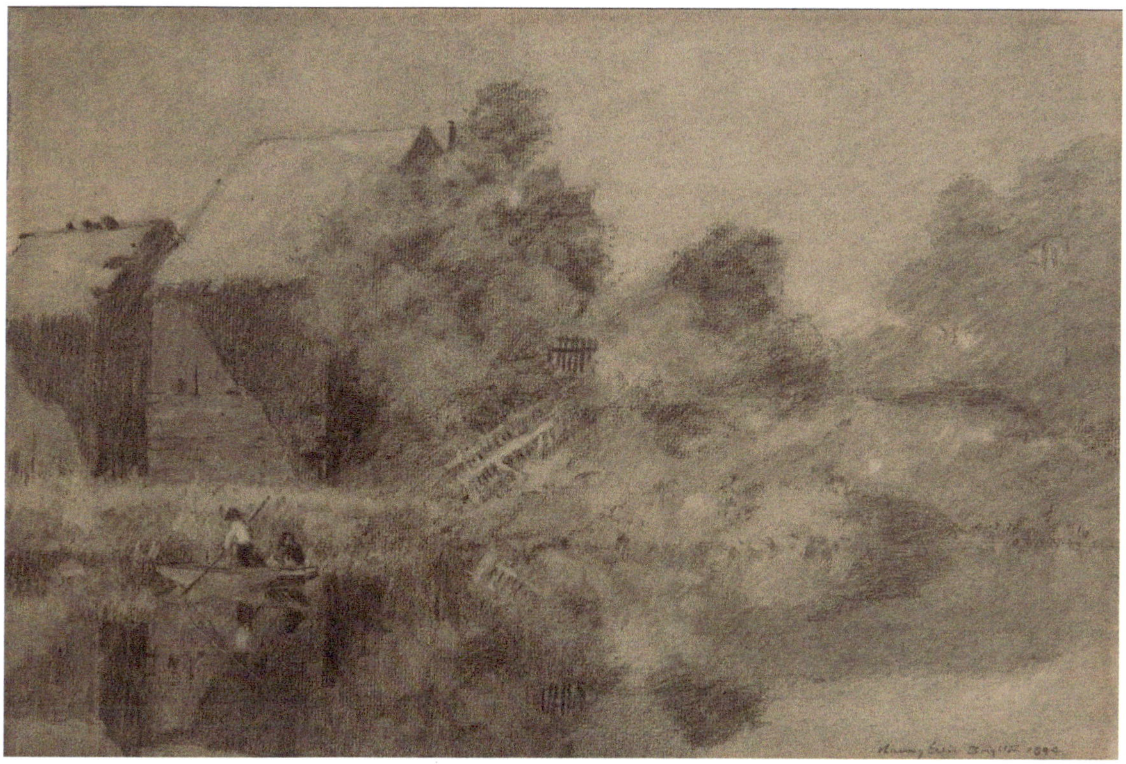

Harvey Ellis, *Landscape Along a Stream*, 1894. Charcoal on laid paper. 2016.44

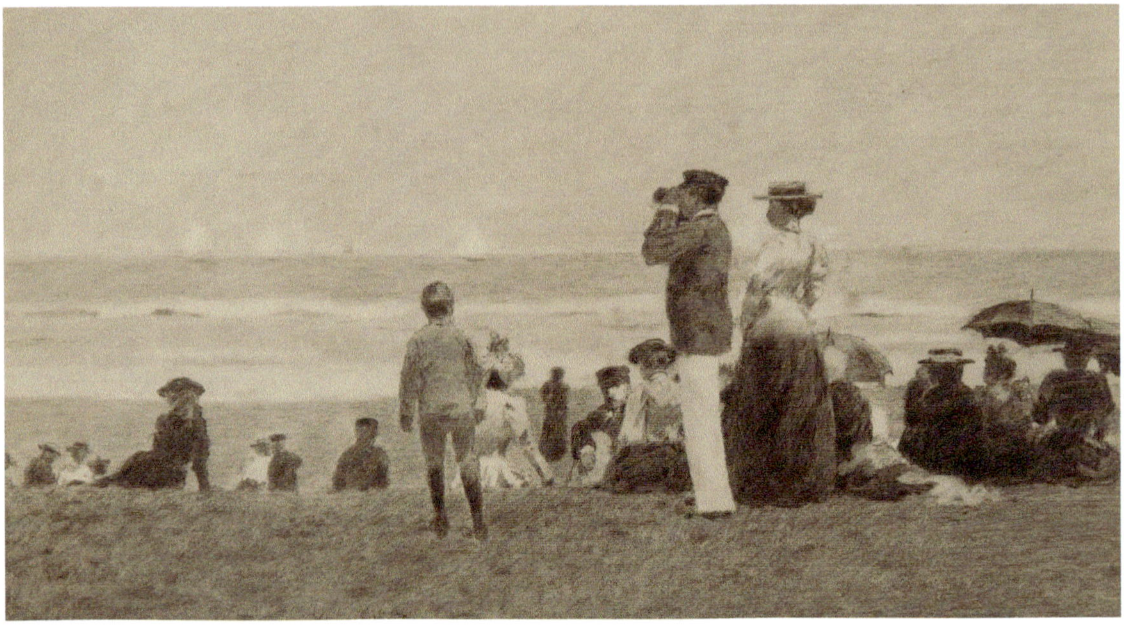

Harvey Ellis, *Regatta Scene*, 1894. Charcoal on paper. 2016.50

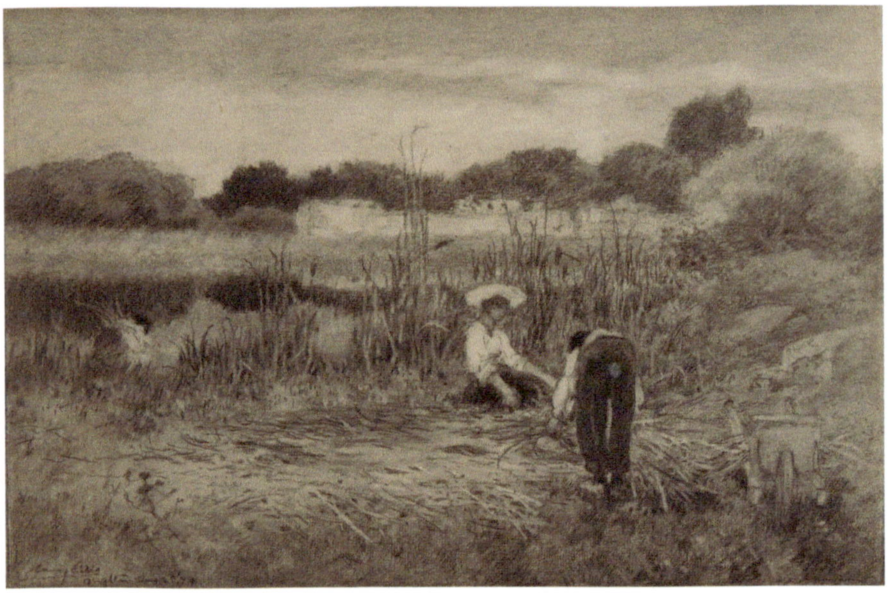

Harvey Ellis, *Three Figures in a Field*, 1894. Charcoal on buff laid paper. Anonymous gift, 1972.92

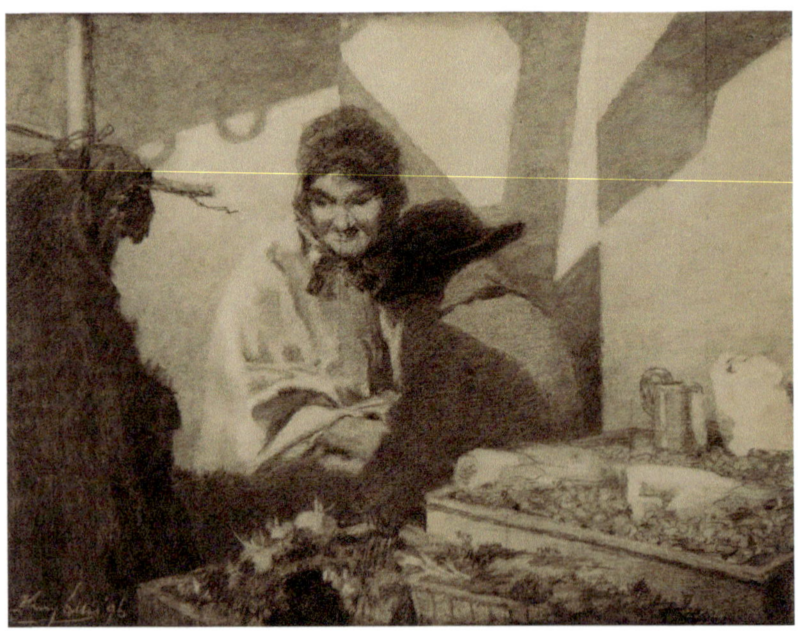

Harvey Ellis, *Vegetable Sellers*, 1896. Charcoal on laid paper. 2016.49

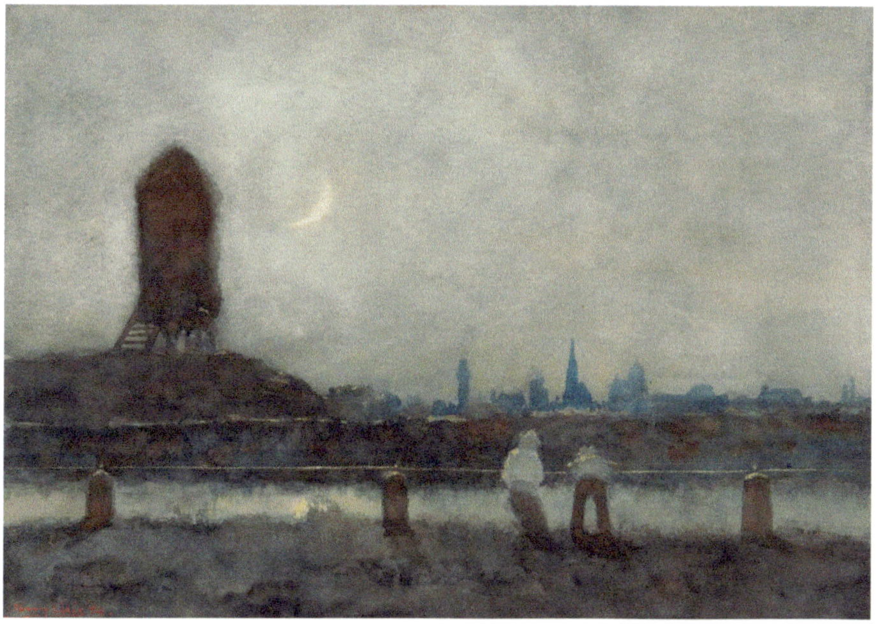

Harvey Ellis, *River Scene with Crescent Moon*, 1894. Watercolor and pastel on paper. 2016.59

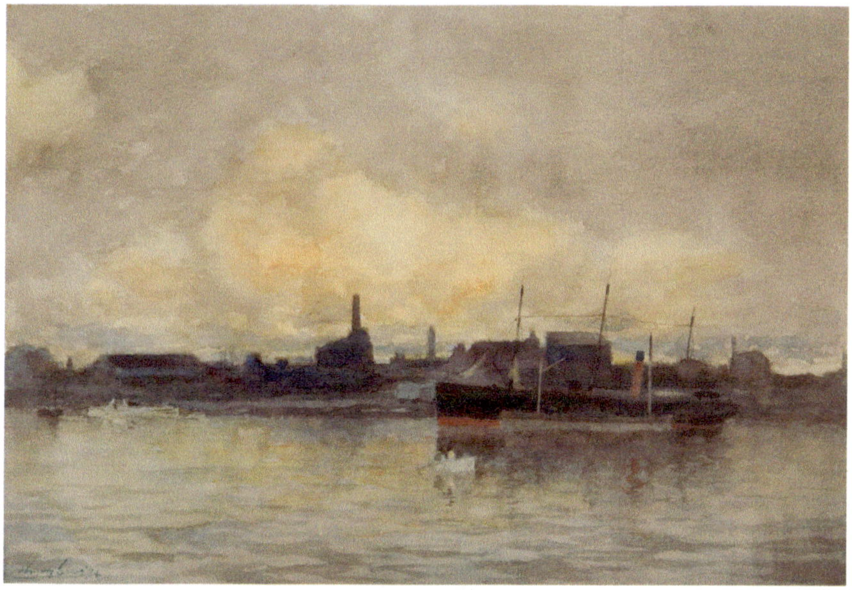

Harvey Ellis, *Harbor at Sunset*, 1894. Watercolor on paper. 2016.60

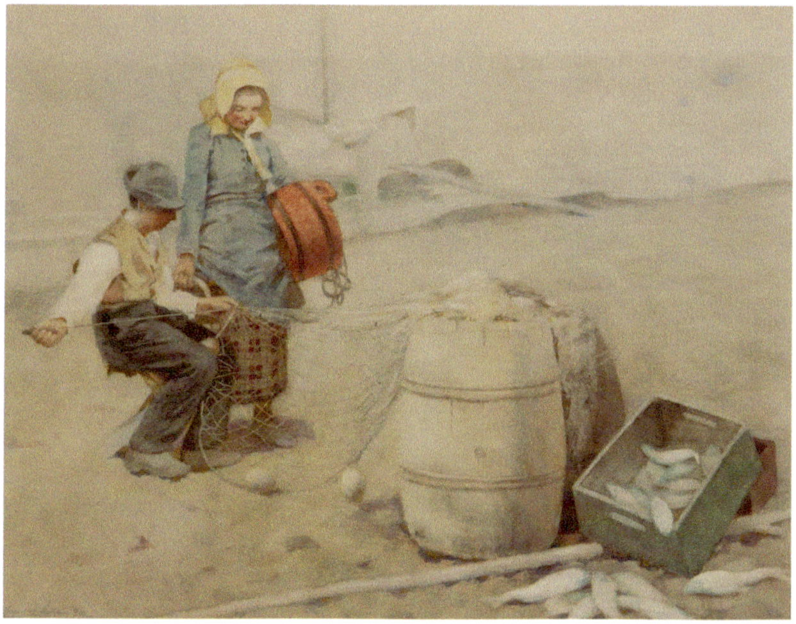

Harvey Ellis, *Mending Nets*, 1894. Watercolor on paper. Gift of Mr. James G. Cutler, 1914.2

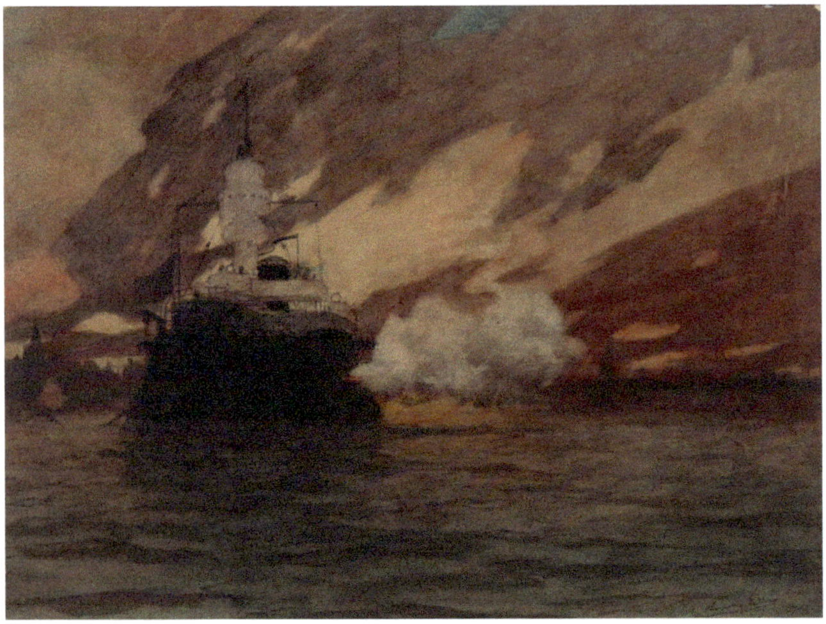

Harvey Ellis, *The Evening Gun*, 1894. Watercolor and pastel on board. 2016.79

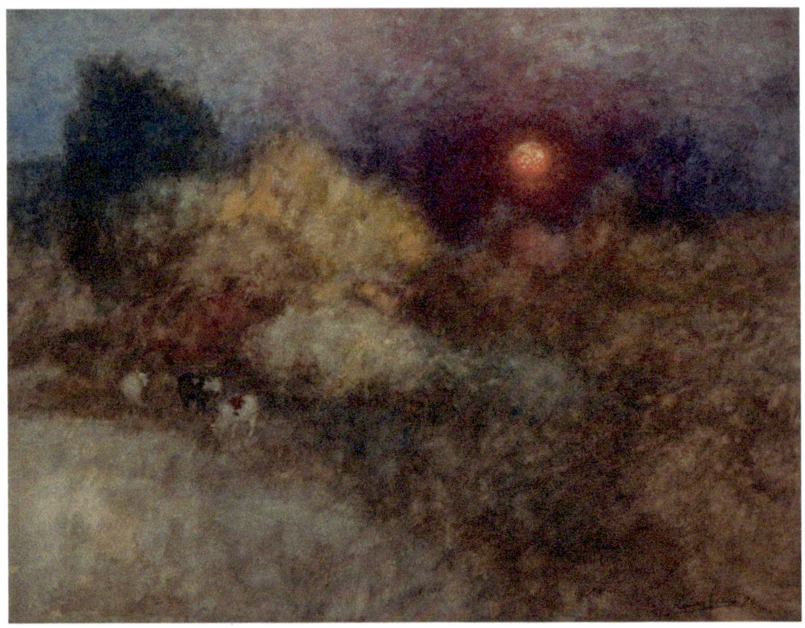

Harvey Ellis, *Cows in a Hazy Landscape*, 1894. Watercolor, gouache, and pastel on paper. 2016.53

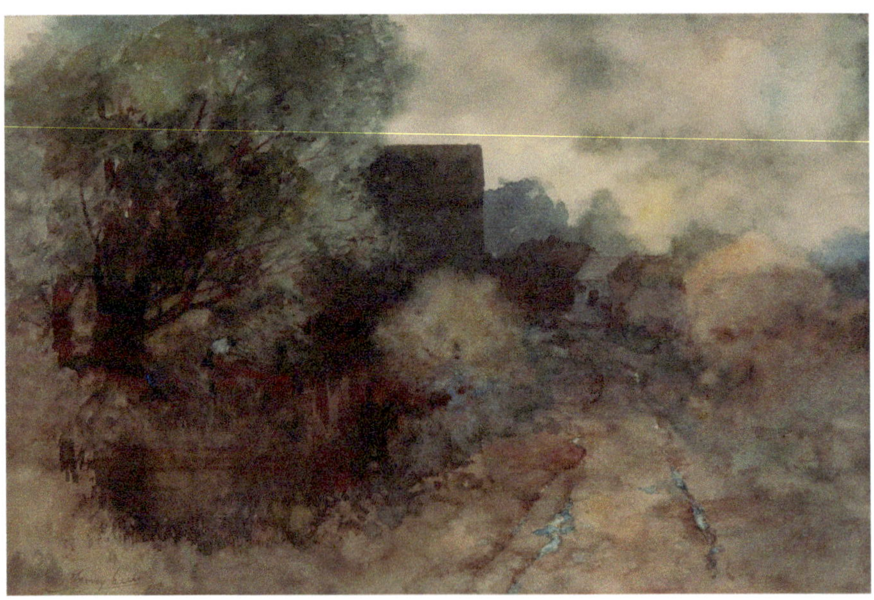

Harvey Ellis, *Farm Pond, Evening*, 1894. Watercolor on paper Gift of Mrs. Charles Wright Dodge, 1942.67

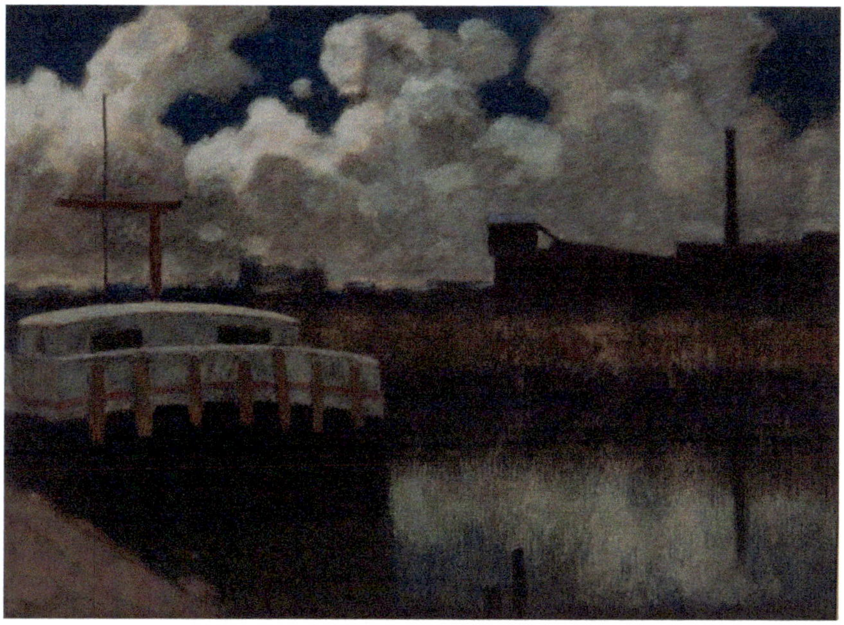

Harvey Ellis, *Canal Docks at Night*, 1895. Pastel on paper. 2016.47

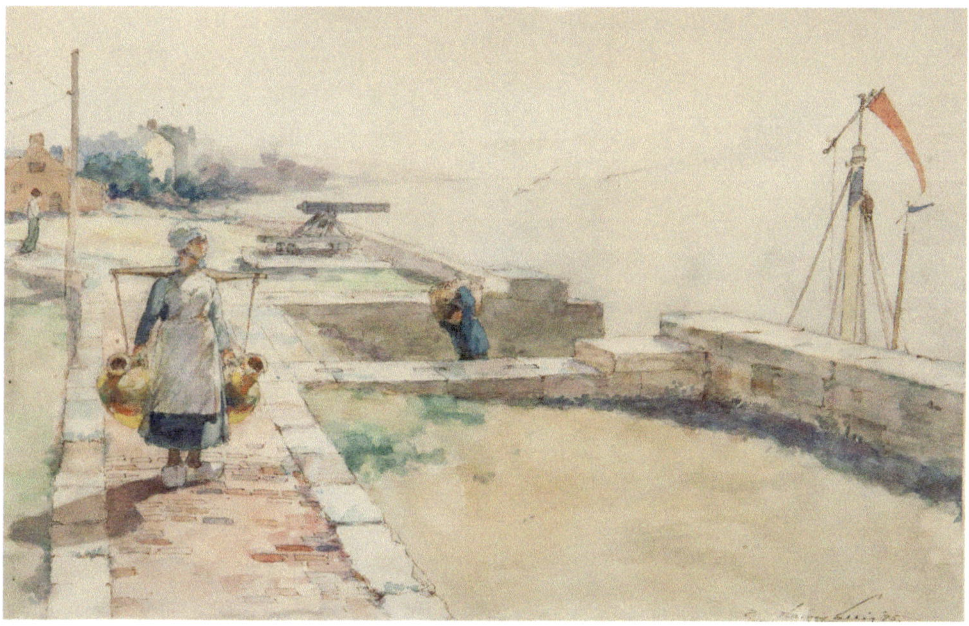

Harvey Ellis, *By the Sea*, 1895 Watercolor, brown ink, gouache, and graphite on paper. 2016.13

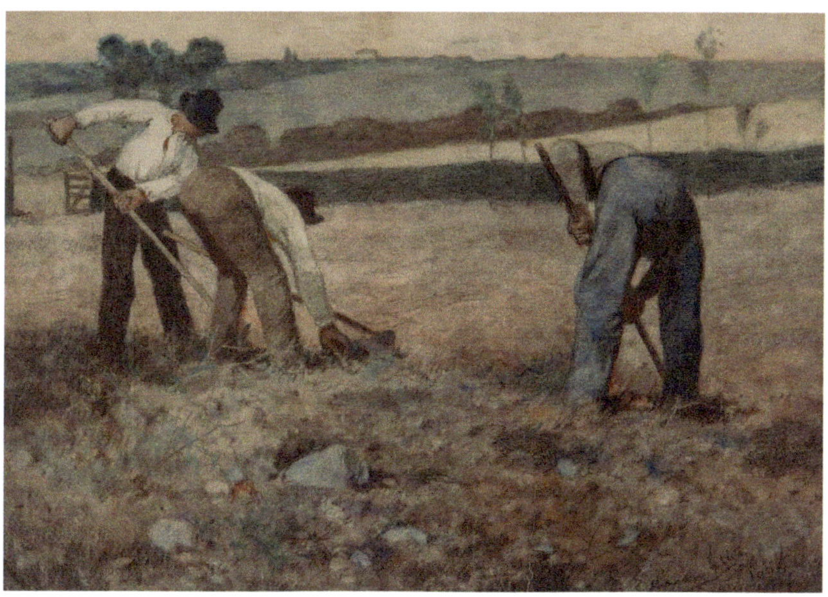

Harvey Ellis, *Three Men Hoeing a Field*, 1896. Watercolor, pastel, and charcoal on laid paper. 2016.48

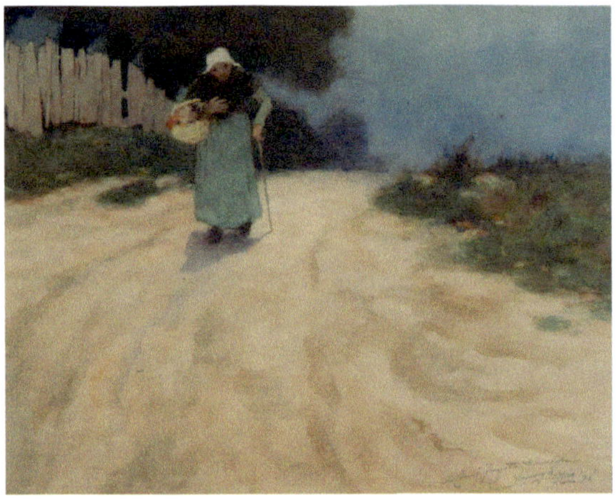

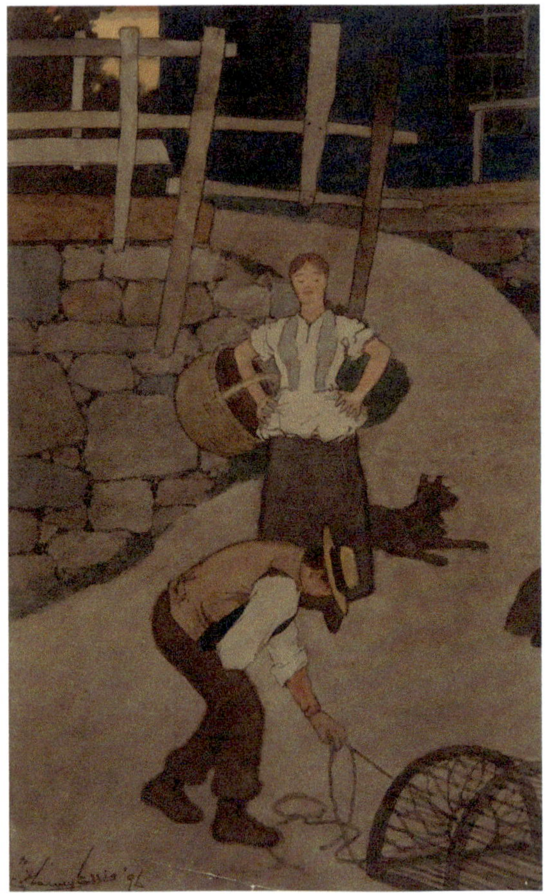

Left: Harvey Ellis, *Road to Market*, 1896. Watercolor on paper Gift of Chandler Bragdon in memory of his father, Claude Fayette Bragdon, 1956.83

Right: Harvey Ellis, *The Trap*, 1896. Watercolor on wove paper Gift of James B. Arnold, 1958.114

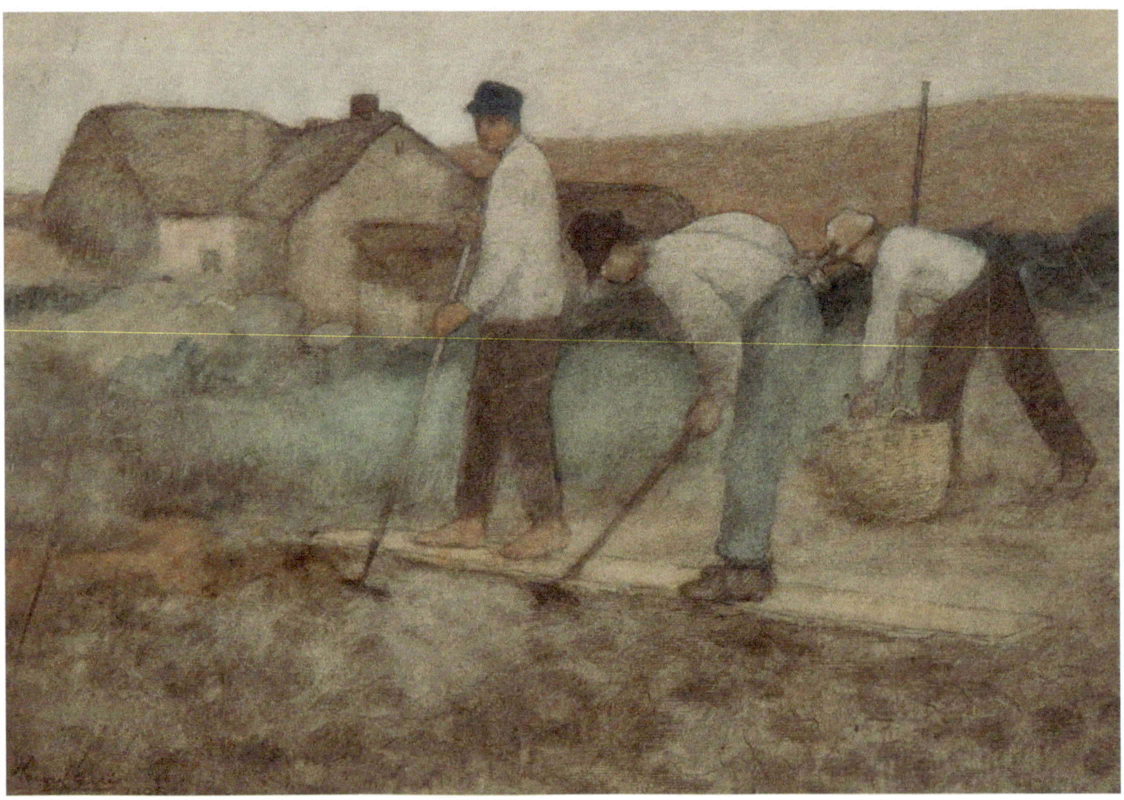

Harvey Ellis, *Men Working*, 1896. Pastel, charcoal, and watercolor on paper. 2016.26

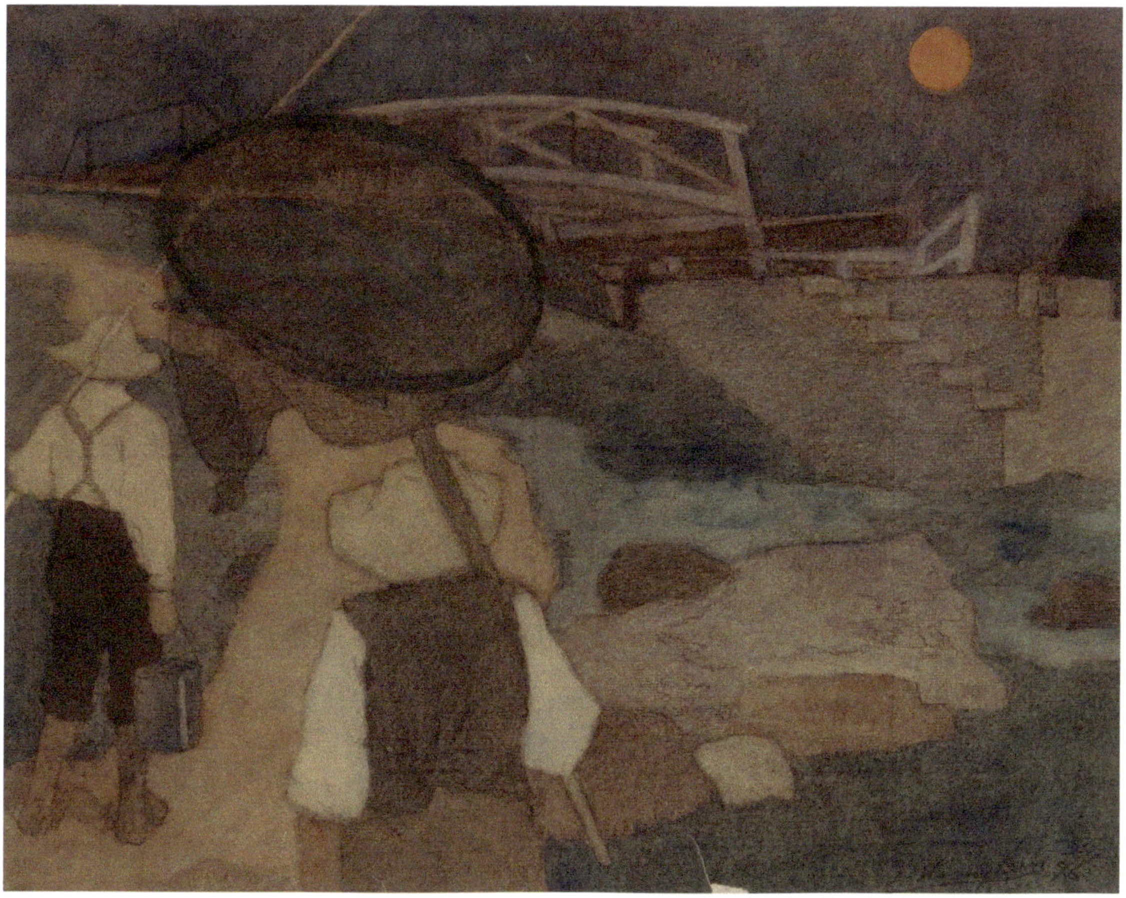

Harvey Ellis, *Fishermen at the Canal Lock*, 1896. Watercolor and charcoal on paper. 2016.56

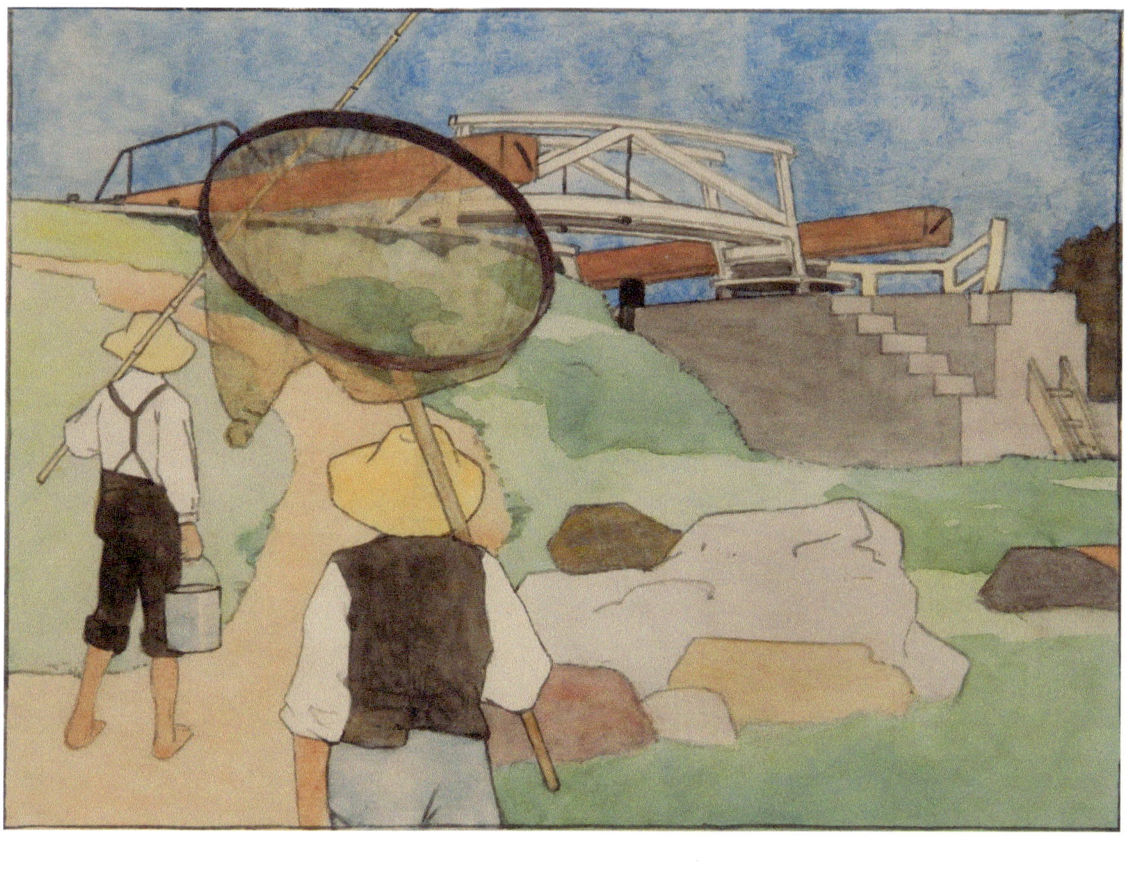

Harvey Ellis, *Fishermen at the Canal Lock*, 1896. Watercolor and graphite on paper. 2016.57

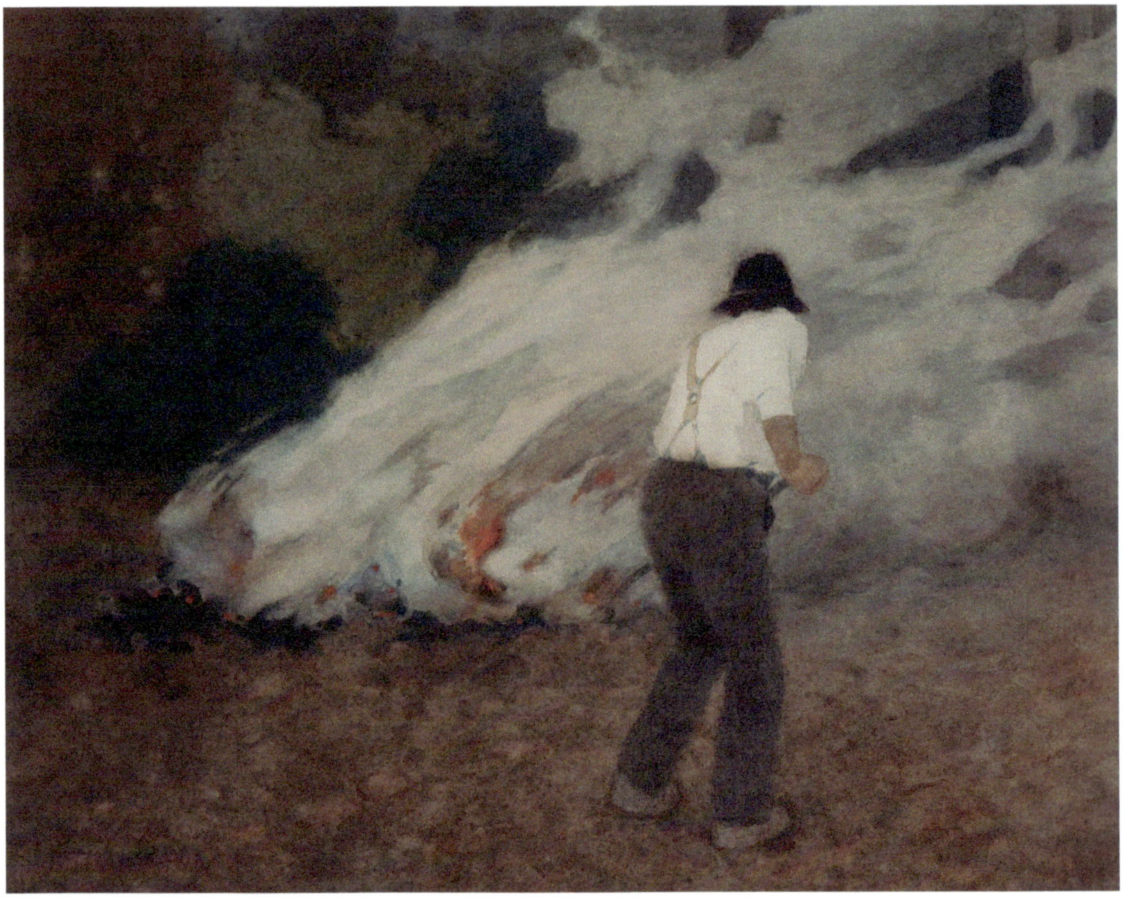

Harvey Ellis, *Burning Brush*, 1896. Watercolor on paper. Gift of Erickson Perkins, 1914.44

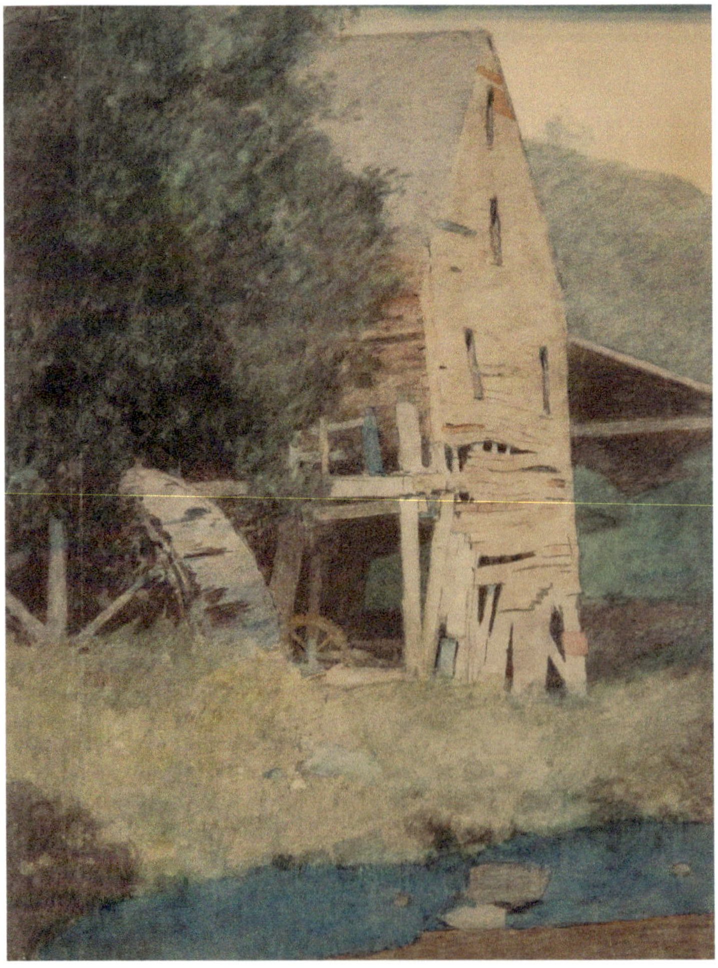

Harvey Ellis, *The Old Mill*, 1896. Watercolor, pastel, charcoal, and graphite on paper. 2016.76

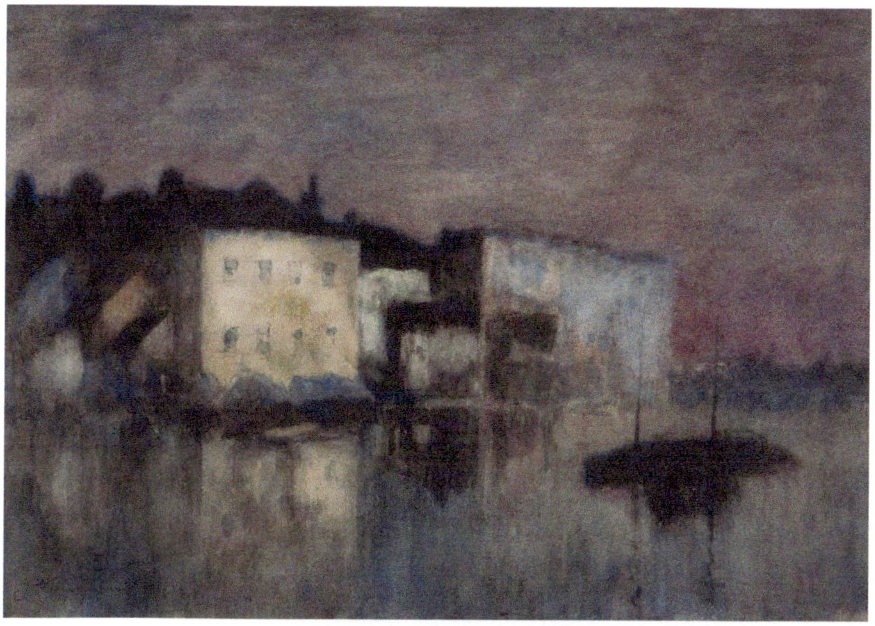

Harvey Ellis, *Canal Scene at Night*, 1897. Watercolor, charcoal, and gouache on paper. 2016.46

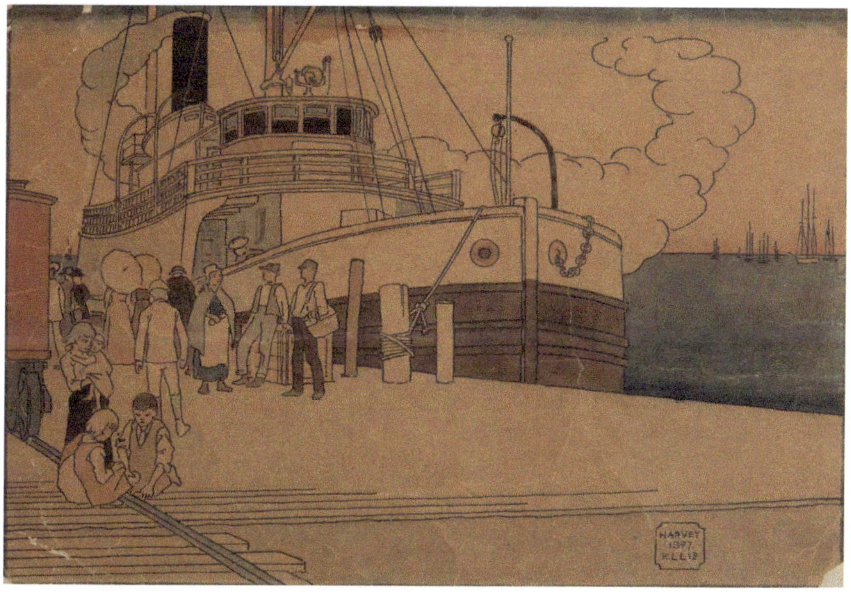

Harvey Ellis, *Charlotte-Cobourg Ferry*, 1897. Ink and watercolor on paper. Gift of Henry Bragdon, 1970.51

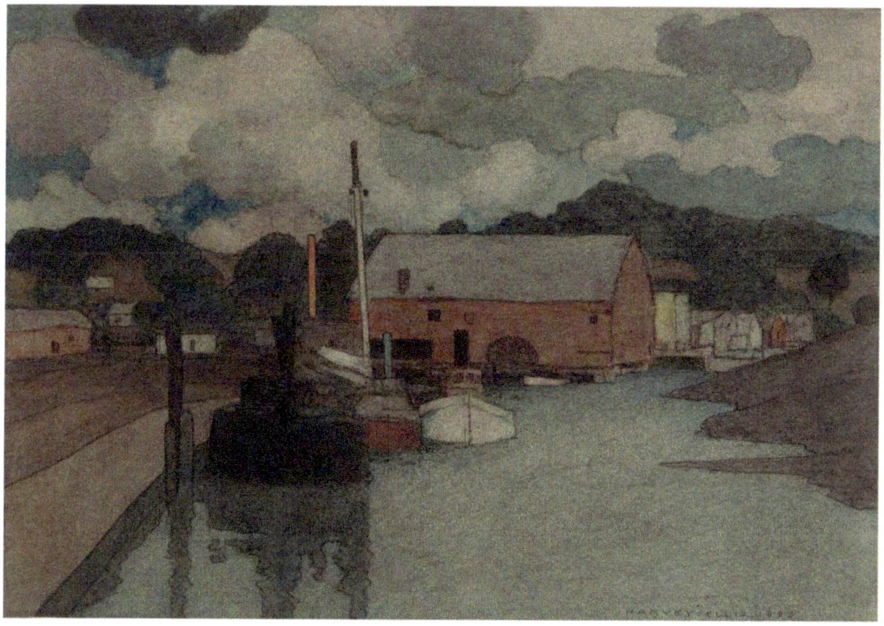

Harvey Ellis, *Little Harbor*, 1898. Watercolor, pastel, and charcoal on paper. Gift of Elmer Adler, 1922.43

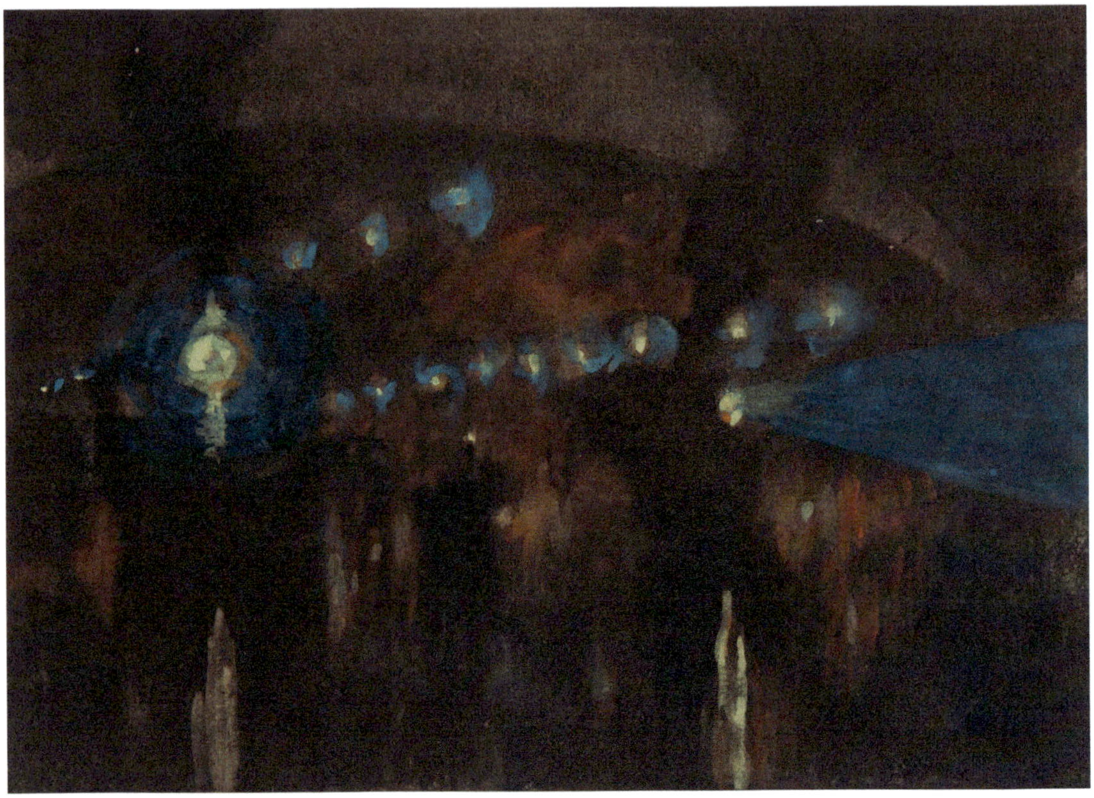

Harvey Ellis, *Night Study of the New York Central and Hudson River Railroad Station, Rochester*, 1899 Pastel and watercolor on paper Gift of James B. Arnold, 1958.113

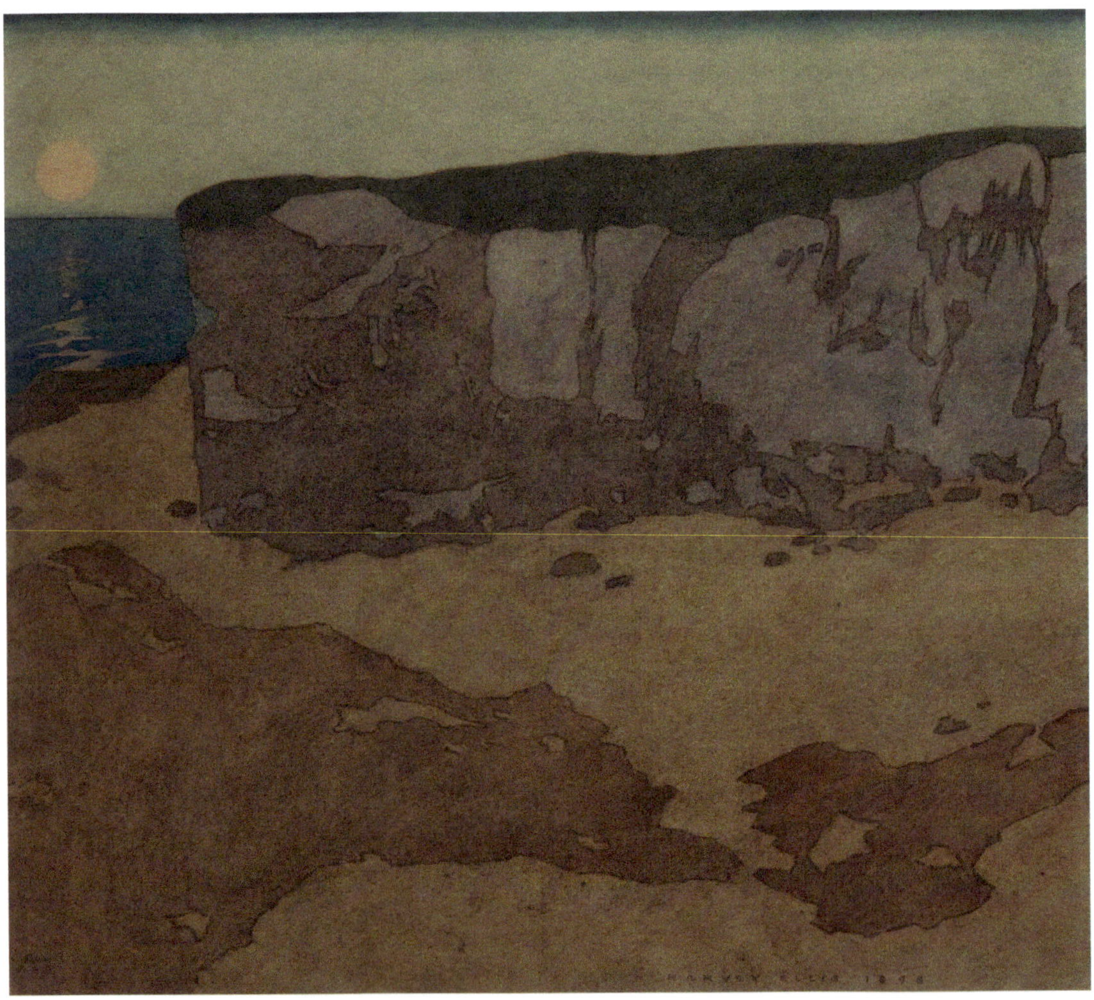

Harvey Ellis, *Sandy Bay*, 1898. Watercolor and pastel on paper. 2016.11

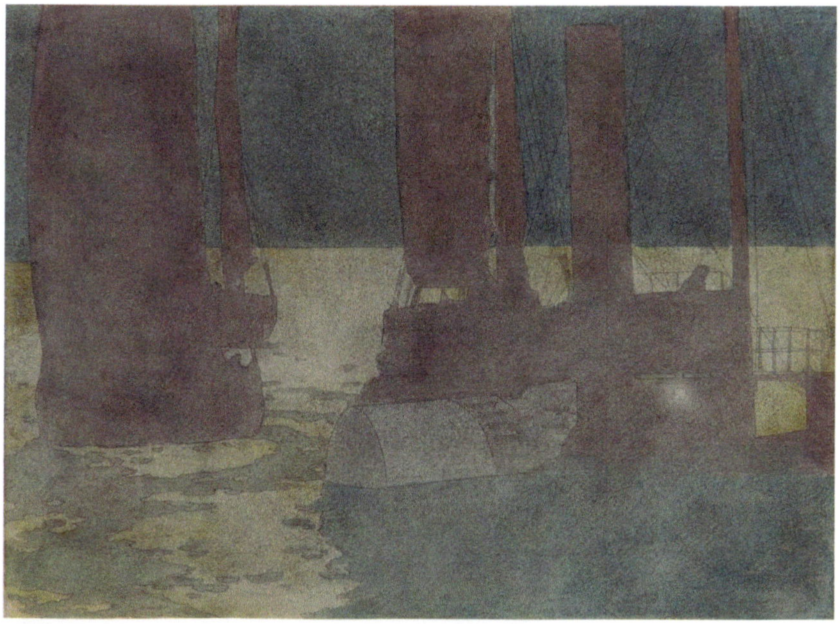

Harvey Ellis, *Study for "Silhouettes–Boats,"* 1899. Watercolor, charcoal, and ink on paper. 2016.41
*See related work on page 18.*

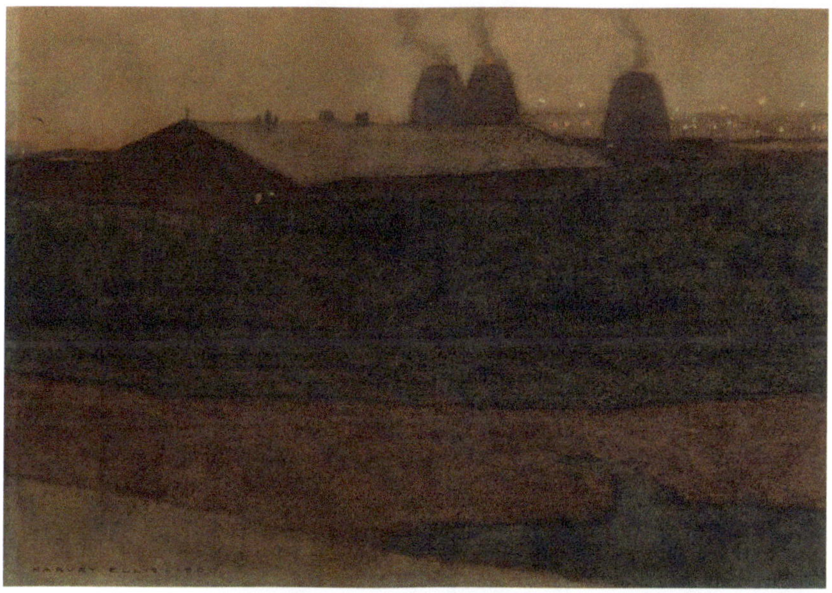

Harvey Ellis, *Skyline with Three Smokestacks*, 1900. Watercolor and charcoal with touches of gouache on paper. 2016.58

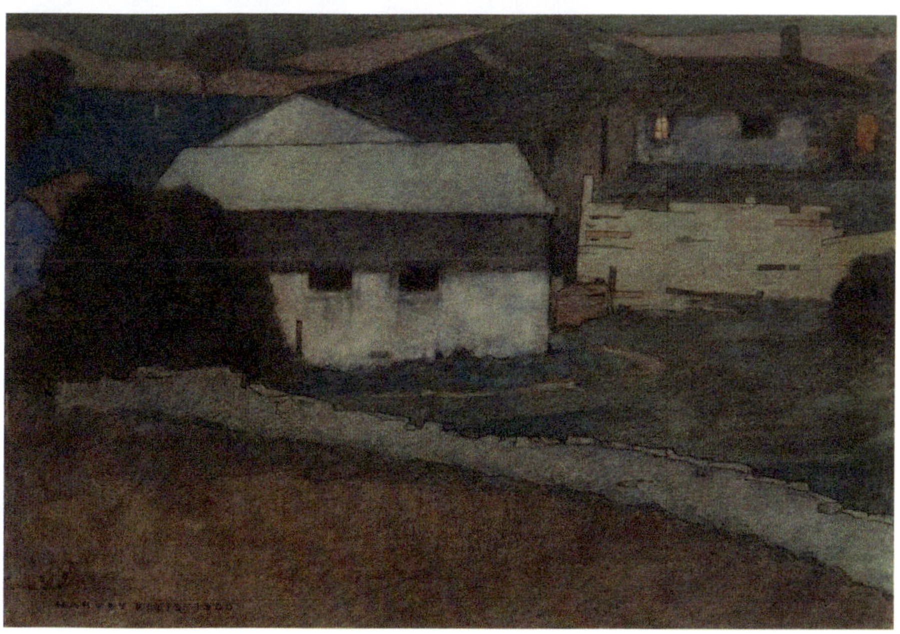

Harvey Ellis, *Evening*, 1900 20th century. Pastel on laid paper. Gift of William Balkan, 1914.1

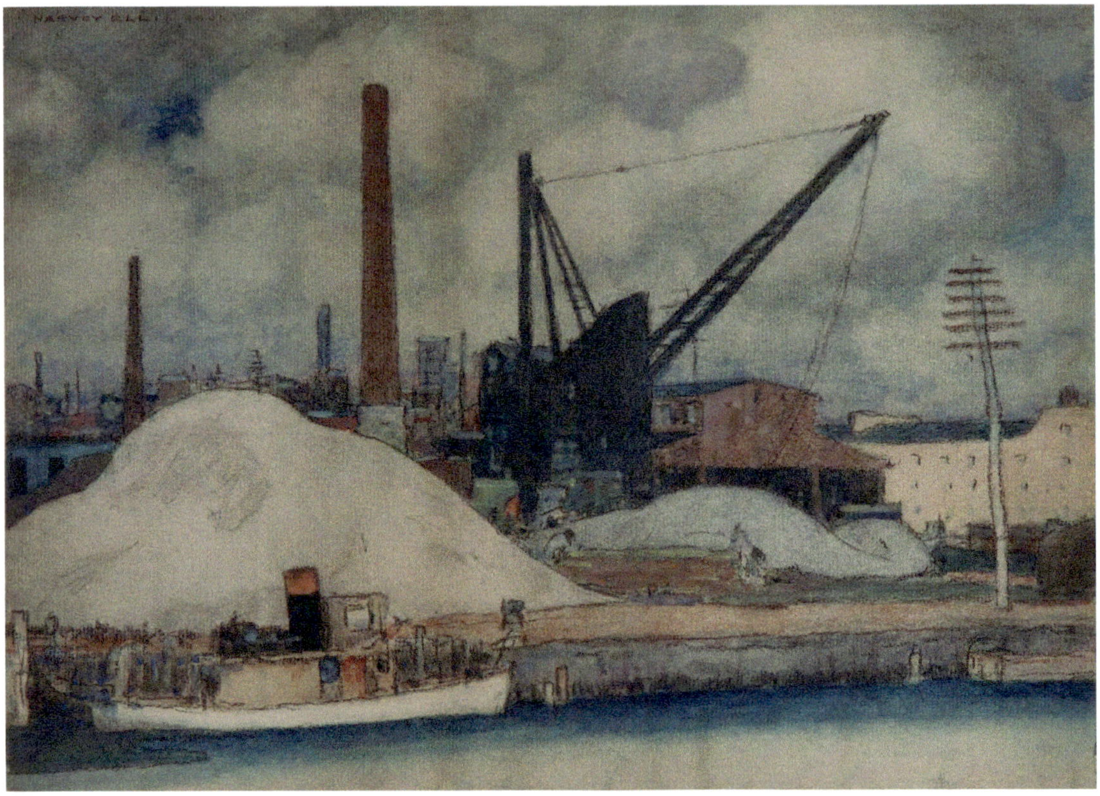

Harvey Ellis, *Port Scene*, 1901. Watercolor, pastel, gouache, and charcoal on paper. 2016.33

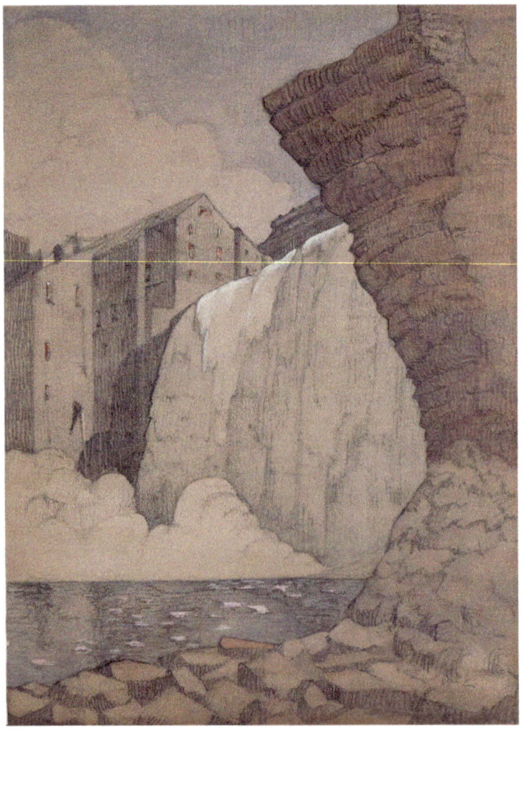

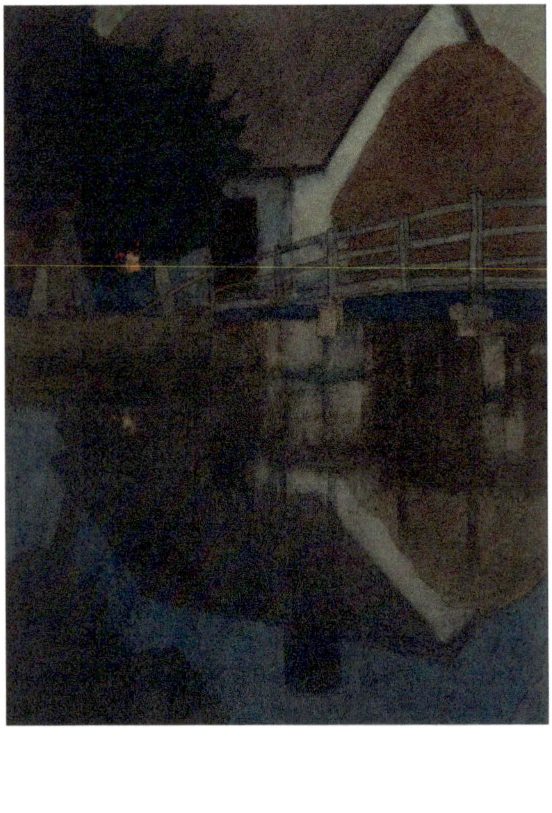

Left: Attributed to Harvey Ellis, *Waterfall Scene*, 19th–20th centuries. Watercolor, chalk, and charcoal on paper. Gift of Jean R. France, Architectural Historian, 2022.4

Right: Harvey Ellis, *Farm at Twilight*, 1900. Ink, charcoal, and watercolor on paper. Gift of the Estate of Emily and James Sibley Watson, 1951.107

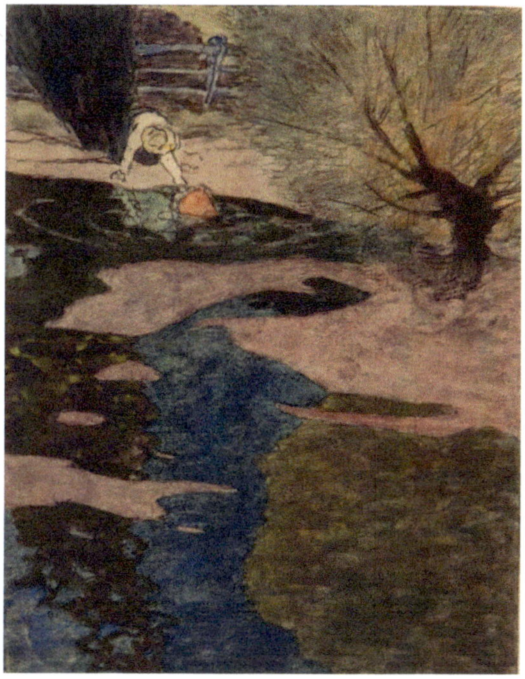

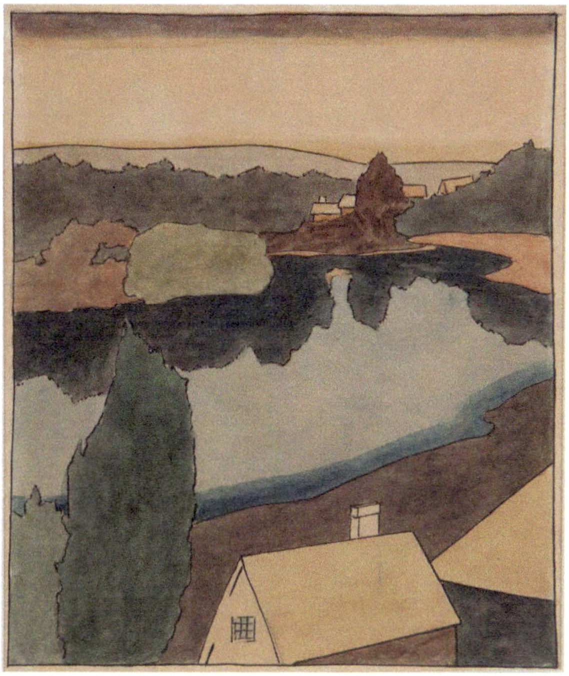

Left: Attributed to Harvey Ellis, *The Water Hole*, 19th–20th centuries. Watercolor and pastel on paper. 2016.51

Right: Attributed to Harvey Ellis, *Landscape with Pond*, 19th–20th centuries. Watercolor and ink on thin paper. 2016.61

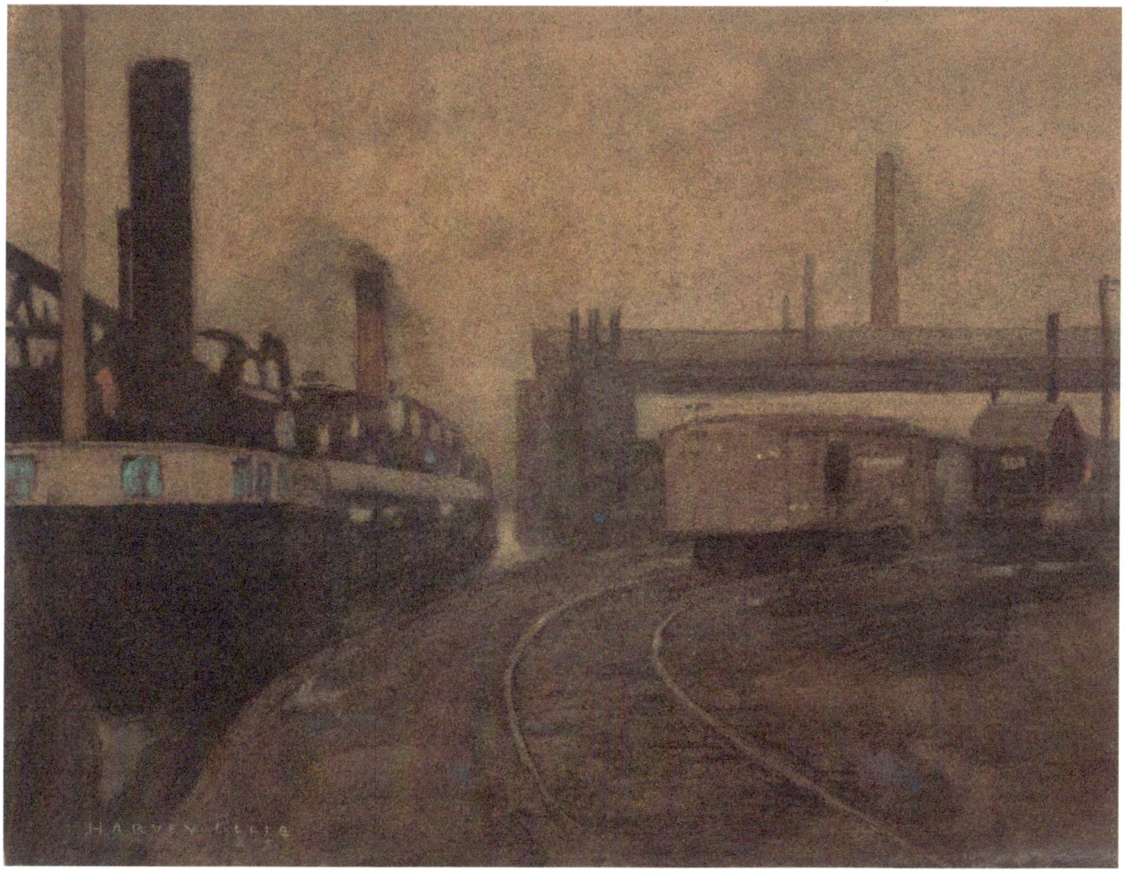


Harvey Ellis, *Port Scene*, 19th–20th centuries. Gouache, pastel, and charcoal on thin board. 2016.35

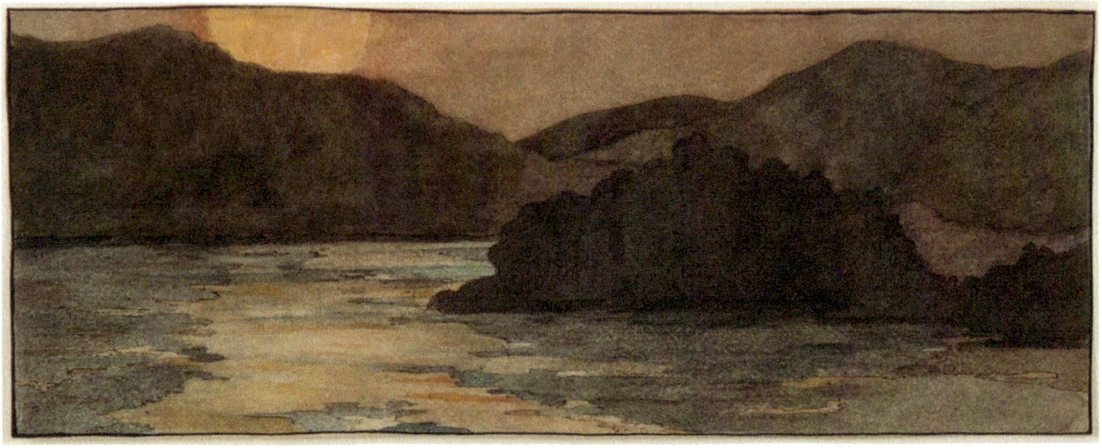

Attributed to Harvey Ellis, *Moonlit Mountain Lake*, 19th–20th centuries. Watercolor, charcoal, and black ink on paper. 2016.36

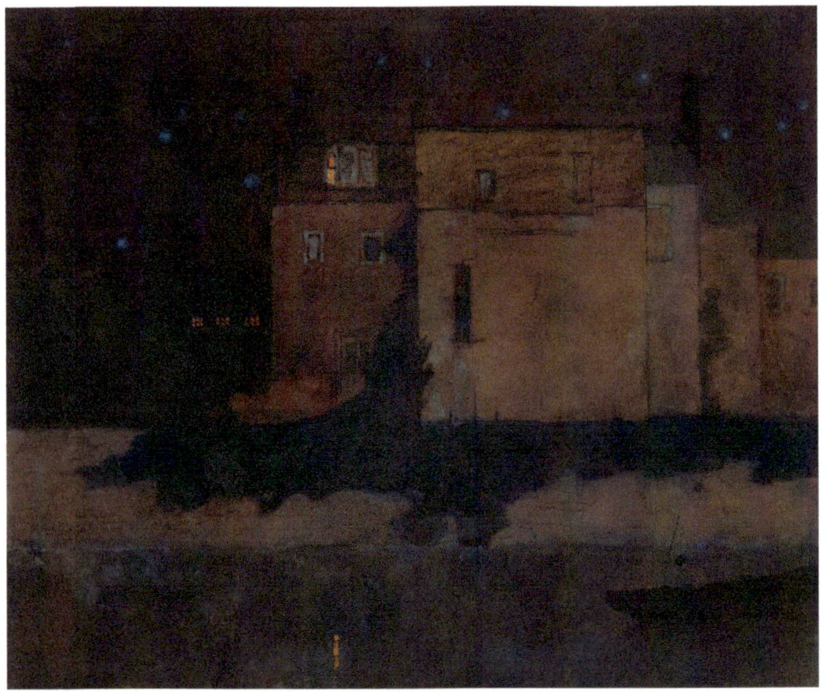

Harvey Ellis, *Nocturne–Houses*, 19th–20th centuries. Watercolor, chalk, and gouache on paper. 2016.28

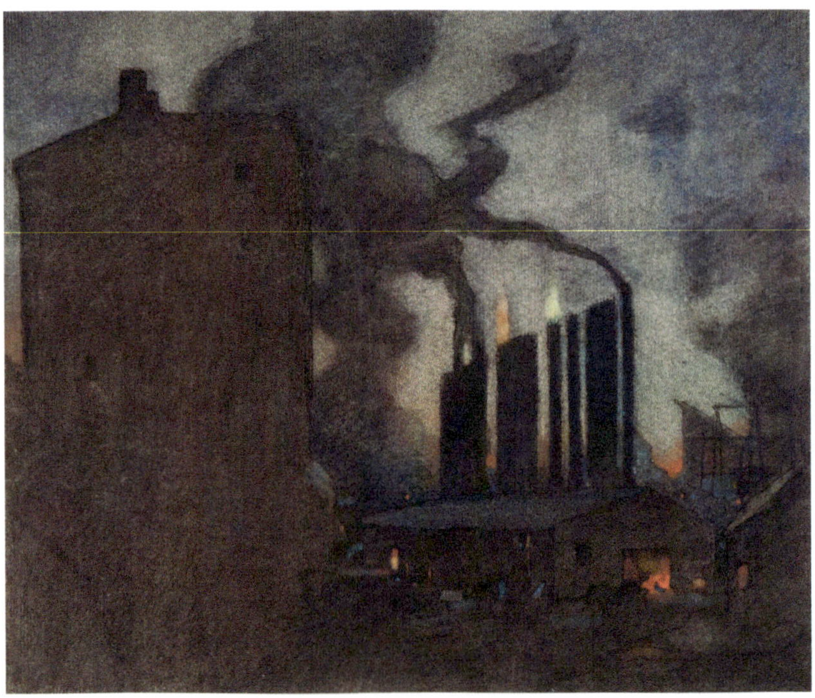

Harvey Ellis, *Furnaces at Night*, 19th–20th centuries. Gouache, pastel, and charcoal on laid paper. 2016.22

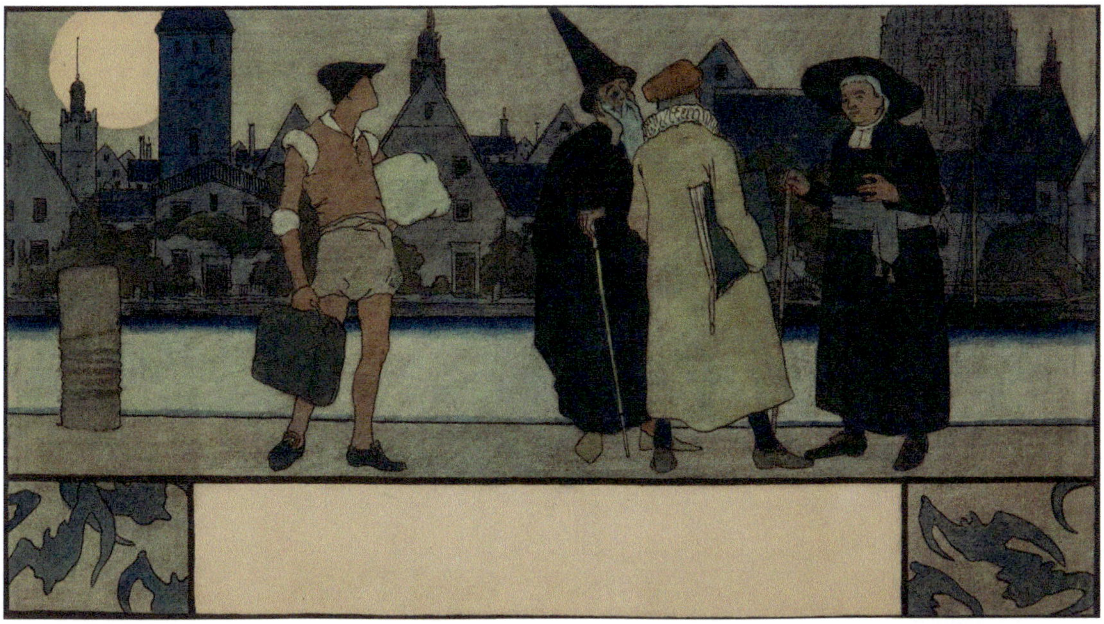

Attributed to Harvey Ellis, *Design for a Mural*, 19th–20th centuries. Watercolor, charcoal, and black ink on laid paper. 2016.69

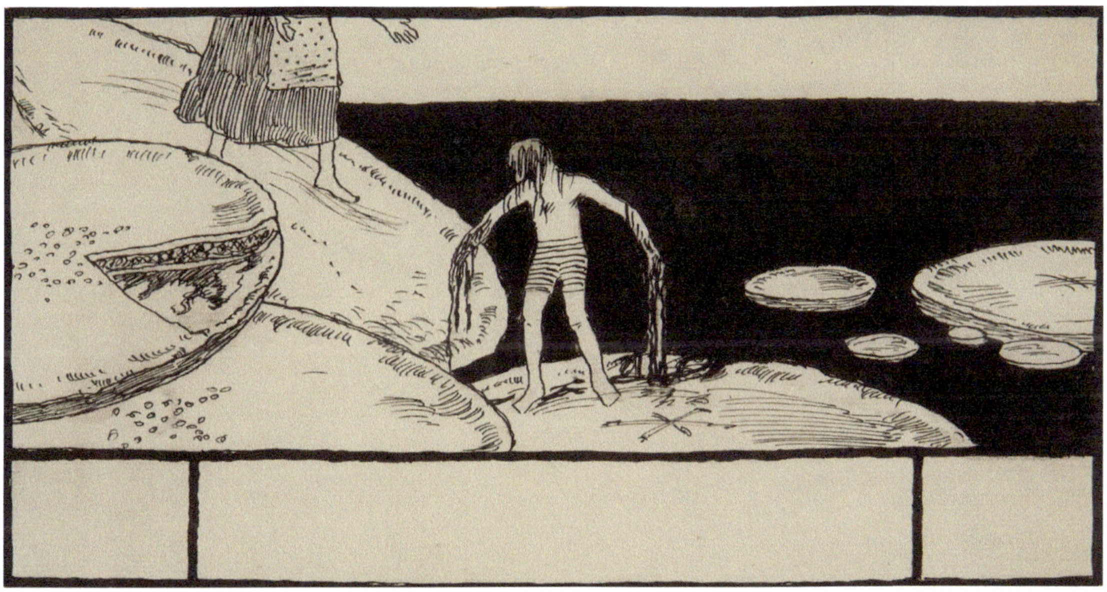

Harvey Ellis, *The Pie Eater*, 19th–20th centuries. Black ink on paper. 2016.82

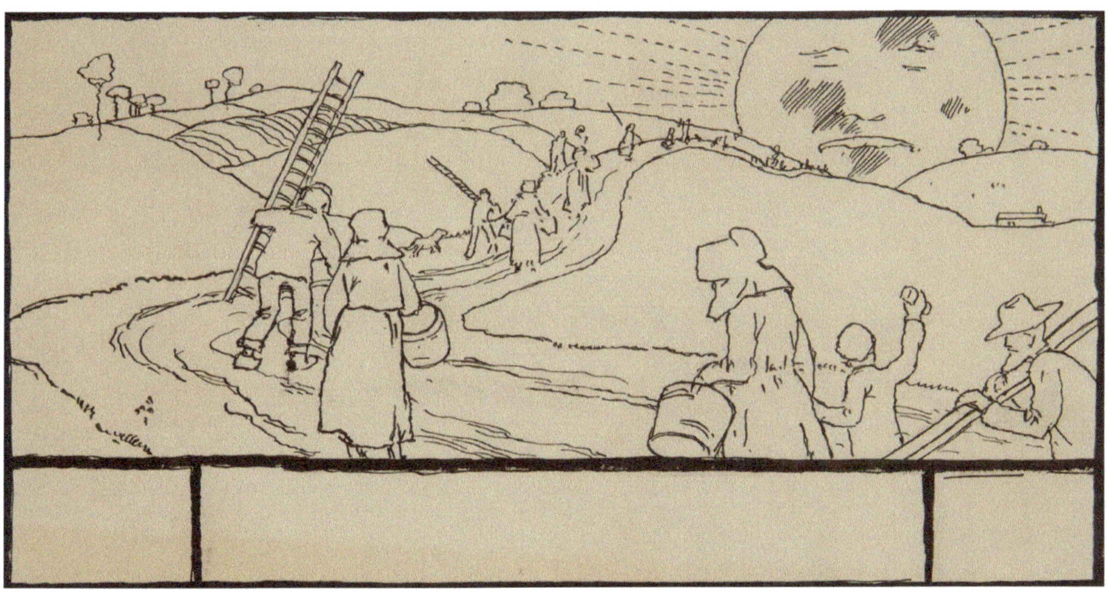

Harvey Ellis, *The Cherry Pickers*, 19th–20th centuries. Black ink on paper. 2016.81

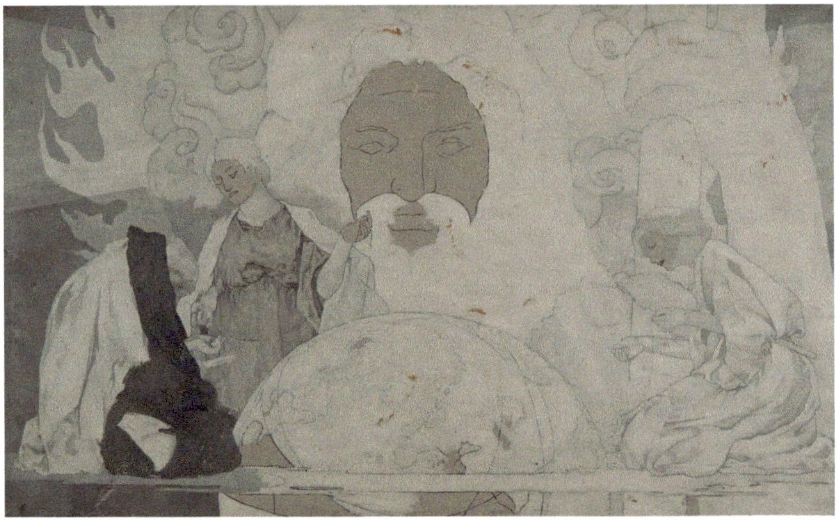

Attributed to Harvey Ellis, *Cartoon for a Mural*, 19th–20th centuries. Oil on canvas. 2016.70

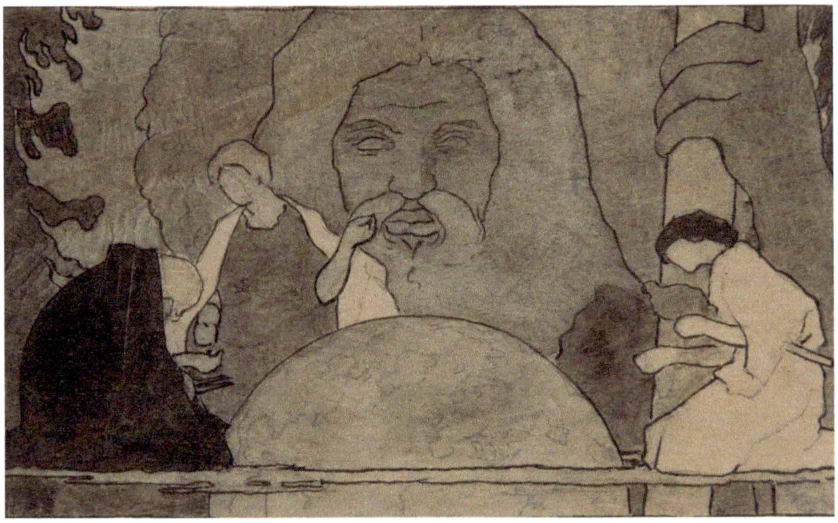

Attributed to Harvey Ellis, *Preliminary Sketch for Mural*, 19th–20th centuries. Ink and wash on paper. 2016.71

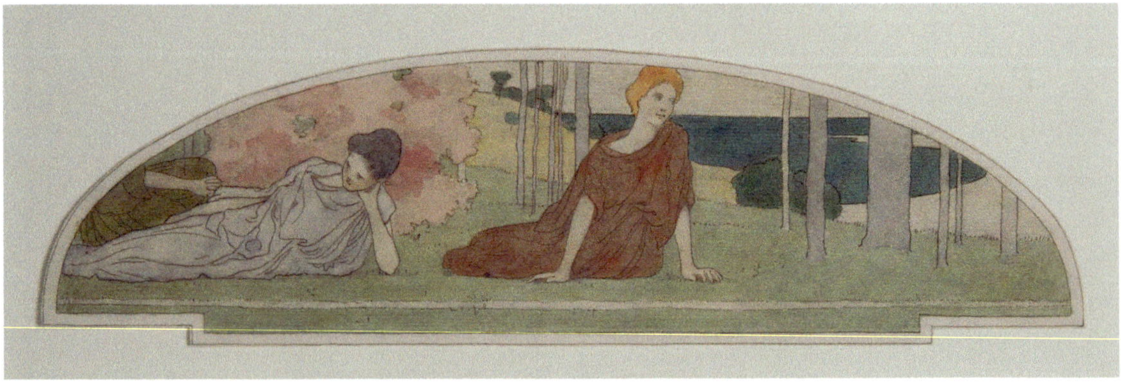

Harvey Ellis, *Studies for a Mural*, 1895. Watercolor and brown ink on paper. 2016.68.1

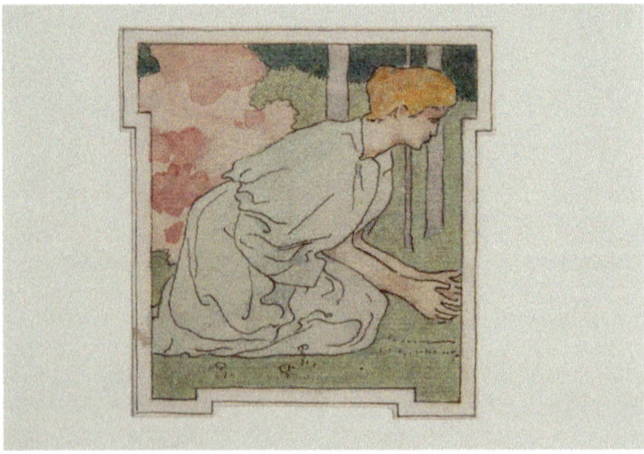

Harvey Ellis, *Studies for a Mural*, 1895. Watercolor and brown ink on paper. 2016.68.2

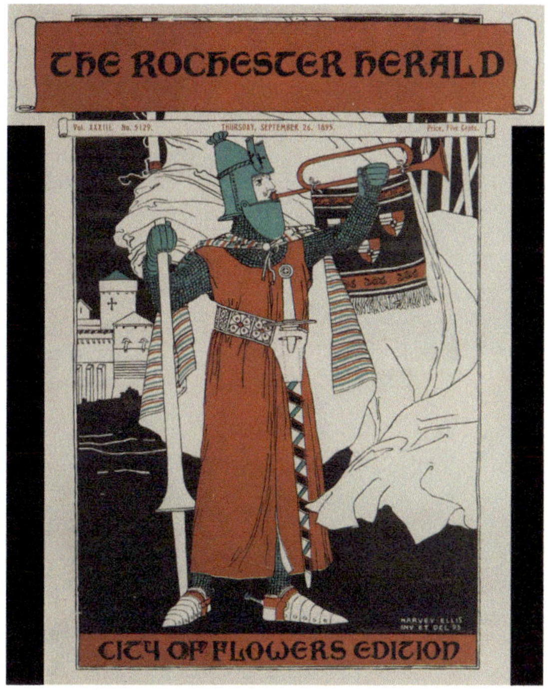


Harvey Ellis, *Cover of the Rochester Herald for September 26, 1895*
Lithograph. Gift of the James Somerville family, 1972.15

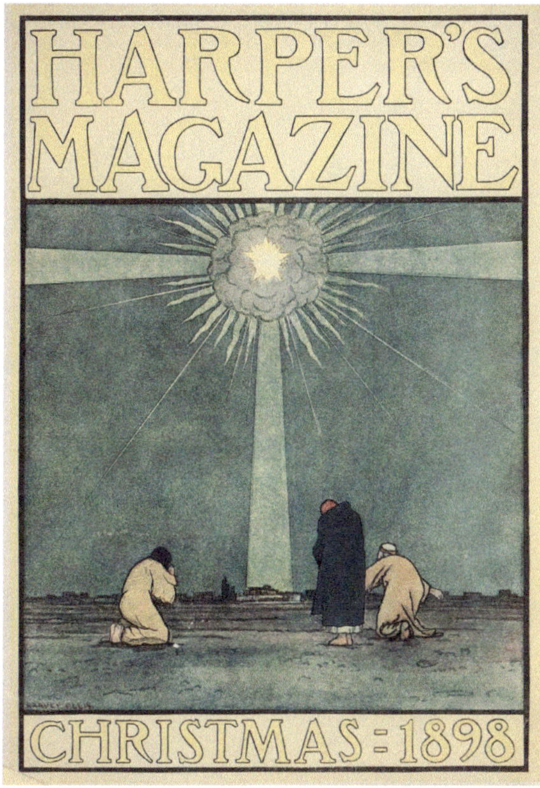


Left: Harvey Ellis, *Harper's Magazine Christmas Cover*, 1898. Color lithograph. Gift of Jean R. France, Architectural Historian, 2022.3

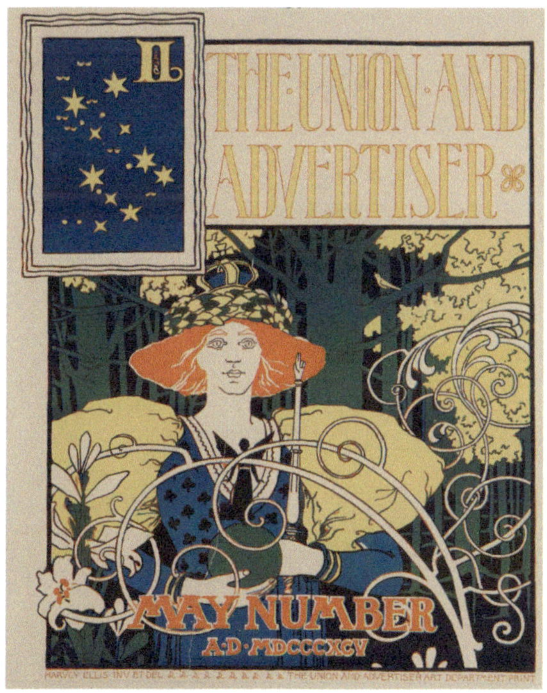


Harvey Ellis, *Cover of the Rochester Union and Advertiser for May 4, 1895.*
Lithograph. Gift of the James Somerville family, 1972.16

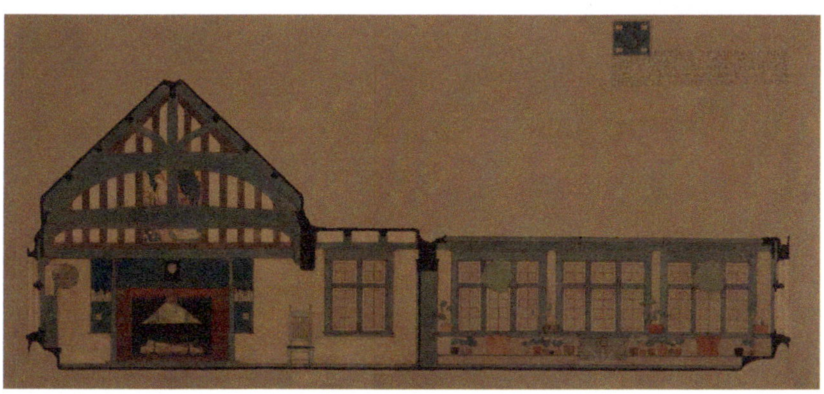

Harvey Ellis, *Library and Conservatory of Joseph T. Cunningham*, 1900.
Watercolor, ink, and graphite on brown paper. 2016.55

Left: Harvey Ellis, *Joan of Arc*, 1890. Watercolor, pastel, and charcoal on laid paper. 2016.23

Right: Harvey Ellis, *Study for "The Odyssey,"* 1895. Charcoal on laid paper. 2016.73

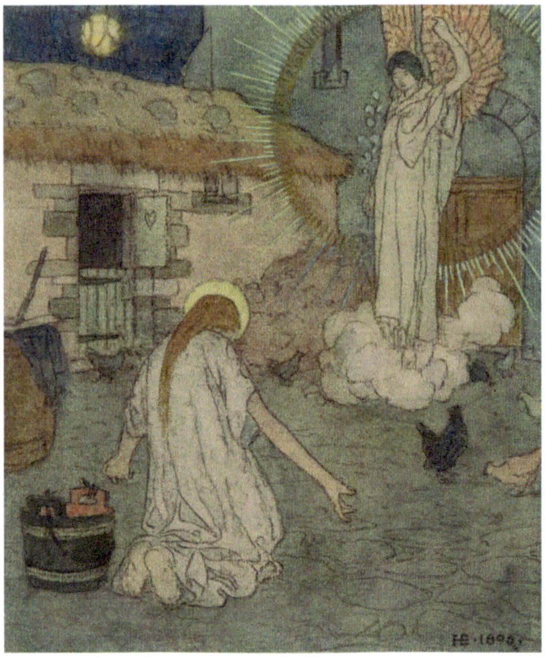

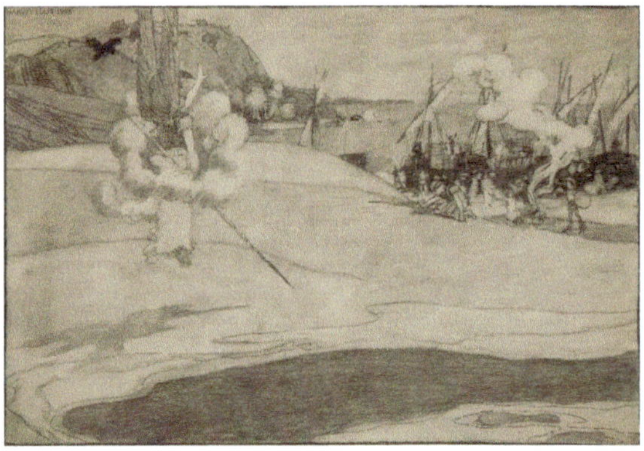

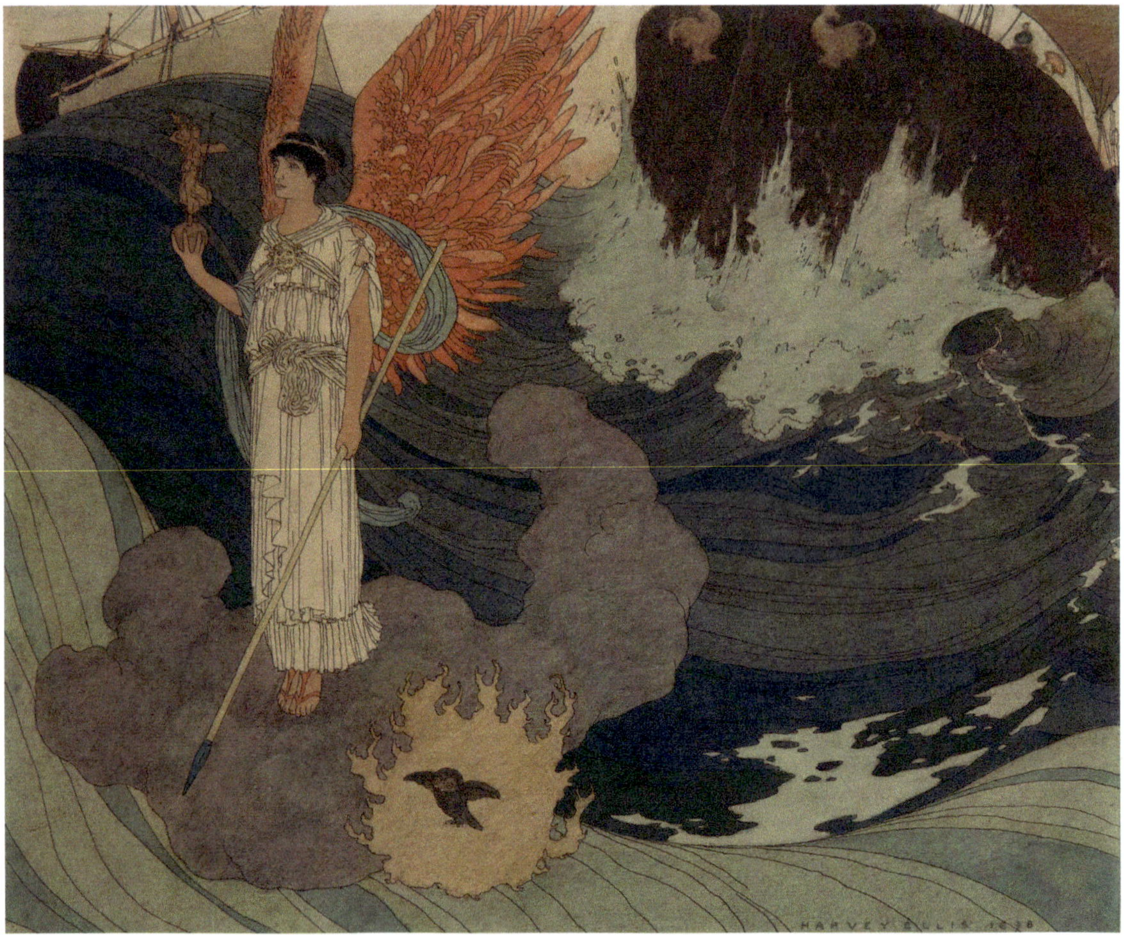

Harvey Ellis, *The Odyssey*, 1898. Watercolor, charcoal, and black ink on laid paper. 2016.32

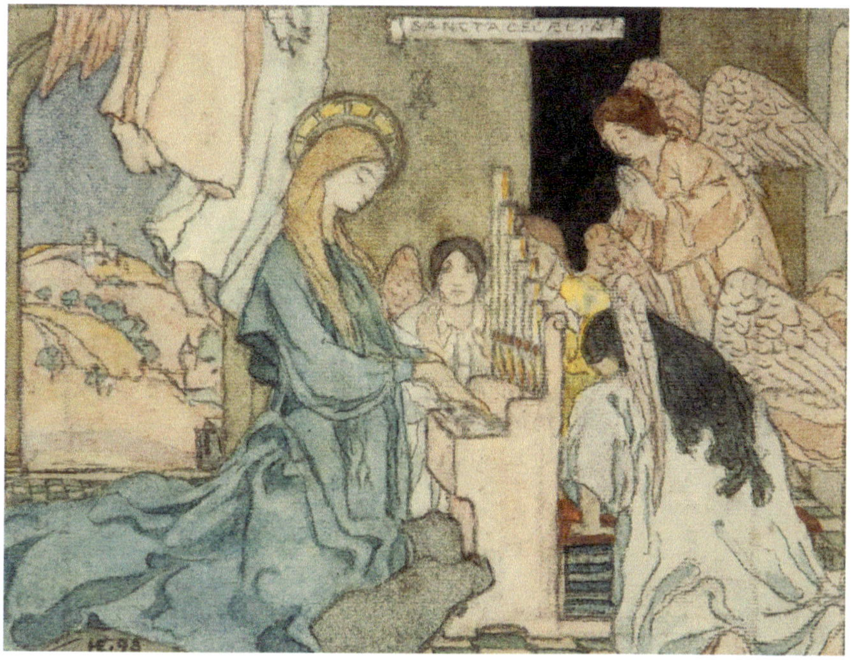


Harvey Ellis, *Sancta Cecilia*, 1898. Watercolor, pastel, and graphite on laid paper. 2016.74

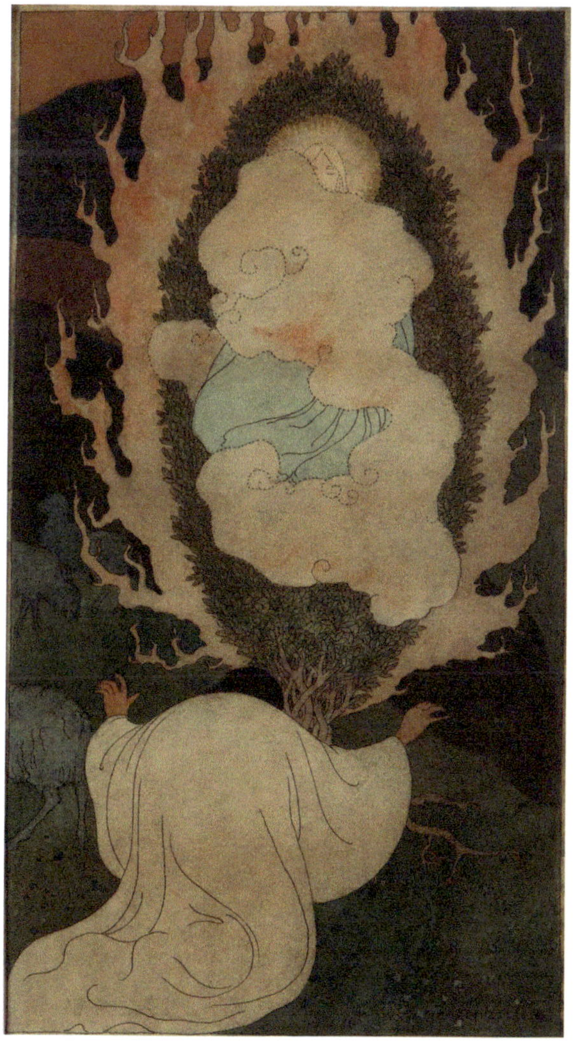

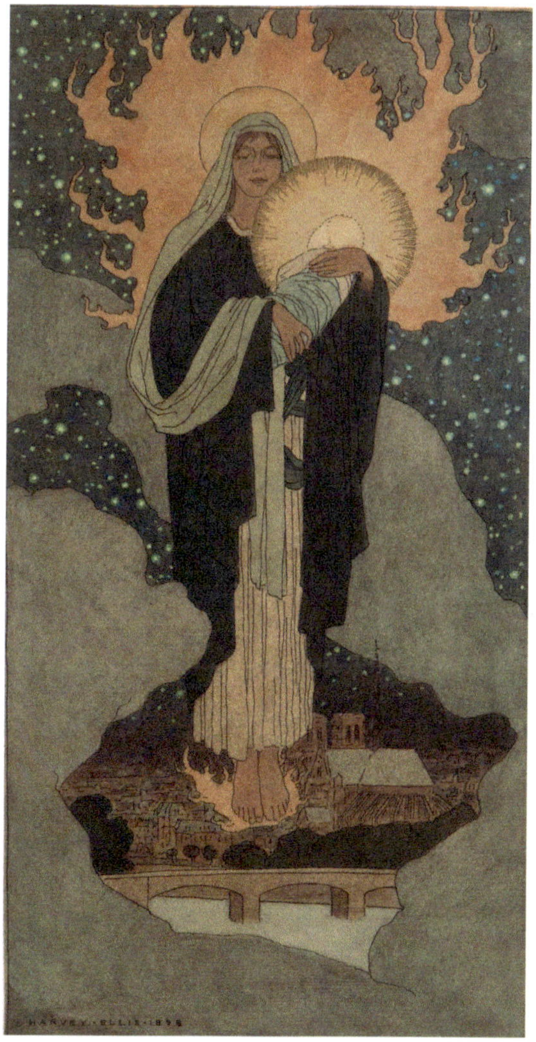

Left: Harvey Ellis, *The Burning Bush*, 1898. Watercolor, charcoal, and black ink on paper. 2016.21

Right: Harvey Ellis, *Our Lady of Notre Dame*, 1898. Watercolor, charcoal, black ink, and gouache on laid paper. 2016.24

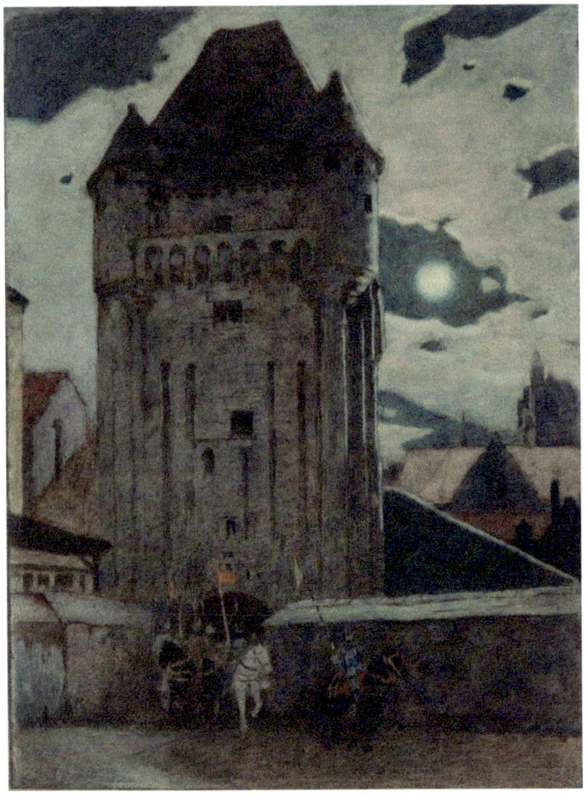

Harvey Ellis, *The Sortie from the Castle*, ca. 1898. Watercolor and pastel on laid paper. 2016.63

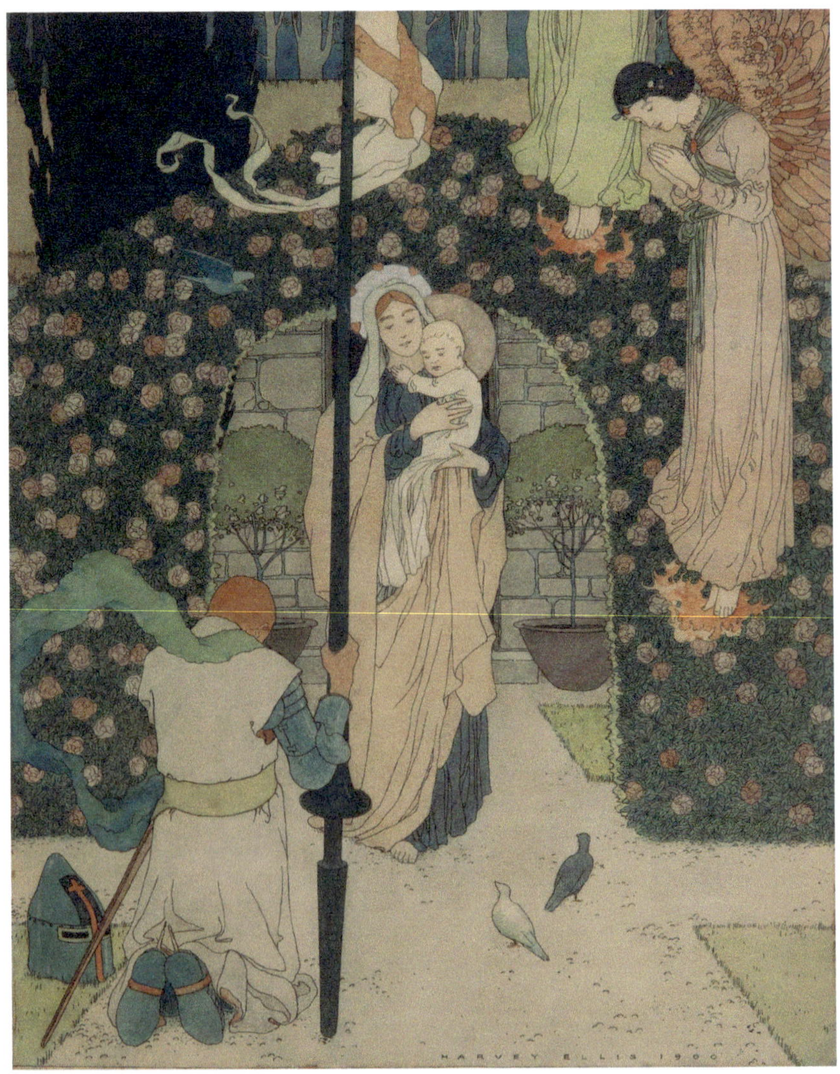


Harvey Ellis, *St. George and the Virgin*, 1900. Watercolor with black ink on paper. 2016.25

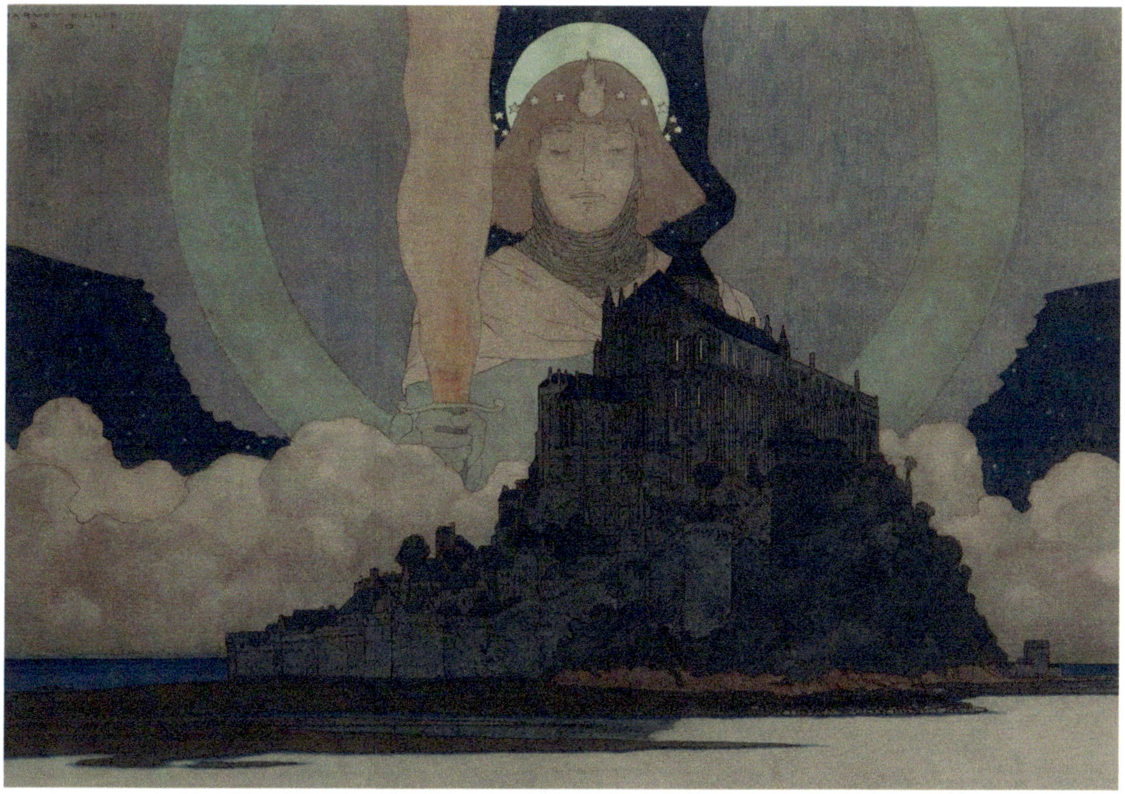

Harvey Ellis, *Mont St. Michel*, 1901. Watercolor, ink, and pastel on paper. 2016.16

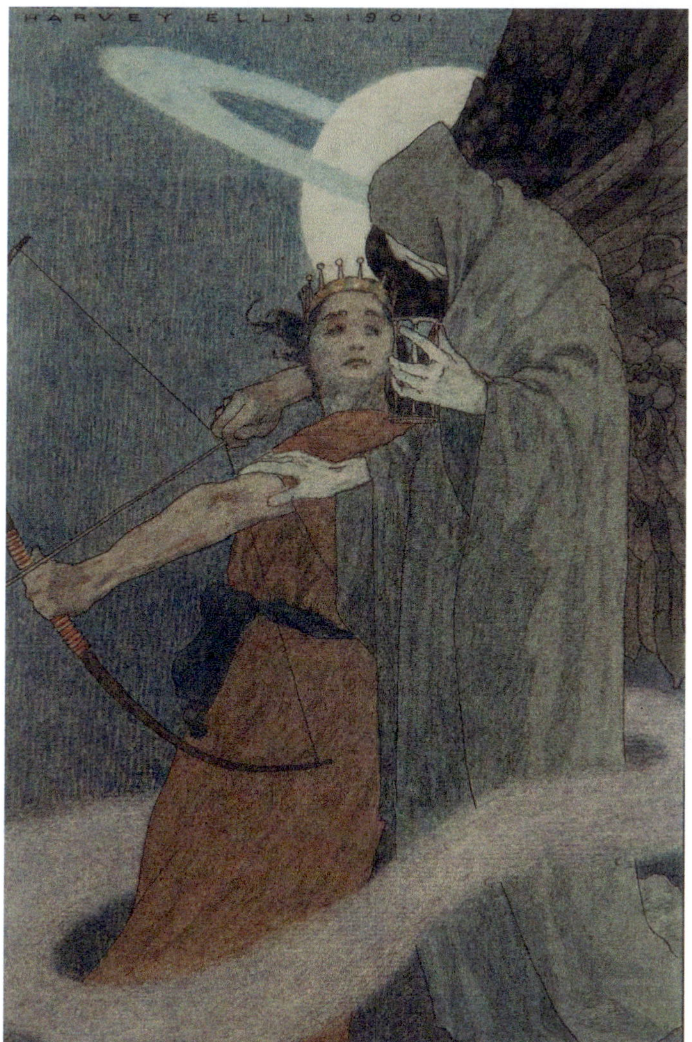


Harvey Ellis, *Time the Beneficent*, 1901. Pastel and ink on paper laid down to board. Gift of Mrs. Kenneth H. Field, 1948.81

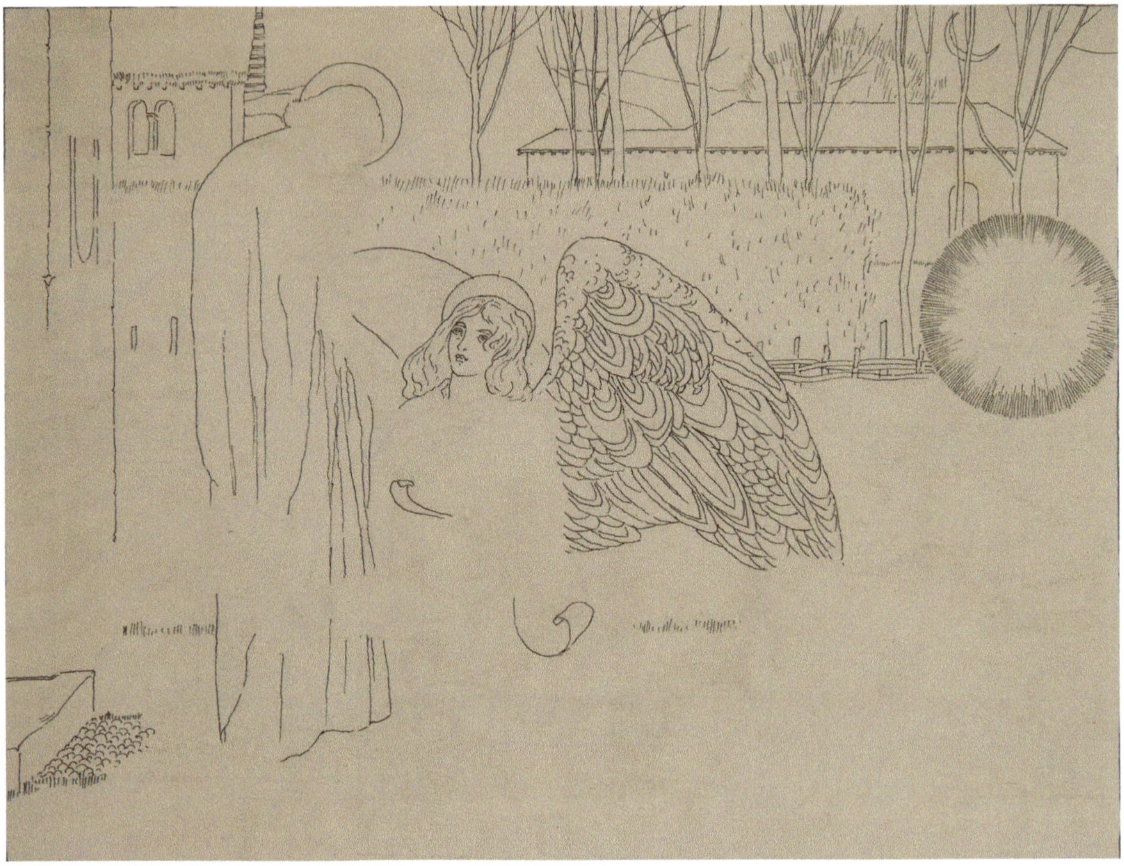

Harvey Ellis, *Unfinished drawing for an Annunciation*, 19th–20th centuries. Black ink and transferred charcoal on laid paper. 2016.64

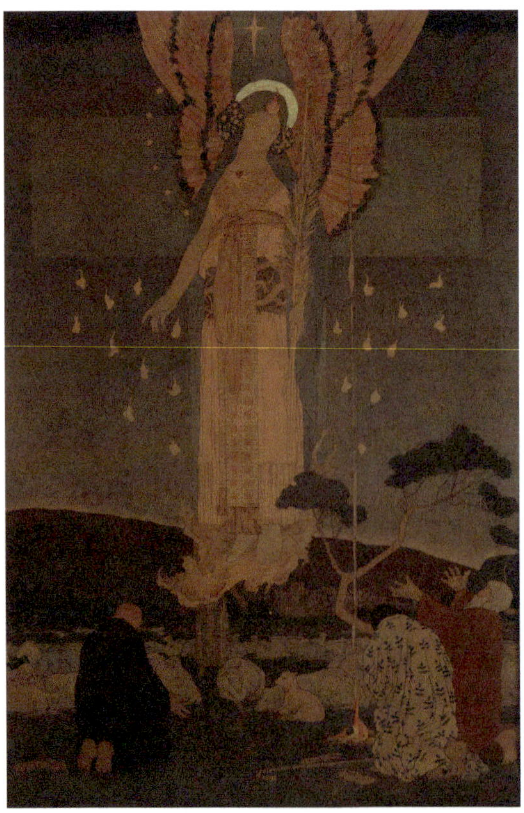

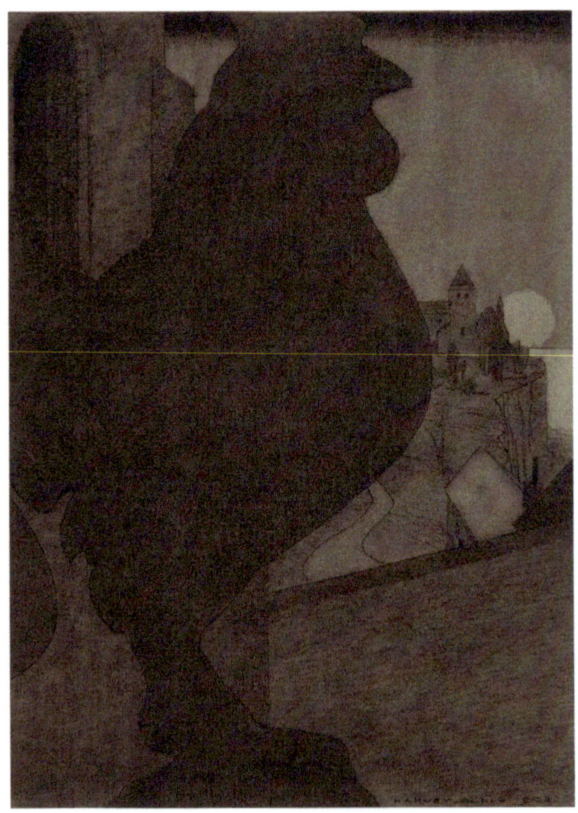

Left: Harvey Ellis, *The Shepherds*, 1901. Watercolor, ink, and pastel on paper. 2016.34

Right: Harvey Ellis, *Rooster and Castle*, 1902. Charcoal and ink on laid paper. 2016.40

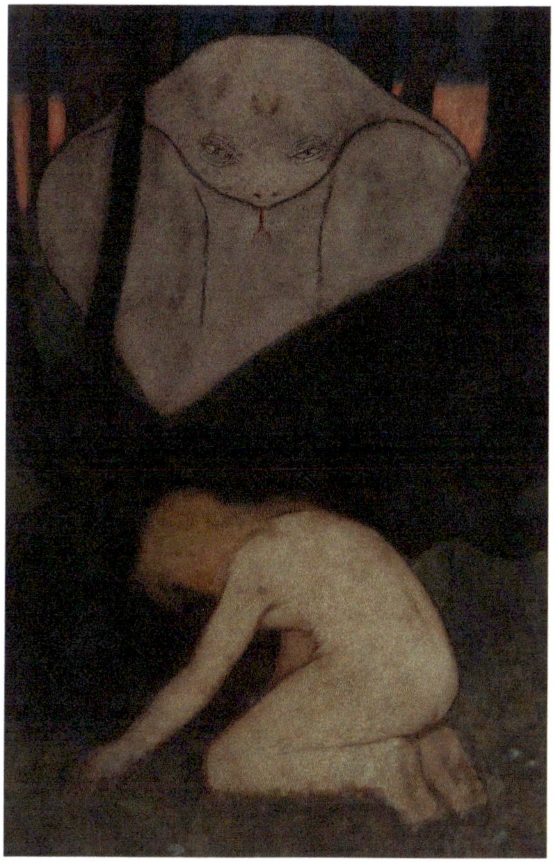

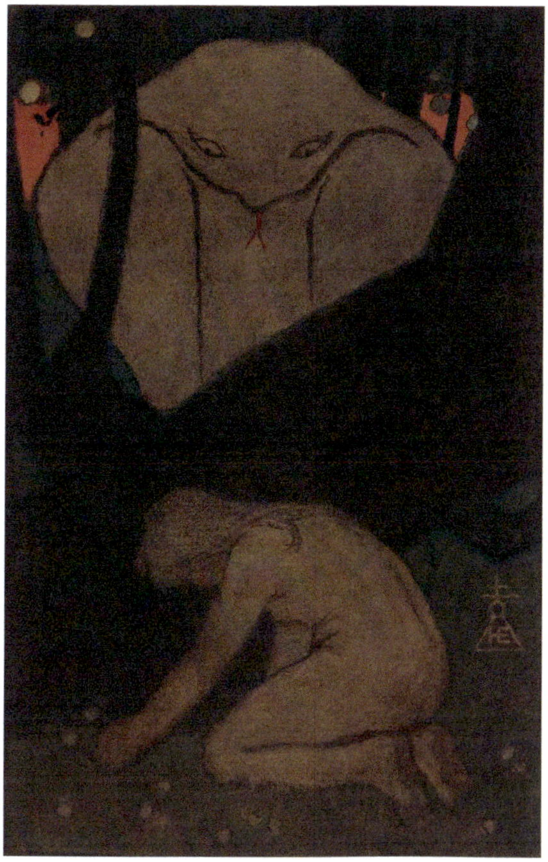

Left: Harvey Ellis, *Study for "The Temptation of Eve,"* 19th–20th centuries. Watercolor, pastel and charcoal on paper. 2016.19

Right: Harvey Ellis, *The Temptation of Eve*, 19th–20th centuries. Watercolor and charcoal on laid paper. 2016.18

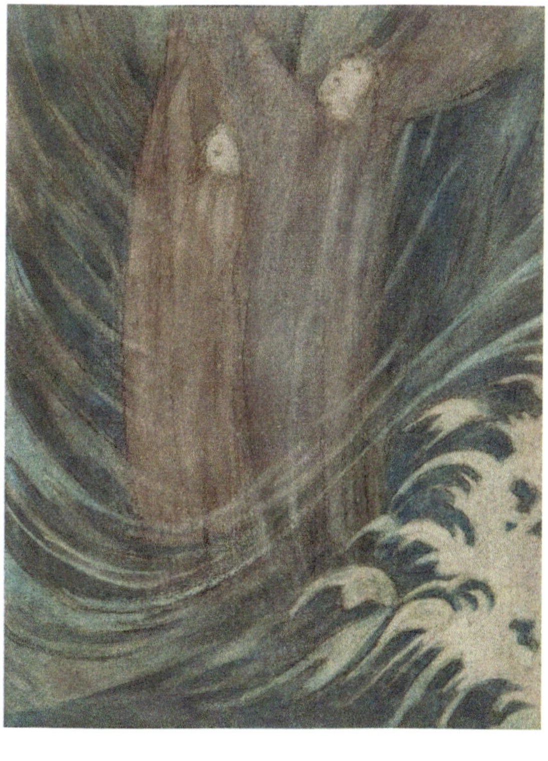

Attributed to Harvey Ellis, *Spirits Rising from the Sea*, 19th–20th centuries. Watercolor and charcoal on laid paper. 2016.66

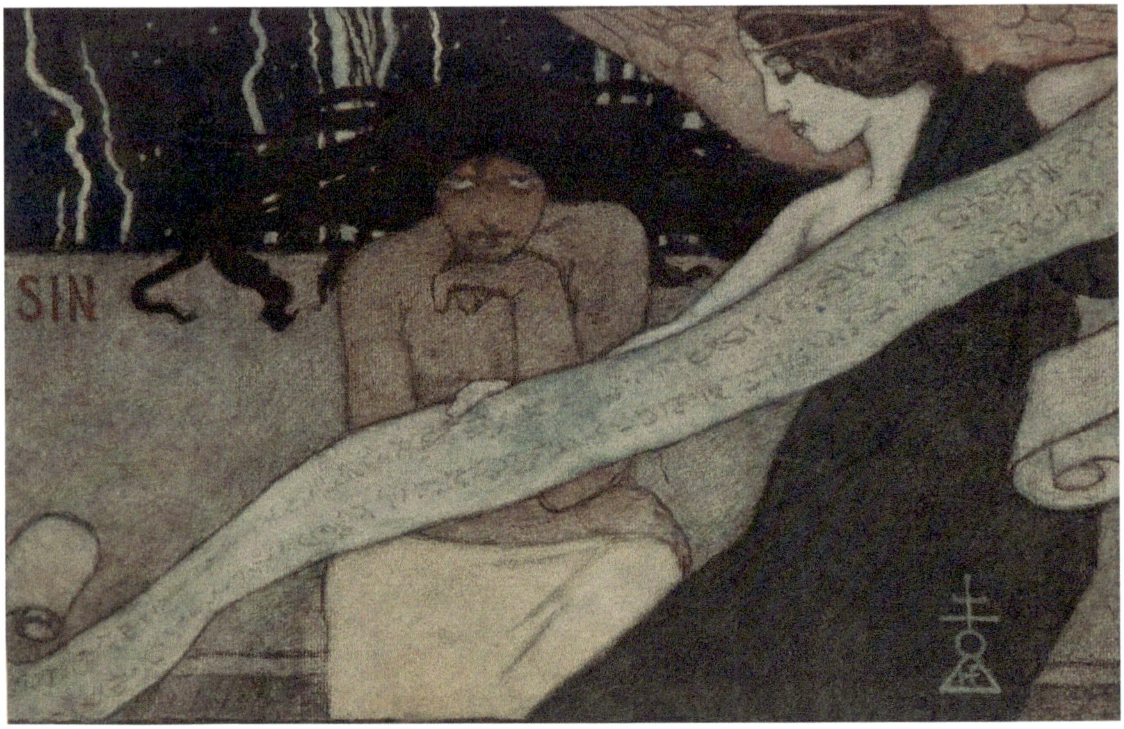


Harvey Ellis, *Sin*, 19th–20th centuries. Pastel, watercolor, and charcoal on laid paper. 2016.12

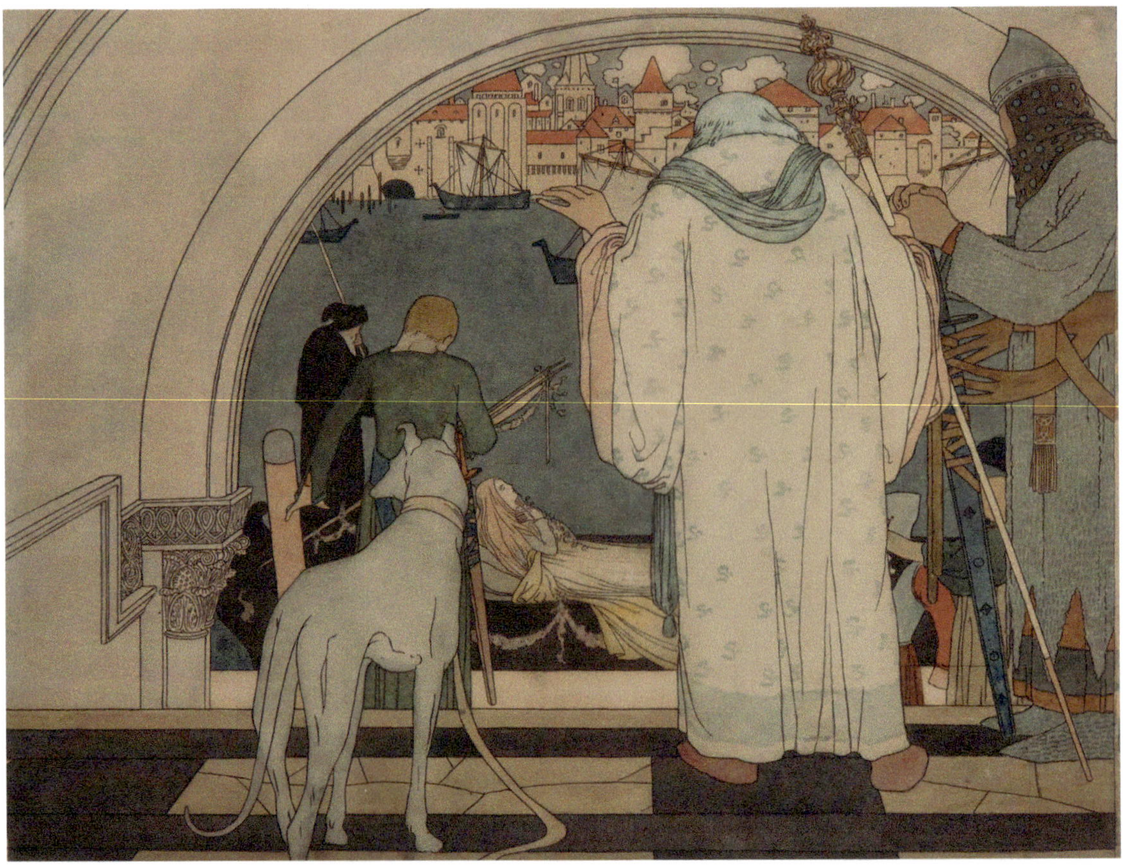

Harvey Ellis, *The Lady of Shalott*, 19th–20th centuries. Watercolor and black ink on paper. 2016.15

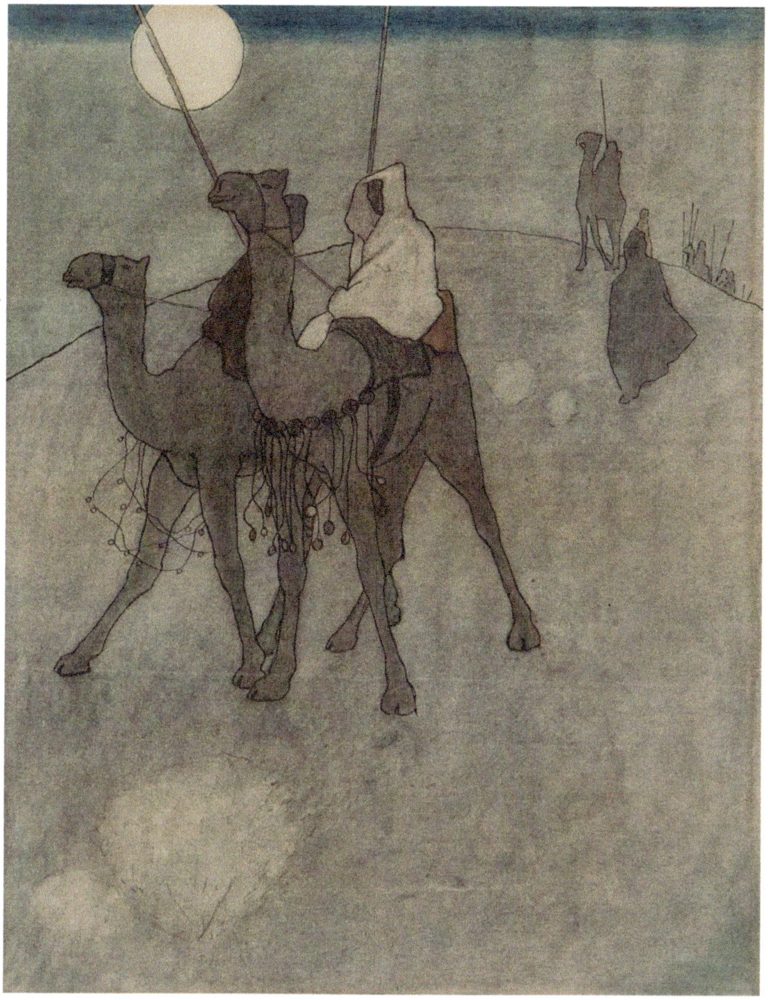

Harvey Ellis, *Camel Caravan*, 19th–20th centuries. Watercolor, charcoal, and black ink on paper. 2016.20

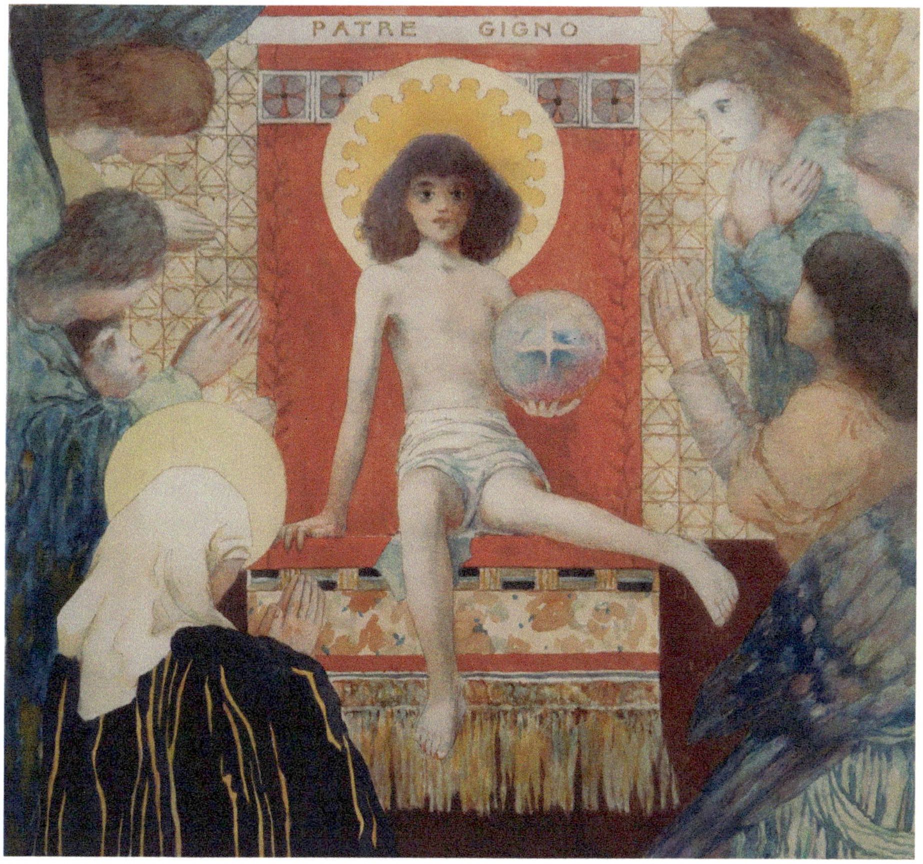


Attributed to Harvey Ellis, *Patre Gigno*, 19th–20th centuries. Watercolor and brown ink on paper. 2016.72

# Colophon

*Editor*
Alexandra Hoff

*Copy Editor*
Mary Safford Curioli

*Design*
Marnie Soom

*Printing and Binding*
Lulu.com

*Typefaces*
Della Robbia, Minion Pro,
and Avenir Next Condensed